SPECIAL REPORT

Salary or Hourly?

Are You Breaking the Law With your Telephone Sales Compensation Program?

What You Don't Know Could Cost You

By Lee R. Van Vechten

—Special Report—

Dear Fellow Inside Sales Professional,

Nearly $200,000.

That's what it cost Cooper Electric Supply recently in fines and legal fees for violations of the Fair Labor and Standards Act (FLSA) relating to the firm's Inside Sales unit.

Think this couldn't happen to you? Think you could beat an audit by the Department of Labor?

That's what this Collingswood, NJ electrical parts distributor thought before learning some of the harsher realities of the FLSA. Let's take an inside look at this case and what it can teach us about wage and hour regulations for telephone-based employees.

First, Cooper Electric was not alone in this fight. The firm was backed by the National Association of Wholesale Distributors and the National Association of Electrical Distributors, who were named as co-defendants in the case.

Cooper also had what it thought was a pretty strong defense:

The firm's Inside Sales representatives are highly trained, specialized technicians who should be exempted from wage and hour restrictions because they are salaried "professionals."

Wholly responsible for a territory, each inside sales rep performs a host of administrative functions and is therefore exempt from hourly wage and record keeping regulations as an "administrative" employee.

Cooper Electric relies on its Inside Sales reps as the firm's main sales distribution channel.

They are, therefore, exempt as "sales professionals."

Cooper lost this litigation on all three counts. The distributor was fined $74,144 for unpaid overtime and the DOL sought an equal amount in punitive damages. Cooper later lost an appeal contending the infractions were not deliberate.

What can we, as managers of phone staffs, learn from Cooper's harrowing experience? Let's look at a few more examples:

At the GE Answer Center, reps must be trained to advise customers on a wide range of product knowledge. Everything from how to get marbles out of the ice maker to trouble shooting vibrations on the intake of a GE jet engine. Does GE need professionals who can be trained for these demanding assignments? You bet they do!

Another example: Call 911 for help. The operator responds to a wide variety of big and small emergencies with a calming, caring attitude. Do we need trained professionals for these positions? I would most certainly hope so.

Example number three: As an engineer who designs equipment using laser components, you call Hamamatsu Corporation for technical assistance. A certified engineer answers the phone and guides you step-by-step until your problem is resolved. You would probably consider this technically trained representative as a "Professional" because he holds an advanced degree in the sciences.

However, if this person then sells you an electrical component you need over the telephone (and, in truth, that's the assignment: to sell over the phone), then is this rep considered a professional by the Department of labor, Wage & Hour Division?

Who cares, you ask?

You and your company should.

Why? Because this distinction between a "professional" and a plain old "'inside sales" or "telemarketing" representative form the basis for how you can and CANNOT compensate such employees under the law.

According to the U.S. Department of Labor (DOL), four categories of employees may be considered "exempt" from wage and hour guidelines: executives, professionals, administrative staff, and outside sales representatives. These positions are exempt from these regulations because they are salaried and not eligible for additional compensation for working over 40 hours per week. When employees are "nonexempt," overtime and a whole host of other concerns come into play.

Fact is, your--and your employees'--perceptions about what is or isn't a professional position has little to do with the FLSA regulations. College grads or others with specialized techniques, skills, and job knowledge tend to think of themselves as professional employees and not as "hourly" employees. This is largely due to class perceptions about "blue collar" and "white collar" workers, and factory and office employees.

But, like it or not, these biases have nothing whatsoever to do with the law.

The Simple Facts of Life, According to the FLSA

Let me tell you the facts of life right up front. If you employ inside sales and service representatives who take incoming or make outgoing calls, they may not be exempted from the wage and hour guidelines of the DOL. Secondly, their exemption has nothing to do with common sense definitions of "executive," "administrative," "Professional," or "outside sales" positions.

The legally binding definitions are outlined in detail in Title 29, Part 541 of the Code of Federal Regulations, DOL,(WH Publication 1281, Revised 6/83). I encourage you to send for this important document. If you are exempting your staff when they should be classified as non-exempt, both you and your company may be in violation of the FLSA and liable for serious fines, penalties, imprisonment or all of the above.

Just one infraction will result in an inspection for compliance for all areas of your company, in addition to the area in question.

A survey of compensation practices compiled by our former publication, *The Van Vechten Report October 1990*), revealed this startling fact: 92.13% of our entire subscriber base was in violation of FLSA regulations, specifically, the exempt and non-exempt issue. The primary cause was a misinterpretation of the "professional" exemption. The second problem was the assumption that if outside sales people are considered exempt, then inside sales reps must also be exempt from wage and hour regulations. No such exemption exists for your telephone staffs. Period.

Let me try to clarify this a little further. The "professional" exemption requires a degree in advanced sciences; learning of specialized, intellectual instruction; and more than a general academic education. This includes such professionals as doctors, lawyers, scientists and engineers who spend less than 20% of their time on tasks. The term has nothing to do with doing a "Professional" job. It is simply a definition of a class of employee.

Here's another clue. The only reason outside sales representatives are exempt is because they work outside--not because they are professionals or because they are sales types. And, if they work inside for more than 20% of their total time performing sales tasks other then selling, they could lose their exemption according to FLSA regulations.

Therefore, if any of your phone reps are 100% salaried and their compensation is not computed by the hour as documented by time logs you have a problem. Hours worked over 40 in any one week should be compensated at time and one-half. Furthermore, employees may not surrender their rights under the FLSA by working at home, or finding some other way around these hourly restrictions.

Whether you agree or disagree with the regulations, they will not go away. Violating them intentionally could mean you will "Go directly to Jail—Do not pass Go, do not collect $200!"

How easy is it to get caught? All it takes is one employee complaint that leads to a DOL investigation. That's it.

What CAN You Do?

Now that we've scared the daylights out of you (and if you're not scared, you should be), what can you and your company do to operate within the FLSA guidelines? Plenty.

· The first thing you should do is send for the regulations, circulate them among your legal and upper management staffs, and plan a course of action. Write for them to: The U.S. Department of Labor, Employment Standards Administration, Washington, DC, 20210. (This document is free)

· Secondly, don't fool yourselves into thinking you can fight these regulations and win. As the case history on Cooper Electric has shown, many others have tried and failed. It's far easier to live within the guidelines than to try to change them.

By law, one misinterpretation of the regulations should not get you into trouble if you are audited. Everybody makes mistakes!

However, willful, intentional violation could result in serious damage.

When all is said and done, you CAN compensate

your inside sales people on a salaried basis. The key is in how you do it, and how you document it. Just make sure their time is computed on an hourly basis and don't allow them to work either on or off site more than 40 hours per week.

Remember that they can't surrender their rights under these regulations, *even if they want to*.

Lastly, if you've studied the regulations and are still in doubt on this issue, you could certainly write the DOL for their opinion about your particular situation. Just remember, in our experience, the DOL always wins!

If you are exempting your staff when they should be classified as non-exempt, both you and your company may be in violation of the FLSA and liable for serious fines, penalties, imprisonment or all of the above.

Lee R. Van Vechten

> *"When all is said and done, you CAN compensate your inside sales people on a salaried basis. The key is in how you do it, and how you document it."*

Important Note

This information is provided with the understanding that the author and publisher are not engaged in rendering legal or other professional services. The author and publisher disclaim any liability, loss or risk incurred as a consequence, directly or indirectly, of the use and application of any of the contents of this information. This information is not a substitute for the advice of a competent legal or other professional person.

Business By Phone Inc. • 13254 Stevens St. • Omaha, NE • 68137 • (402)895-9399

The Successful Sales Manager's Guide to Business-to-Business Telephone Sales

Everything You Need to Start, Reposition, and Manage a Telesales Department

Lee R. Van Vechten

Business By Phone Inc.

13254 Stevens St., Omaha, NE 68137   402-895-9399   Fax: 402-896-3353
www.businessbyphone.com

The Successful Sales Manager's Guide to
Business-to-Business Telephone Sales
Everything You Need to Start, Reposition, and Manage a Telesales Department

By Lee R. Van Vechten

Cover design by George Foster, Foster & Foster, Fairfield, IA

Special thanks for editing and layout: Frank Treu; Bob Van Voorhis

ISBN 1-881081-09-5

Published By:

Business By Phone Inc.
13254 Stevens St.
Omaha, NE 68137.
(402)895-9399
Fax:(402)896-3353
E-mail arts@businessbyphone.com
www.businessbyphone.com

The Successful Sales Manager's Guide
to
Business-to-Business
Telephone Sales

Telemarketing:

Tele – from the Greek "τελε," meaning far; used in the formation of compound words meaning "distant", especially "transmission over a distance".

Market — (n), a meeting of people for selling and buying.

Telemarketing — (n), intensive use of the telephone worldwide, for a variety of selling and buying objectives, more often than not in a business environment.

Telesales — (n), conducting selling activities over the telephone using the medium of telemarketing.

Dedication

This book is 100% dedicated to my wife Tanya and working moms everywhere. I also would like to acknowledge my colleagues, clients and friends. Their combined help and encouragement allowed me to finish the work started a few years back. To all of you my heartfelt thanks.

Van Vechten

Vincit qui Patitur.

"HE WHO PERSISTS SHALL CONQUER"

About the Author

Lee R. Van Vechten, has spent the bulk of his adult working career in sales and marketing (since 1962) and since 1975 has been specifically involved in the medium called telemarketing. When you ask him how long he has been in telemarketing he says with a smile, "Since 1962, only then we called it, using the phone a lot."

Since 1977, Lee is President of F.G.I., Freehold, New Jersey, a management consulting and sales training firm. The company specializes in turnkey, telephone marketing installations and repositioning for businesses, specifically the creation of telephone selling resources for clients. A recipient of the DMA's Telemarketing Council's Pioneer Award, Lee is also the co-founder of the American Telemarketing Association and served on its Board of Directors. In October 1997 Lee received the TeleProfessional Magazine's Top Ten TelePros of The Year award.

He is a past Vice President of Sales and Marketing with AMR International, where he developed and implemented his first successful telephone marketing and sales organization. Under Lee's direction, that unit's telesales volume increased from 1.6 million to 8.5 million dollars in a 30-month period.

Lee spent 14 years with Dun & Bradstreet in various sales and management assignments. He worked with Duns Marketing Services Division, utilizing the 250 sales representatives to sell primary and secondary research services. His final position with D & B was as Senior Manager of Research Sales and Fulfillment.

He is the past publisher of THE VAN VECHTEN REPORT and EXTENSIONS. Both publications were proactive telephone sales skill newsletters for management. Lee is also the publisher of TSR HOTLINE, a training reinforcement program for Telephone Sales Representative (TSRs) and CSR HOTLINE, a skills publication for Customer Service Representatives (CSRs). His organization also conducts management and sales representative seminars. The Black Belt I, II, and III series of Sales and Operation Management Seminars are reported to be unique and motivational, as well as educational, by hundreds of managers worldwide.

Lee has performed consulting services for over 200 companies including Perkin Elmer, Dun & Bradstreet (U.S. and Canada), Honeywell, Inc., General Electric, Champion Paper, UPS, Westvaco, Peterbilt, AT&T Corporate, General Foods, Smith Corona, Coca Cola, Inc., Blue Cross/Blue Shield (Maryland and Massachusetts), Rayovac Corporation, Polaroid, Rohm & Haas, Boehringer Mannheim, and "The Telephone Doctor". His impact on the business to business catalogers and their multi-medium marketing is evidenced by the successful start-up of over 26 inside sales operations for catalogers in the past 20 years.

Lee is a contributor of many articles for industry publications. He has been a regular featured writer for DM News, TeleProfessional Magazine, Operations and Fulfillment, and contributed the Compensation chapter for Prentice Hall's Encyclopedia of Telemarketing, as well as Dartnell's Marketing Managers Handbook. He is a frequent speaker at trade conferences and has presented skill seminars for AMA, DMA, ATA, Target Marketing Conference Corporation (DMB & NCOF), Dartnell, Direct Media, Marketing Publications, Inc. (Customer Service), and the Universities of Alabama, Minnesota, Georgia, and Syracuse. Lee majored in Labor Management at the College of Business, Pennsylvania State University and served as a non-commissioned communications officer with the 3rd Armored Division, U. S. Army, in Germany. He continues as a successful business consultant and developer of client specific corporate sales training programs. His wife Tanya is a partner in his business, and his son Derrick is following in the same career field.

Introduction

I know of no one who when asked what they wanted to be when they grew up answered, "I want to be a telemarketing manager or call center manager." By the same token, I can count on one hand the professional sales representatives and managers, who, at the outset of their careers declared, "Count me in. A sales career is for me... for sure!" Most of us come into these fields from other endeavors, or other professions and studies.

Even more interesting than that are the conversations one overhears at a variety of social events, at local watering holes, ball games, church, conferences, and the like. They usually start off something like this, "What is it that you do at your company?" And the response is... "I'm involved in (hand to the mouth, mumble, mumble) "marketing."

Not that long ago there was some interest in changing the American Telemarketing Association's (ATA) name to the American (mumble, mumble) Association. Finally, in 1999, the ATA did change its name from Telemarketing to Teleservices. What we seem to have is an occasional image problem. If there really is a problem, then it isn't that complicated. Both the American Teleservices Association and the DMA Telemarketing Council can manage it very well. They stand for professionalism, have codes of ethics, and educate legislators at all levels on a continuing basis. My personal opinion is that the definition of who we are and what we do is unclear, and to a larger degree, "much ado about nothing".

Those of us who are professional managers know what we do, why we do it, and generally are proud of our contributions. That's what is really important. It's to this end that this book is written. I agree with my good friend Rudy Oetting of Oetting & Company, NYC, when he ended his keynote speech for the ATA in Monterey, California a few years back by saying, "You'll know that we have finally arrived when the Wall Street Journal carries a feature article noting the promotion of a top executive to the office of president for a top 500 company, who got his or her start as a telemarketer." I agree.

For the purpose of definition and clarity I will use the following definition of the medium, and as you will see, it follows the K.I.S.S. principal (keep it simple, stupid!).

Telemarketing is the intensive use of the telephone in a business environment.

If I'm not mistaken, that definition covers about everything. Let's see... business-to-business, or business-to-consumer, inbound, and outbound, reactive, and proactive, company owned (captive), or service bureau, call center, customer service provider, outsource agency, and any combination of these things. What we do under these titles, is what we do. How and what we do in this medium falls under the topic of mission, philosophy, and objectives. Finally, it all boils down to the function topics, like selling, customer service, order entry, research, accounts receivable, collection and the like. Returning to the problem of nomenclature, we know many in the field do not like to have their representatives called telemarketers, and they don't need to be, as far as I am concerned. Title them by their function, e.g., inside sales, customer service, product/service consultant, but not tele-anything. Telemarketing is merely a selling channel, and if the title is an issue, change it.

We are in the people business; therefore we are only as good as our people. The management of human resources is the key to our success. Let's not forget that our people are talking to our customers and our prospects, within our spheres of influence. Anything we, or our company, can do to better manage this real time activity most certainly will be a wise investment.

The medium of telemarketing is one of the key answers to positive marketing productivity and simply stated, "the better mousetrap". The more we learn about the medium, the more effective we will be. I trust this work will be helpful to the reader. I most certainly wish each and every one of you tons of success. I think the keys are in this book.

☎ ☎ ☎

Lee R. Van Vechten

The author invites comments, suggestions and questions on this material or any material relating to the GUIDE's subject matter. We can be contacted at:

www.vanvechten.com

Table of Contents

CHAPTER 4
(Applies to U.S. readers only)
Management Concerns: Risks And Dangers

CHAPTER 5
Management Guidelines

CHAPTER 6
Finding And Hiring Your Staff

CHAPTER 7
Compensation Reward And Recognition Systems

CHAPTER 8
Understanding Sales Staff Motivations

CHAPTER 9
Telephone Skills And Training Techniques

CHAPTER 10
Training, Workbook Design, Format And Examples

CHAPTER 11
Performance And Performance Appraisals

CHAPTER 12
The Sales Center Facility

CHAPTER 13
Conflict Resolutions

CHAPTER 14
Publications, Associations, Conferences

CHAPTER 15
Marketing, Budgeting and Consultants

CHAPTER 1
Yesterday, Today and Tomorrow

1

Industry Buzzwords

The genesis of multi-phased marketing is interesting from a number of perspectives. It's often described in fad words. Fad is defined as current public fancy. The fad-word, integrated marketing, is used to describe a variety of marketing channels, actions, or methods, working together to accomplish a total marketing objective. Integrated marketing seems to have replaced other fad words in the Direct Marketing, Direct Response industry; synergy, synergistic, synergism, which appear to be out of vogue in the 90's. I am reminded of an old adage that comes to bear, "When you ask someone for an opinion, you will get one". The same is true here. If you ask someone for a definition of integrated marketing, you'll get one. Try these on for size:

Integrated Marketing: "Using techniques of response marketing wrapped around any and all information and information sources in order to make a sale."

> *Don Libby*
> *The Libby Consultancy*

Integrated Marketing: "Does that mean there is a status or situation called non-integrated marketing or better yet is the term redundant, as in marketing marketing?"

> *Geri Gantman, Partner*
> *Oetting & Company, Inc.*

During a coffee break while presenting at a DMA seminar, Rudy Oetting called and agreed with his partner, Geri Gantman. "Multiple marketing strategies and techniques is Marketing!"

> *Rudy Oetting, Partner*
> *Oetting & Associates*

"Integrated Marketing: A lot of people talk about it. No, I don't have a definition. Nothing more than multiple strategies or tactics working in tandem toward an objective. That's marketing. I think I'll write a book about it."

> *Bernie Goldberg*
> *Direct Marketing Publishers*

I'm sorry I asked!

More Buzzwords

I suppose that when peers meet at industry training conferences it is paramount that they be able to communicate and use the so-called "in" buzzwords. Doing so must be a signal to others that you're on top of your game.

I receive no less than 20 industry conference brochures a month. These announcements are loaded with the latest buzzwords. Try these on for size. CTI, CSP, IVR, Enterprise Business Center, Blended Environment, Skills Based on Routing, and Telephony; Even the term Call Center has changed in the final years of this century.

Terminology has gotten so complex that I had to purchase the *Telcom Dictionary* for $35, and a book entitled *Introduction to Computer Telephony*, (Carlton Carden, Flatiron Publishing, Inc., 1997) for $30. And yet, these books change yearly. But really, all I want to do is advise companies how to sell stuff over the telephone, especially in proactive, business to business sales channels. So, without all the complex nonsense, that is what this book is all about.

A Classic Case Example

Since I am involved in the sales operational side of the medium, I tend not to get fancy or academic. Fad words don't help me pay for a Jaguar, results do. If I can bring the costs down and the results up, I'm happy, and so are my clients. Let me relate one of my case histories that might be considered as integrated marketing, or simply, "selling something".

The UCCEL Affair

About ten years ago a woman attended one of my management seminars, "Telephone Sales, Should You, and How," a three-day presentation in Birmingham, Alabama. Susan McKenna brought her financial backer with her. They were going to do something very uncommon for that time. Susan wanted to sell software for IBM mainframes over the telephone, without any assistance from rep organizations, and without employing field sales representatives. They wanted to know how to set the unit up, and how to make it work.

To make a long story short, she did exactly that, and became so successful, that five years later she sold the company, Software Corporation of America, to UCCEL Corporation, for $11,000,000. She and her partner split the proceeds down the middle, and as she exited the business world for her global cruise, she said thanks to me, and noted that she had given my name to UCCEL Corporation as a referral for an international opportunity.

Time passed and I find myself in Oxbridge, England (just outside Heathrow Airport), talking to the Director of International Operations about selling software over the telephone.

Needless to say, the "Brits" were very hospitable to this Yank. However, they were not thrilled that "Corporate" had sent them a U.S. consultant to assist them with their telemarketing. The first objection revealed itself with comments like, "We don't do business like you Yanks do. It just would not work in the UK or any other European Country." It sounded like an objection to me and my methods. It's appropriate to note that they had been doing this telemarketing thing for a full year, and had not sold a thing. So much for success patterns.

Here comes what might be called the "integrated example". After sizing up the situation and rolling up my sleeves, I asked for a phone and a prospect company to call in Holland (after all, my last name is of Dutch origin). There was near rebellion at my request, and some fear to boot. The "Yank" was going to muddle things up for sure.

I had designed a ten-step calling process that allowed the last three steps to accept an "in-person visit". But, you could not go from step to step unless the prior one was completed. The "Brits", after much convincing, let me dial up Philips, NV (the electronics giant). I asked to speak to the controller of finance, and, you guessed it, he took my call.

After that (in my mind) it was simple. Develop interest and determine who would make the decision. The call went something like this: (please keep in mind that IBM mainframe users were easy to identify and that throughout the ten-step process support mailings were used)

Lee Van Vechten:	Mr. Van Dyke? Lee Van Vechten from UCCEL Corporation, U.S. headquarters. How are you?
Phillips:	Thank you for asking, I'm just fine, how are you? (and in perfect English)
Lee Van Vechten:	Great Hans, just great!! Need your help today... I'm curious ... if your accounts payable program overrode your payroll program in a processing run and everything was dumped and or destroyed, who would lose their job at Phillips?
Phillips:	(After a lengthy pause) I would.
Lee Van Vechten:	Do you know that it can't happen at Phillips?
Phillips:	No.
Lee Van Vechten:	Do you think it's important to find out and take appropriate action?
Phillips:	Yes.
Lee Van Vechten:	Do you want to delegate the investigation or should we be talking to you?
Phillips:	I think talking to me would be fine.
Lee Van Vechten:	Good. I'll have our Amsterdam people get a package to you and call you Monday of next week. Does that make sense?
Phillips:	Yes, thank you. I'll look forward to the contact.
Lee Van Vechten:	I appreciate your time and we will be in touch Hans.

(Call Ended)

Exactly five and one-half weeks later, UCCEL Corporation closed a 1.8 million-dollar site license for the "product" with a package that included installation and training.

Today we call that, a call, mail, call, call, Field Tech Representative, FSR program. It consists of seven specific telephone call objectives using a lot of phone calls, and supported by mailings. That's integrated marketing in my book, and it worked.

War Story epilogue: The British, not wanting to lose face, noted to me on my next visit that they were correct. A field rep closed the contract not a telemarketing rep. That's when I went to the nearest pub to collect my sanity. Really, who cares who closed the deal? The deal was closed, and the use of the telephone in the sales event was an important marketing element. I believe it's called prospecting.

Yesterday, Today And Tomorrow -- The History Of The Telesales Medium

It appears to me that we should not have a hang-up on academic or fad words and phrases for this work. I agree with the Oetting partners, what we really need to concentrate upon is marketing. The objective is sales productivity, which means the cost of programs when compared to the desired results, i.e., cost of sales. But herein lies another problem. The business world likes to see activities in defined blocks. Enterprises seem to say, "I've got an idea, let's sell Data-Comm equipment. We can get a list, mail some stuff, and call them on the phone and make a fortune. Anything that's really big we can take away from an inside sales rep and have our field team work."

That's a good idea as far as it goes, but it is necessary to have a marketing

Figure 1.1 -- Early 1970s

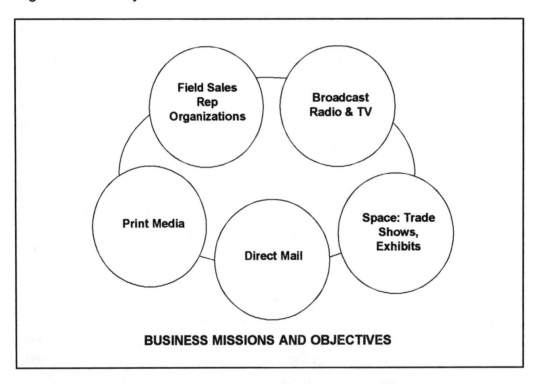

BUSINESS MISSIONS AND OBJECTIVES

plan. Obviously, there is more to the facilitation of a plan or an idea than just the doing of it. Now thinking specifically about what we are calling telemarketing, and its genesis, please review Figure 1.1 .

The exhibit suggests that during the 70s these tools were available, and business objectives were accomplished. Mail was reasonably inexpensive, especially prior to the 70's. While the energy crisis was having an impact, and business life was getting progressively more difficult, our other circles and functions were in fair shape. As a matter of fact, we were even using the telephone as a tool. Note that there is no circle (a clear box) for the telephone. In the old days (my son, Derrick notes that anything prior to 1972 is the "olden days") we said that using the telephone a lot, was called, "Using the phone a lot." But, the energy crisis (brought on by the oil cartels)

Figure 1.2 -- Late 1970's & most of the 80's

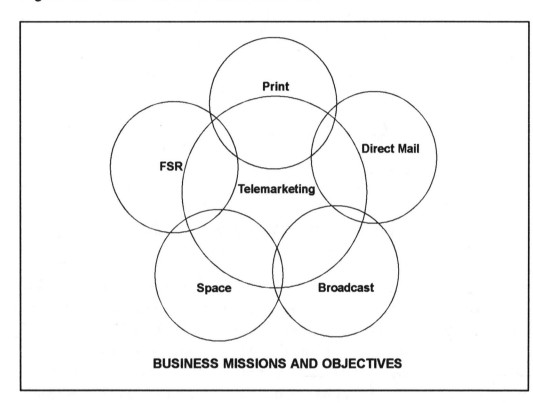

BUSINESS MISSIONS AND OBJECTIVES

was having a stronger effect on the economy than anyone ever expected, and you know the rest... a deep recession. The cost of paper and ink exploded. Fuel prices (gasoline) went sky high, and resulted in the infamous service station waiting lines.

Field sales reps were unable to cover their territory, and there were incremental postage price hikes. Enter telemarketing. Both the telemarketing function and its intensive use were now at work. Now, please review Figure 1.2 .

This is what business thought they wanted.

Curiously enough, many had a different view of their wants. If you were a field sales manager, you would most likely have the FSR circle as a center block, etc. But, since I am biased, we'll leave it like it is. At about this time the marketing fad word was synergism or synergistic, or synergy. Yes, the sum of the parts are or will be greater

7

Figure 1.3 -- In the late 80s and early 1990s, business ended-up with

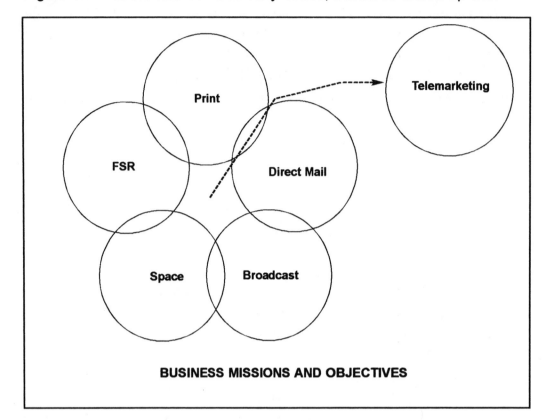

BUSINESS MISSIONS AND OBJECTIVES

than the whole. That's good for me and the question is, "Is it good for you?" You bet!

There were a ton of case examples at the time demonstrating how telemarketing was the "in thing", and productive at that. The business to consumer folks jumped on it like free tickets on United Airlines. Murray Roman, founder of Campaign Communications, had saved the Chrysler Corporation (the first time) with an exciting telemarketing campaign. Even I helped to move a seminar company's sales results (AMR International), from 1.65 million, to 8.5 million in revenue, in less than 30 months in the late 70's. All this with an inside sales unit.

In the late 80's and early 90's both the worldwide recession, and the U.S. national debt crisis, encouraged marketers to get a bigger bang for their marketing buck. But, quite often we would see the aberration noted in Figure 1.3.

As you will note, the telemarketing medium was isolated, off in the wings, outside the main flow, the recipient of the marketing plan as opposed to being involved in the front-end of the planning cycle, in other words, not in control of their destiny.

Understanding the medium was half the problem. You still hear comments like these in the phone sales area:

- "Did I tell you that last week we mailed 112,000 letters with your 800 number

on the response card's call to action section? Oops! Sorry..."
- "Stop what you're doing. The boss wants to know if our coffee brewing systems are being used for the competitor's products instead of ours."
- "If we get those people to make 200 calls a day each we can get through this list in 210 days."
- "Do me a favor, can you slip in another 3,000 calls for my pet project?"
- "What do you mean you can't do my project! Hell, those people are only on the phone two hours a day."

Figure 1.2 is where we want to be (with a dotted line), literally using a variety of marketing methods in tandem, to accomplish our business objectives. This resource works very effectively if its designed use is understood at the front-end of the planning cycle, but not if it is used after a plan has been designed by others in a planning vacuum.

Future Trends

The term telemarketing is a catch-all description that occasionally is an emotional word. In fact, it's so emotional it's being replaced with terms like Call Center, Inside Sales, or Telesales. It's more than a profession of out-of-work actors, or those people who will do this task until they can find a "real job". These customer contact positions are important, all of them. Remember that you have two major categories of employees at your firm.

- Those who have contact with the customer
- And *all* other staff

We know that the people who have contact with customers are important, as reported in a number of research projects and in the industry press, each and every day that we are in business.

Take the study *Future Trends in Wholesale Distribution* from the Distribution Research & Education Foundation, Washington, DC. It was designed as an on-going device investigating and tracking best practice trends. I believe the survey sample was sizable and statistically significant. Although dealing in perceptions (and perceptions can change), we believe that there is a plus or minus 3.5% confidence factor in the results. Thus, it's good stuff.

Before you review the exhibit, please understand some of the research methodologies. First, the survey was one that ranked preference. In other words, captions with brief descriptions were provided in alphabetical order. The participant then decided which was more, and which was less, important. Other service topics were a part of the research, but not listed or shown here, because the data was not really relevant for this work.

Second, the sample was from all lines of business (service, retail, manufacturing, construction, wholesale) and all sizes of business (ranked by employee size). Finally, representative locations all over the U.S. were used. I recognize you may not want to bet the farm on the result, but remember this was not a telemarketing survey. This data popped up out of the blue from a distribution study. Please review the exhibit (Figure 1.4) with me, and let me interpret the findings; in turn you will understand my perspective.

Figure 1.4

SERVICE	1970	1980	1985	1990
Contact with Outside Sales person	First	Third	Fifth	Eighth
Frequency and Speed of Delivery	Second	First	First	Second
Price	Third	Second	Third	Fourth [2]
Range of Available Products	Fourth	Fifth	Fourth	Third
Capable Inside Salespersons	Fifth	Fourth	Second	First [1]

1995(*) See notes below
Source: "Future Trends in Wholesale Distribution," from Distribution Research & Education Foundation, Washington, DC. Survey conducted by Arthur Andersen & Co.

What Customers Want Most... the Survey

First, let me tell you what this study does not suggest. Notice that contact with an outside sales person moves from first in 1970, to eighth in 1990. This trend does not mean that field selling organizations are being replaced by inside selling resources. When you investigate in detail, you find that the issue is *time*, and *selling expenses*, as in cost of sales. Customers and selling organizations alike are being pressed to use time more efficiently and effectively. Buyers (customers) can't afford, indeed don't want to afford, spending an hour in a routine sales call. And along those same lines, not all sales calls warrant the expense of having a field sales rep make the call. And finally, field sales reps migrate towards the big spenders and only cover the mix of smaller spenders if time and quota conditions allow, or if their jobs are in jeopardy. All of the aforementioned conditions encourage the use of the telemarketing, telesales medium, both inbound and outbound, and even demand that segments of account structure be assigned to an inside sales selling asset. What we are seeing here is an adjustment in selling accountabilities, not a replacement.

Unfortunately, the research format changed for 1995, and for all future studies. The new title, *Facing the Forces of Change; Transforming Your Business with Best Practices* was also funded by the NAW (National Association of Wholesalers), and addressed the same issues, but did not use the same methodology.

First, the 1995 result, and the forecast for the year 2000 revealed that the trends only adjusted modestly. The adjustment was directly related to wireless phone technology. It takes into account the fact that we could all be in touch with each other at a moment's notice, via cellular phones. That we have the ability to be in instant contact was only half the requirement, being able to make "things" happen immediately was the other half of the requirement. Now, through CTI (computer telephony integration), the database for an account is available with the phone call. But, the CTI feature still appears to be difficult from a field location, and may not be the most effective tool for field agents anyway. Thus, the inside sales agent is still the number one selection, i.e., the most important category. (1)

Second, when something is sold, the customer's expectation level peaks. The "I want it now" prevails. In this age of instantaneous communications, the customer assumes everything is instantaneous, and wants it that way. This is one reason why Federal Express has been so successful. They fulfill the rapidity requirement that business perceives it needs. Let me suggest this, this speed of service has forced United Parcel Service and the U.S. Post Office to rethink what business they are in. Both organizations have moved up to meet the Federal Express challenge. It's amazing and almost an oxymoron, Priority Mail is a US Post Office service option, rather than the standard.

11

Third, price. Every sales person in the world anticipates and fears the price objection. Yet customers' answers in this research, was that price is important, but not the number one consideration. I think so highly of this data that I have nearly convinced myself there is no such thing as a price objection. Most price objections are either phony, or the result of poor probing. However, that's another chapter. (2)

Finally, the inside rep is filling the time management requirement, and in most cases, favorably for buying influences. The selling company's sales expenses are also reduced, which in turn keep costs at their best ratio.

The question that might be asked, to demonstrate the value of telephone selling and the staff involved in making the medium a valuable tool for all business is, "who does business with whom?" For example, answer the following:

True or False

1.	Business conducts business with other business	T	F
2.	Business conducts business with people	T	F
3.	People conduct business with other people	T	F

Answers: 1 False; 2 False; 3 True.

And now you can see why we can't just put anybody on the phone communicating with our customers. We need well trained, highly skilled, deeply motivated staff for these assignments. That's why this work has been created. It's not that this medium or channel is less expensive, it's what our customers want.

What is a telemarketing sales manager and why are they different from other management types?

I suppose I can get into trouble with this analysis, but let me try anyway. An argument could be presented that the points I am trying to make are true for all managers. No matter what the function of the telemarketing resource is, or its objective, management people must spend an inordinate amount of time with their people. By that I mean it's constant hands-on management. It's not one of those functions where on Monday you say to your reps, "Okay, you got it? Good. I'll see you on Friday." It's monitoring, coaching, and counseling reps 40% to 65% of the time. It's motivating. It's being a parent. It's defending the unit and disciplining the staff. It's victory celebrations, and it's the agony of defeat. I have compared the entire function to the submarine Navy as compared to the regular Navy. It's a team and teamwork, within a controlled environment, all working together to make the system optimal. The function is intense, and can go down the wrong path quickly. It also can thrive on its own success.

Managers who spend over 50% of their time in meetings and not with their staff always have problems. I am reminded of my experience with my last employee assignment. I was hired as the telemarketing sales manager, also title "VP Sales." The company required I be in every key meeting they had, and the place was meeting crazed. In less than 90 days I was in big trouble. I could not impact the resource itself. The solution? Inside/Outside! I hired my best friend from my previous assignment, and cut a deal. I handled the company; he handled the telephone sales department. I told him not to attend any staff meetings. I would present our needs, translate meeting agendas into objectives for the department, and stay out of his way. He could manage the unit 100% of the time. This inside/outside managing partnership blew sales budgets and meaningful compensation objectives clean out of the water.

Simply stated, telemarketing is a people business. It's not an operation, and it's not a process. It's people. And, when we forget that, trouble is not far behind. Telemarketing managers are highly skilled people managers, handling a variety of functions, e.g., customer service, sales, etc.

I asked my good friend, Dick Fisk at Seton Company (a highly successful business to business catalog marketing firm in Branford, CT), "What makes your telemarketing operation successful?" His response was, "Three important points. The manager, the manager, the manager." We concur. The managers are human resource, sales management specialists.

Why Call The Function Inside Sales?

This is more of an explanation of why we don't call it telesales, telemarketing, or "tele" anything. Please keep in mind, that using the telephone is only how we do it, not what we do. Basically, what you do when using the phone to communicate is how your function should be described. Thus, these functions come to mind, and are reasonable descriptions for departments or functions:

- **Inside Sales**
- Customer Service
- Accounts Receivable Collections
- Marketing Research
- Credit
- Stockholder relations
- Order Entry
- Customer Relations
- National Accounts
- Government Relations
- Tech service/sales

There is no need to call your reps tele-anything. The titles of the decade are Product Consultant, Service Consultant, plus all the standards, i.e., Client Service Rep, Account Manager, Account Executive, and believe it or not, no designation at all.

Chapter 1 -- Yesterday, Today and Tomorrow

Your Business Structure ... "Where Does It Fit?"

The answer can be a book by itself, but there are a few pointers to keep in mind.

1. If the function has anything to do with revenue generation, either on an inbound or outbound basis, it needs to report to a sales executive on the highest level of your line staff chart, but,

- Not to the Distribution Managers,
- Not to the Finance Director,
- Not to the marketing executive (unless no sales executive exists),
- Not to the credit manager,
- Not to a part-time manager (one who has several other areas of accountability),
- Not to the Customer Service Manager,
- Not to the Direct Mail Manager,
- Not to the Vice President of Manufacturing.

2. If you don't have a sales executive, the function should report to the CEO of that function, division, branch, etc. If it is a non-sales function, then wherever the reporting relationship works best.

3. Spans of control are extremely important. How many people can one manage, (reporting directly) before one starts to lose control, or impacts results unfavorably?

- Inbound, 12 to 15 representatives
- Outbound, 7 to 9 representatives

After an organization expands into three teams of eight proactive inside sales reps, or 45 reactive inbound reps, you'll need a supervisor for each team. The same is true with supervisors, no more than eight under one manager. Span of control is one of those items that doesn't seem like a big deal, but it really is.

You might ask why? It is because the requirement is that as a manager/supervisor, you will want to spend a minimum of 40 to 65% of your time doing people things. It's the people that make or break your career, not the tasks or objectives.

4. Location is important. Centralization, as much as possible, is a positive factor. But, keeping the unit out of harm's way is also paramount. Thus, where is the best place to locate a resource? Where it will **work** best is the answer. You do not need to be at the headquarters location or in a large call center city. Phone lines go everywhere, and data can go anywhere. Distraction for this function can have a killer influence.

15

Because people are what makes this thing work, locate where you can obtain the best staff with a good work ethic, and who are career minded. Incidentally, the above reason is why service bureau organizations have moved to the mid-West, from the East Coast. Conversely, in Tucson, Arizona it's hard to maintain staff levels. There, the population that applies for these assignments appears to be on the move, in other words, transient. Tucson apparently is one of the stopping points before the reps move on to something else.

The nature of a sales activity may be somewhat distracting and that is why it's generally not located inside another department's space. It's distraction in reverse. Those of you who still have plenty of room to expand will find that the function starts to resemble a company within a company. Please see Figures 1.5 and 1.6 to show both ends of the spectrum. This is yet another reason to be proficient in human resource skills, because it can resemble a company within a company.

5. If you decide to locate the activity away from the headquarters/main office, etc., you tend to take the group away from the total picture (the action at headquarters), causing a potential recognition void. Knowing that this feature can be a problem directs you to the answer to the problem. Insure that the perception of isolation is kept at a minimum.

Positions; Are They Careers?

I know of no other field that has as many rapid growth opportunities as this one does. That can be both a blessing and a nightmare. Let me review:

- Telemarketing or center directors, managers, supervisors, and representatives are in great demand. There is not, and will not be an over-supply of these human assets for decades. Good ones can practically name their price. Most have been in their assignment under three years.
- The good reps who are achievers and like what they do, are promoted so fast, that they know little of all other work experience topics. That too can be a nightmare. It's not unlike the old joke; "Yesterday I couldn't spell consultant! Today I are one!"

I am reminded of my first assignment with Dun & Bradstreet in May 1962. I started as a Country Business Information Reporter at age 27. The top manager in my office was 56. He had moved eight times with the company, and held ten different positions to get to his current title. Today you can start in an inside sales function and if you show promise, jump into the top slot they have in three years or less. Management seasoning is just not reasonable in that short period of time.

As companies become more comfortable with the medium itself, and recognize its true contribution, they pay more and more for the assignments. On average, in the past five years incomes have jumped at close to 50% a year from where they were. More on that later.

The Future: "Looking Good"

I am the eternal optimist and do not have a pessimistic bone in my body. I always see the future as rosy. For the most part, the medium, channel of distribution, and profession has arrived, and is being accepted by the North American business community as the way to go. Technology, attitude, and global interests all lend themselves to this function. But again, there appears to be one pitfall, and that is the less-than-full understanding about the people side of this business. When we master the people topic, we can say, "Look out Japan, North America, and European Common Market, we are just a phone call away."

Figure 1.5

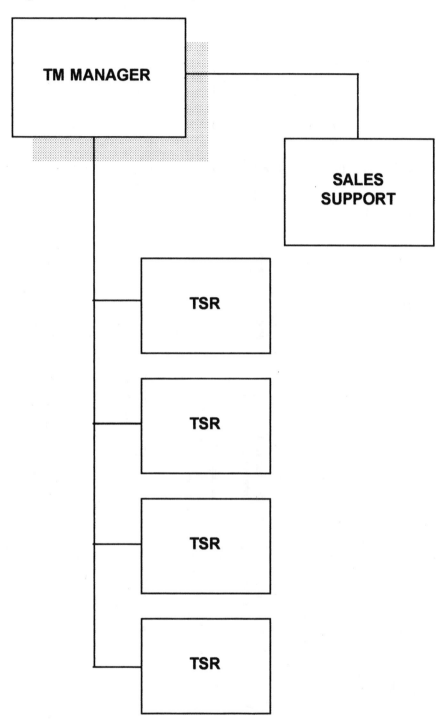

BASIC START-UP TELEMARKETING

FGI030598

Figure 1.6

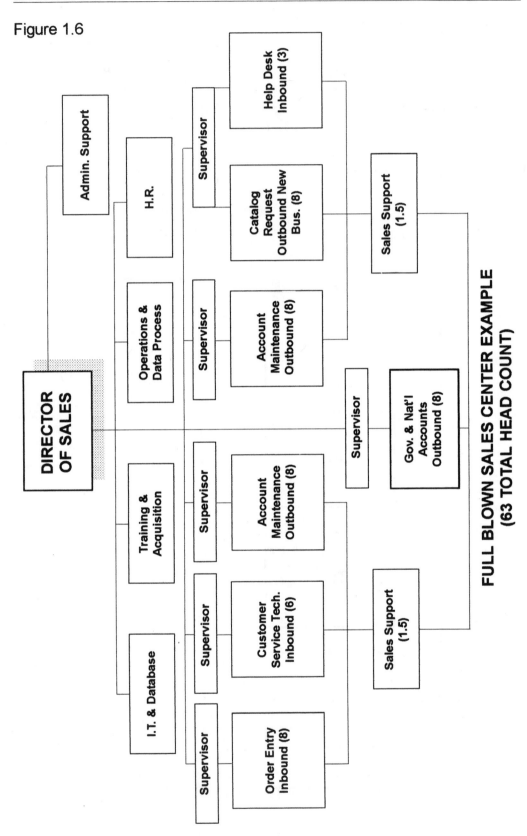

FULL BLOWN SALES CENTER EXAMPLE
(63 TOTAL HEAD COUNT)

CHAPTER 2

Telephone Sales and Its Risks

Introduction -- "Your Place or Mine?"

The title of the chapter itself begs two questions before one can make the decision to start, or further develop an inside sales department.

The first question is the ever popular 5 W's: what, where, why, when, and who, and then how. The second question is, "Should we outsource* or do it ourselves". Outsourcing is emotional to some, and is really hard to do in some cases, but it is an important consideration.

Believe it or not, these are very complicated questions, especially so for the sales center organization just getting started. The financial risks for staff and company are paramount with a new sales center. Failure for a five-person team can cost upwards of $180,000, hard cash, in a one-year period. There are several pitfalls for the organization that can be avoided assuming we know what to avoid. I'll list those later in this chapter.

---

* Programs handled by service contractors acting on your behalf.

67% Failure Rate For Start-ups!

Over a twelve-year period of publishing *The Van Vechten Report*, an inside sales management report, careful statistics were kept on subscription cancellations. Each year we lost about 15% of the total paid subscription base. The management report was entirely sold via the telephone, to a business-to-business clientele. When a cancellation request was received, one of our phone sales people, a Product Consultant, would call and attempt to reinstate/resell the subscription. Here are some of the interesting statistics gathered from that effort:

One-Year Cancellation Statistics for The Van Vechten Report

☎ Average length of subscription terms	2 years
☎ Cancellations for the year	135
☎ Trading area: entire US, 5% International	
☎ Average cost of of subscription	$204 US
☎ Number of subscriptions (two year) canceled	15
☎ Number of subscriptions (one year) canceled	120
☎ Number of subscriptions saved because of change in management and resold to new manager, etc.	15
☎ Reasons stated for cancellation	
● Too expensive, non-applicable, outsourced telesales	20
● No longer functioning, discontinued telephone sales, "didn't work," failed, etc.	100

Conclusion: Telephone Sales Department Start-up failure rate
(100 ÷ 150) = 67%

This data repeated itself over the twelve year life of the publication. The reasons for failure appeared to be repetitive year after year, and suggested that start-ups are indeed risky.

Nine Reasons for Failure

1) No Real Objective or Plan

Management literally asked several members of the staff (when they weren't busy with other duties) to, "make some calls and drum-up some business." Often these people were reactive, customer service types, or inbound order entry staff. They did not know their call objectives, and had no training. They had no ability to measure the results against the expenses. There was no consistent effort. They were not well managed. They died a slow and unnatural death.

2) No Manager

This effort requires 100% of a sales manager's job. The investment in staff takes a consistent 40% of the manager's time (if not more), in monitoring, and literally keeping the staff on the phones. Part-time management is a disaster here. Murphy's Law, rules: "If anything can go wrong, it will."

3) Sales Channel Conflict

Anytime another sales channel is a part of the selling process, a chance for major conflict arises. Direct Mail Managers don't want incentives paid to Inside Sales reps for sales that the mail normally brings in anyway. Field Sales Management and their sales teams are notoriously suspicious of a new telephone sales operation. They often feel that the accounts for the new sales team once belonged to them. Why the suspicion, you might ask. The answer is, because the existing compensation culture may change, and most likely will. How this change will affect Field Sales Management compensation, and upward mobility, may make them look bad. Of course it all depends on your perspective. A politically strong Field Sales organization can literally bury a new inside sales group if it feels threatened. Naturally that will become a major problem. Trust me on this point.

4) The Eternal Challenge

The entire company will continually ask, "Is this really worthwhile? Wouldn't we have gotten this business anyway?" For whatever reasons, as soon as one of the reps is seen not on the phone (for any reason), you will be challenged as to the true benefits of your endeavor. The need for a control group must be a part of your plan. A control group answers the questions of real worth. It compares telephone selling activities/mission(s) in a defined cell to **no** telephone sales activities in a similar cell. This shows the true incremental gain, and value. However, if you can't track your effort, then you're dead-in-the-water anyway.

5) Call those 2,000 accounts

Of course it depends on the mission(s) of your sales resource, but if it's an account maintenance program (penetrating the customer base), then only 400 of these accounts (20%) will get any serious attention. The rest of the accounts tend to fend for themselves. Not recognizing that this task highly mirrors a field sales task is going to be a problem with your planning. In addition, maintaining 2,000 accounts is absolutely impossible. A better condition is 350 to 500 accounts.

6) Staffing Mistakes

Not all reps can make outbound calls consistently, and/or effectively. One of the biggest mistakes made by management is to promote customer service reps handling inbound calls to outbound sales assignments. It hardly ever works, and is the cause of great stress to the promoted reps. The behavior styles needed for the positions (outbound vs. inbound) can be in conflict. Expressive persuasive styles are required, as opposed to the amiable styles which literally dislike proactive behavior, but who enjoy being reactive.

7) Sales and Phone Techniques Training

These are just plain non-existent. Product training may happen, but little if any skills training on selling or phone technique occurs. Remember, we are talking to our customers, not the walls! I hate to say it, but even less training occurs on the so-called follow-up instruction. That is a disaster waiting to happen.

8) Management

There is none or it's part-time. You might as well kiss the program off to *win a few lose a few.*

9) The Opportunities

If one can get out of the mind-set that this is a stand-alone marketing tool, one will have already taken a very large step towards a successful venture. The best and most singularly successful case examples of telephone sales, are the ones that have, or have had, a continuing relationship with a customer. An active or inactive customer, a prospect, a request for information such as catalogs and samples, or inquiries and a very carefully planned lead generation program, are all highly productive opportunities. What does not work well is the pure cold call program. It's just too expensive, and the results are almost always minimal. The cold call program is hard on the reps (resulting in turnover) as well as on the recipients of these calls. Your customers don't like it either.

All of the above opportunities, in tandem with other channels, or even on a stand-alone basis, can and do work well for your new and improved sales program. Who should run the show is another good question. We see problems galore when the sales unit reports to other than a sales executive, i.e., the Operations Manager, the Customer Service Manager, even the Marketing Manager. If it is a selling assignment, the function should report to the senior sales executive at that site. If no one is available, then the top manager at the site or location will do. Problem solving and arbitration are the rules of the day with newly planned units, and a top manager is needed for their influence.

A word of caution: Do not have one lonely inside sales rep reporting to the branch sales manager at a satellite location. That person will end-up as an administrative staffer, and will not be able to sell a free product sample in a room full of buyers.

Here is a case in point: Several years ago a 3M Visual-Aids corporate product manager asked me to assist with the development of a telesales force. One rep was planned for each district sales office, which at that time consisted of over 30 field offices. Politics required that the rep be left in the control of the field sales branch manager at that site, in other words, one rep per office. I politely refused the assignment, but gave the appropriate warning: "When this goes down, it will go down in flames and quickly." It lasted less than nine months. The staff product manager lost his assignment, and the reps went back to whatever they did, or were discharged. It was sad for sure.

All of the above combined makes the 67% failure rate an almost sure thing, and that's the bad news. In fact, any one of the above reasons can cause the demise of an entire program.

The good news though, is, "If it's thought out, and well-planned, the benefits are enormous to the using company."

Central Facilities Make Sense

The prior case example would have worked well and would not have violated the field sales territory culture and control at all if it had been located at a centralized resource. There are economies of scale when the organization is centralized. In addition, reps are with peers, not at the bottom of the office pecking order. We are aware of a sales facility -- and a big one at that -- at Lanier in Atlanta, GA that is a positive case-in-point. The Lanier people sell a large amount of office equipment and ancillary supplies over the phones in tandem with their field sales organization. This is a major operation, on the scale of tens of millions of dollars.

There are at least 75 reps on the sales phones. They compete with each other, and they are geographically assigned to their respective sales districts. They serve the customer, and are a part of the total sales team. They make their enhanced objectives yearly, and without fail. It's selling and teamwork in motion. Curiously enough, they don't think of themselves as telemarketers. They think of themselves as sales people. Inside sales people.

They call their customer base. No cold calls. They also have a specialized unit led by qualified field sales reps, who directly sell the office equipment for which Lanier is famous. No sales channel conflict here; inside sales is partnered with its field counterparts. Both teams are rewarded for reaching the assigned objectives and both teams attend national sales meetings. And, to the best of my knowledge, they don't call it tele-anything.

Opportunities in a Nutshell

If a company starts a unit with the major objective being to save money, a problem will quickly occur.

A business that is cutting away field sales representatives and replacing them in one fashion or another with mail and telephone sales campaigns has lost sight of the business objective.

The objective should be quite simple. ***Partner with the customer, serve the customer, fulfill the customer's needs, and make the customer feel we are there for him.*** That's not only good selling, that's good customer service.

When we say that it doesn't make sense to have a field rep personally call on a small $500-a-year account that calls us anyway when they need something, it's true. But, it's not totally the expense thing we are talking about. The field reps, if they have any brains at all, will work from the largest account down. If there is any time left over, they will work the lower end of the account structure or search for new business. It's easy to see who gets the short end of the stick: the smaller customer. The correct way is, service and sell them on a proactive basis, fulfill their needs, and do it on the telephone.

Case in Point

I asked Revere Chemical & Maintenance Products Company in Solon, Ohio, to define a smaller account. They described it as one who had ordered under $50 in the previous quarter. The inference was that they will mail to the account once in a while, but that's it. I asked to see an Nth* factor selection of names fitting the criteria of "small accounts." Lo and behold, there were big company names laced throughout the list. One of them was Westinghouse, 6900 Elmwood Ave., Philadelphia, Pennsylvania. They had ordered Miracle Seal (a roof patch kit) for $30. This turbine manufacturing division had acres of buildings, parking lots for thousands of employees, and should have been a prime target for Revere. It wasn't targeted under the current definition of "small account."

The end result was that they were called by the inside rep, and after reasonable effort, turned the account into a $9,000 per-quarter customer. And it was all based on an intelligent inside sales calling program. The program was simple. The call plan determined;

- In addition to yourself, who else makes decisions on products like we (Revere) sell?
- How big are you? (Size questions.)
- What else can you use? (Need questions.) Then ...
- Start closing on the discovered needs.
  It wasn't all that complicated, was it?

* Nth, a random sampling technique, i.e., select every tenth name.

28

The Management Position(s) as a Career

There isn't a week that goes by that I am not asked to refer a management candidate to someone. What were $35,000 positions 10 years ago are now $75,000 positions. Additionally, the managers stay in touch with me as well. If their company does not have the perceived appropriate opportunity, then they are going to move to a company that does have the opportunity.

These career fields appear to be fast tracked as well. Achievers can move quite quickly up the so-called management ranks. This opportunity is both good news, and bad news. Many have not had the opportunity to truly learn their managing skills. They are great on the phone, but may not have a clue on how to manage others. This is a people intensive business. The HR (Human Resources) side of this is paramount. In fact, that is the entire assignment, managing sales people.

What separates these management fields appears to be function. The *Sales Manager*, has always been very well compensated, and commands a lot of respect. The *Call Center Operations Manager* is a mix of management talents, but selling may not be one of them. Both areas are lucrative with reference to compensation. The most highly rewarded one I know of had a mix of the above required skills, and commanded $200,000 yearly, with a $100,000 signing bonus, and a $70,000 incentive program for reaching the assigned targets/objectives. The organization, a worldwide banking influence out of the UK wanted to make a major impact on the US banking market, and apparently money was not an objection.

The difference between the two functions is obviously the size of the facility and whether it was inbound or outbound driven, as well as the overall process. Here are examples:

- Operations Manager, American Express Corporate Customer Service Center, Salt Lake City, Utah. This was mostly an inbound call activity. Required there was an in-depth knowledge of telecommunication equipment, hardware, software, call distribution, and management of the administrative staff. No real proactive sales accountability was needed, although the function may have had some reactive sales results. Big talents were required on managing the process and the operation.

- Director of Inside Sales, Times Mirror Training Group (TMTG). This person has operations people reporting to him/her, but is primarily graded on the maintenance of existing accounts (no bleeding of revenue), and incremental revenue gains. The function is considered as a profit center, and the manager/director understands selling completely. The manager usually comes from a career selling field. Compensation is based on profitability of the program, not just expense management. He/she is not necessarily measured on calls handled, but calls made, and revenue generated. This is a Vice President level position at TMTG.

Other interesting facts about these career fields are that management positions are 60% populated by women, and depending on the calling assignment, 65% plus are in the sales management positions themselves. Here, "equal pay for equal results" is a hallmark.

NOTES –

Outsourcing -- Pro and Con

Outsourcing may be defined as having your business function -- one that was previously performed by employees -- performed by others. Examples are customer service, order entry, etc., and they are done for a defined fee or cost. The American business community has recently welcomed the opportunity to outsource entire departments/functions to very sophisticated Service Bureau Organizations or Customer Service Providers (SBOs or CSPs). One reason is because risk is acceptable, and costs are equal to, or less than, the existing departmental expense. The issue, more often then not, is employee head count, and run-away employee benefit expenses. Second, the ability to take advantage of technology advances, without capital investment, is a given. Finally, the benefit of downsizing via outsourcing, when and where necessary, without fear of repercussion (unions, employees, government, etc.), is also exciting.

In many cases the contracted servicing agency can do the job better. What you want accomplished, is really their business *specialty*, as opposed to having just another department in your company. The SBO can fill in gaps by moving staff to the appropriate project on an as-needed basis. There usually is a cost benefit passed directly to you, the customer. The same is true with computers, software, and phone charges. It is less expensive, and the savings can be passed along to the customer.

The largest benefit, of course, goes to the customer, and that's what it is all about. It's not about saving dollars, or head count, or any other perceived company benefit. It's about lifetime customer relationships. All other benefits are great, but should be considered as "in addition to", not the main benefit.

One can get SBOs and CSPs to compete for your business quite easily. The main objective is well-treated, happy and ongoing customer relationships. If they fail, they are easier to replace than customers.

Words of Advice

With all of the aforementioned being said and believed, there are some rules of thumb to guide you through this important decision. Remember, these people are going to have direct contact with your customers.

1. Task-type activities are suitable for outsourcing. These tasks are usually repetitive in nature.

2. Product knowledge, especially if it is in-depth and complicated, requires a more complicated solution, which may be prohibitive. For example, engineering scenarios, products and application responses to and for the end-user (the customer/prospect) require a massive database of FAQs (frequently asked questions).

3. Some applications and responses can be mounted in computerized response-software answers, i.e., "4 oz. of glue for your Better Bilt glue gun is $17.00 per cartridge." A screen pop-up here can increase your average order.

4. Insist that the staff handling your application at the SBO is your staff, and not working on 50 other projects at the same time. Of course, there is some wiggle-room here, but be careful not to over-extend.

5. Ask the SBO for clear evidences of excellent hiring practices, and the ability to handle major training programs with reasonable facilities. This is important.

6. You have the ability to monitor, offsite, at will, and ...

7. You have full-time staff monitoring the program 100% of the time.

8. Your application is tested side-by-side with your onsite results, in depth and appears seamless.

9. The task is most certainly suitable for outsourcing if it's an inbound application.

10. Also appropriate, are seasonal applications, i.e., holiday cataloguers, horticulture products, etc.

Remember, this handbook is mostly about selling... units that sell, proactive, outbound, etc. In my mind, very few applications fit outsourced opportunities for a selling discipline, i.e., blitzes, proactive customer service, etc.

☎ If the nature of your business is campaign or blitz based, outsourcing is possible.

    Example: "Mr. Vee you ordered promotional pens last year. I've called to see if we can re-run your order on a two for one offer."

                        "Maxell HD Disks are on sale this week at a 35% discount. You have ordered them before, how many boxes do you want today?"

☎ Lead qualification routines make sense as well, but only if it is an ongoing task as opposed to occasional.

☎ Customer satisfaction surveys, ongoing.

☎ List cleansing routines, ongoing.

Words of Warning

The more creative the task the more risky outsourcing is. Non-scripted, outbound sales calls, with major probing sequences are creative tasks. Anything to do with identifying needs and multiple call closing sequences are very difficult, or near impossible to outsource.

Account maintenance programs where the customer has a personal rep who represents the entire resources of your company are very difficult or near impossible to outsource. Park Seed of Greenwood, South Carolina conducted research with its customer base. The answer to what customers wanted most was to not have their sales reps churned/changed, etc. Changing reps proved to be deadly to customer lifetime values. Outsourcing cannot effectively deal with this concern. However, inbound, seasonal order entry programs may be entertained for outsourcing.

Rep and Management Profiles

Profiles are fairly easy to review. The answer comes with some bias from your author. There are none! Everything works to one degree or another.

There used to be profiles for everything, but I believe that they may have been politically motivated. Let's review some tongue-in-cheek, albeit real, examples.

☎ You can't sell skyscrapers over the phone. Well, yes you can. I helped to do it, and in fact, $200 million dollars worth. Did I actually close the order? No. Did I find a need, and the decision-maker via the telephone? Yes. Can you get the president of AT&T on the telephone and talk to him about buying a building? You sure can!

☎ You can't sell big ticket, highly technical products over the telephone. Yes you can. I did it with $1,680,000 dollars worth of IBM mainframe software to Phillips Corporation, NV, Holland. Did I take the close/order and get the signature? No. Did I talk to the decision-maker, the corporate controller? Yes. Did I create the interest? Yes. Did he buy? Yes. Ten phone calls later and three onsite visits, and it was a done deal. All within six weeks.

Remember that this is a synergistic medium. Stand-alone, or as a part of the total selling process, both are OK. To try and say, "Oh no you don't, that was not sold over the telephone" is ludicrous. Any line of business and size of business has the opportunity to use the telephone as an effective selling tool either in total or in part.

Representatives and Managers at one time were perceived to be the transients of the work force. Their motto seemed to be, "I'll do this until I can get a real job".

That is not so prevalent anymore. Reps and managers do tend to be younger, with men and women alike equally populating the field. The good-old-boys club is not prevalent here either. Compensation levels are less than field sales units in many cases. However, that's natural. Compensation depends on the degree of difficulty, and field sales is more complicated, as well as physically difficult. Travel, and limited time for decision-maker contacts has made this selling medium very expensive. McGraw Hill reported that the average sales call cost over $250 per presentation in the early 1990's. It must be over $350 now.

Surveys taken in the late 90's suggest that both managers and inside sales reps are now well-educated, and choosing this career field, as opposed to backing into it. Rep incomes are traditionally incentivized, and in the US have risen to median levels of $38,000 as of the turn of the century. Of course, the product, profitability, and market place have a great impact on incomes. Your financials will tell you how much to compensate. Both the hiring and compensation chapters will give you the step-by-step data that you will need to create and support a realistic inside sales program, as well as the compensation requirements.

The TM Manager is the Last to Know

If that is the case, it is a big mistake. This position always needs to be on the front-end of the sales planning cycle. ALWAYS! Unfortunately, the medium is occasionally treated like it's a manufacturing process. How many times have you been notified that your 800 number has been placed in a space ad the day before the ad impacted your sales unit? Or, "We need six of your reps to call our coffee customers and find out if they are still using the Binford 200 brewing system. Today". That's a matter of, "Get in line and take a number".

I am reminded of a disaster that took place in New York, for AMR International, a business seminar firm. The Chairman of the Board asked the VP of Sales and Marketing (me) for telemarketing support, for a new seminar called *Conflict Resolution*. On average we were enjoying three sales a day per rep, with 62 reps, valued at $450 a unit, for a variety of products. Mr. White wanted two seminars filled with attendees (locations, San Francisco and Chicago) for the new product presentation. I turned the entire sales team loose on the objective. Immediately our call-to-close ratio depreciated, from one close per four presentations, to one close per 15 presentations, over a two-month period. We filled his new seminar at both locations with 45 attendees each. However, we missed our monthly sales budget two months in a row by $175,000 for each month. That impacted our sales budgets, commissions, and bonuses negatively, and created one upset sales department. If I had known further in advance, I would have been able to do both assignments well. So, here is an example of the cost of being the last to know.

Under-utilization

It goes without saying that the units I have had the opportunity to work with are grossly under-utilized. The biggest problem is the database. The Park Seed Wholesale example fits perfectly as an example here.

Seasonal in nature, seeds, plants, etc., can only be ordered at one specific time, for planting at another specific time. Their reps would call and say, "It's time to place your seed order," and that was as far as the call would go.

They never asked or recorded into the database the size of business, what else they do, or who they buy from. Once the program was shifted, and the data entered into the database, two benefits jumped to the forefront immediately.

☎ They started selling hard goods like greenhouses, and cross-sold everything else... plants to seed buyers, seeds to plant buyers, etc.

☎ Promotions designed for specific prospects could now be designed for profiled prospects and customers, as opposed to mailing and calling the entire database. Big savings, as well as enhanced incremental revenues are now realized.

The Three Main Requirements Needed for Success

This is simple, the manager, the manager, the manager. If you have a manager who knows his or her stuff, and you give that person the tools to get the job done, success is guaranteed. They are the ones that create job satisfaction, sales, and profits. A lot of things can be compromised, but your manager is the key to your success.

CHAPTER 3
Now Here is More to Think About!

Worldwide Telemarketing

U.S. marketers who stay on top of their medium via the business press are now receiving a variety of materials proclaiming the virtues of international telemarketing. *DM News, TeleProfessional,* and others provide a continuous flow of information from a variety of sources, and it is readily available for the conscientious manager.

I believe it's a widely accepted fact that the US is a more mature telemarketing market than the rest of the world, thus driving technology and marketing methods to the edge of the envelope. However, the rest of the world is not far behind. The truth of the matter is that the US has tested many concepts, some good, some not so good. That will save others from time-wasting mistakes, both on marketing methods and technology. One thing is for certain: phone expenses, not unlike computer costs, have been coming down, literally on a day-to-day basis. The only element needed to be successful for telephone selling these days is the phone itself. The business culture now accepts the premise that telephone selling is just fine. Of course, the privacy issue still needs to be sorted out, but privacy issues are more of a consumer concern than a business concern. Business has been using the telephone in commerce nearly since its' invention.

Why is this important? Service centers in Ireland call the US all the time for one project or another. Centers in the Caribbean are taking inbound calls for banking institutions on a regular basis. I have had a host of calls from advertising sales people with a variety of magazines, as well as conference presenters serving the European economy, all originating in Europe.

I predict that international business soon will use the phone intensively to conduct business on a fairly routine basis.

The world is a smaller place, and communications tools have helped to make it so. Why can't I buy my Jaguar from the plant in England? What is wrong with securing my business furniture directly from Denmark? Why can't the Germans be sold their chips over the telephone from the Silicon Valley? Global telephone selling is coming. In fact is here right now. It's just seamless, so you don't know it.

Holland, France, Ireland, the UK (and a host of others) are actively courting US businesses, especially those using the catalog medium. They want to enlist your organization in a cradle-to-grave service that allows you to hit the ground running with everything from transportation, finance, tariff recognition and, of course, marketing. That includes call centers. That is impressive. And when the governments participate in the hunt, it's even more impressive. The telephone can assist in creating instant demand, and it is an environmentally clean activity. Who wouldn't want to have a 500-position call center in their country?

What Can Be Sold Over the Telephone?

Most likely this question is not properly structured, or, it's not the real question. Americans tend to want to put issues in a black or white discussion. I suggest that the telephone can do anything if it is handled properly. The real question is, "How can the cost-of-sales be impacted favorably through the sophisticated use of telecommunications?" That sounds academic, doesn't it? Throughout this writing, I use case examples to demonstrate that literally everything and anything can be impacted, even sold directly, via the phone.

The issue is how we formerly marketed, versus how we can, and should, conduct our marketing tomorrow. There are some cultural issues that need to be dealt with, but that's about it. Here is an example of the biggest cultural issue.

Traditionally, the world's goods and services have been sold via one of two methods. We come to you, or you come to us. It was a point of sales issue. We come to you includes the mail and the ever popular field sales representative. Sears, Roebuck Company is reported to be the first cataloger of consequence in the late 1800's, and of course shop owners and other local business have been in place forever.

Now, enter the traveling sales representative. This person was the driver of all growing industry. The best claw hammer in the world is worthless unless someone sells or buys it.

Over the years the territory concept developed. It resulted in the exclusive promise that all activity in a specific geography belonged to the hardworking field sales rep (FSR). The cost of field sales reps increased in a near geometric fashion, right up to the mid 1960's. Then came the energy crisis.

World recession and increased costs, literally changed the course of marketing forever. It's almost that simple. If you can't get to a customer by car, the alternative is that you call them on the telephone. It wasn't called telemarketing in those days. It was called using the phone a lot.

All that history, all that culture, and all the traditions of the field selling mechanism now come into play, when business recognizes that it must find a more effective, efficient way to reach and service its customers. This is when telephone selling enters the question, as does synergistic marketing. It may seem a long way around to get to the point but here it is.

The account structures, the prospects, even potential customers who purchase our product belong to the company, not the selling influences. Thus, if we wish to service our low end or marginal account structure via the phone, we the company can do so. Territories are for convenience of administration, not ownership by the marketing rep. If the business can be maintained at a lower cost-of-sales via the phone, then that's what we should do. And the real eye opener: if we don't, someone else will.

So, in order for you to determine what can be sold via the phone, you need to deal with the who, how, and when, by a variety of coordinated sales channels. Once that is determined you're home free, because anything and everything can be sold via the telephone. You will finally get away from who it belongs to and concentrate on the sale. And in turn the customer.

These are not simple issues to deal with. But the bottom line of the discussion is that it's a compensation and reward issue, that has been in place forever. It will selfishly resist change. That will be your challenge. As President Harry Truman said, "The buck stops here." That's your job. Make the decisions you need to make, or they will be made for you.

What else can you do?

This is a short topic. It's not what you can do, but how you plan to do it. Here is a list, with brief definitions, to make sure you understand the full spectrum.

- **Account maintenance:** The activity of assigning specific account structure, for the purposes of preventing loss of accounts to others, and to fully determine, via consultive probing questions, how all of your products or services fit into the established customer/vendor partnership.

  There is no limit on size of the account eligible for inside sales. It depends on mission and call objective.

  There is a limit to the number of accounts assigned, usually 325 to 500. You will find that this is all the rep can effectively handle.

- **Reactivation of inactive account structure:** The activity of determining what is inactive first, then developing a call strategy to bring the account back to active status. In most business, the definition of an inactive account is zero sales in any 12 consecutive month period.

- **Sample or information request evaluation:** The activity of determining the value and product application of an inquiry. If required, the follow-up for conversion to a customer or sale. The activity usually involves a full database building exercise. It is also where call, mail, call programs become highly effective.

- **Proactive marketing research:** The activity of gathering additional or special information to validate a marketing premise. Sales staff should not be used for this task, unless coordinated with a selling activity. It's often best to outsource activities like this if it's a larger project, and/or assign (usually) new staff to do the research call, if smaller in scope. Remember, never interfere with your revenue flow.

- **Order entry/customer service performance:** The activity of performing these tasks, usually reactive in nature, for your assigned accounts. Use of a decision table is advised. There is a need to determine if the activity should be handled by the proactive sales rep, or others. Remember, selling time is precious. Tasks are easier to delegate.
- **Competitive research:** Same as above.
- **Visit customers in the field:** Occasionally, it is a good idea, but to do so regularly it is not. This by the way, is becoming a trend with FSRs being encouraged to use the phone frequently.
- **National accounts, government accounts, specialty accounts:** The activity of having special teams handle special situations. This is advisable. These accounts and tasks normally have low calling volumes, but higher revenues. The result, or want, is enhanced selling efficiency via special representatives.

Finally, remember to isolate your risks, and enhance your sales victories. Don't make the mistake of experimenting with a productive sales force in motion. Quarantine the new application if you must, test, then move the call objective or mission into your regular sales production function.

Mission Statements and Philosophies

Most companies have mission statements. Not many have *philosophies*. Hardly any call centers have either. These aforementioned exercises are usually seen as useless, that when completed and posted conspicuously on the Company wall, are immediately forgotten. Quite frankly I suspect that is the case most of the time. No matter what you do in your business environment, you need a mission statement. A philosophy makes sense as well.

Simply stated, they are the foundation of your existence. Without them, problem solving is nearly impossible. If anyone has attended a problem solving, decision making, and goal setting course, they will find that the first task is to understand their mission. If none exists, create one. Without one, problems, decisions, and goal setting are extremely difficult.

For example, suppose your mission statement says, *To partner and service all Acme's customers at a reasonable profit*. A rep comes into your office and asks, "Boss, I have an account that wants to buy a large order at 3% margin, as opposed to our 23% margin. Can I tell him it's okay?"

You: "Nope, check your mission statement. It's 'reasonable profit,' not 'go-out-of-business' profit."

Or, with a different example, using the same mission:

Director of TM: "I know this sounds strange, but if we gave away the tape dispenser at cost, and sold the tape cartridges at a 300% margin factor, we would be in excellent shape to make our profit objectives."

VP of Marketing: "Makes sense to me. Your total cost will provide a more than reasonable profit. Go for it."

Your Department's Philosophy

In larger companies, fully 90% of the employees outside your department's direct influence haven't a clue as to what you do, or what telephone sales does. That's a problem, and a disaster waiting to happen. A philosophy will help you immensely. Especially if it's given to everyone who needs to understand what it is that you do. Please find below, an abridged article that I wrote for the industry press (7/30/90, *DM News*, New York). It should be helpful and still applies.

Does Your Firm Need A Philosophy?

The philosophy does not have to be complicated, and although it may appear to be cast in cement, it can be changed. Again, control is the issue. Telephone marketing is powerful. It is also expensive (second only to field selling expense when comparing cost per contact).

Do small companies need a philosophy? You bet! Do larger companies? There is no question about it. You might ask who should develop this philosophy. We suggest that a management representative of each interested area be asked to develop the philosophy. In other words, take ownership of the program. The minute that top management delegates this task to a support staffer, you're on the way to a fistful of trouble. Delegation comes after the philosophy is established. The philosophy should answer these questions, leading to the understanding of the medium. Thinking of what your department does:

- Whom will it serve?
- Whom do we want it to serve?
- What will it do?
- What type of mission is it expected to have or handle?

Furthermore, what are the risks and rewards relating to the answers suggested by this planning module? What will now come forth is a variety of MISSIONS. These missions will fall into two categories. They are:

1. Expense in nature, serving a company need, and ...
2. Revenue in nature, which speaks for itself.

Here are some examples:

Expense Missions
- Build a data bank
- Qualify leads
- Provide customer service

Revenue Missions
- Specific product campaign
- Marginal-account maintenance
- New business programs

> ***The Philosophy does not have to be complicated, and it can be changed.***

The benefits of all of the above are related to dollars: control of expenses, reduction of selling cost, enhancement of margins/profits and expansion of effort, and equally important, planning for the investment.

In establishing a philosophy, which in turn identifies missions, you have now taken control of a potential fire-breathing dragon. Don't kid yourself and don't make any bets on this. You, and your company, most likely are in a reactive environment as opposed to proactive control. We recommend that you gain control of this resource and enjoy this next decade. Establish a telemarketing inside selling philosophy.

43

Technology, Automation, People

This is a touchy subject. The finest technology in your database, telecommunications CTI systems, software, hardware, furniture, and facility are all worthless if you don't have the people to get the job done, or if they are unprepared to get the job done. It's just that simple, but equally as complicated.

The priorities of the call center should be, "What could we do for our people so that they can be all they can be." Of the above topics, what do they need to get the job completed? What will help? How can we give them the advantage when they are communicating, presenting, and selling to our customers? But equally important is, "How do we provide our customers with experiences that they want and enjoy?" What resources do we need for this to happen? Think about it, the answer never starts with a cost-cutting voice response system. It starts with people conducting business with people. Your investment must always have as its highest priority: your people and the customer/prospect.

CHAPTER 4
Management Concerns: Risks and Dangers

(Applies to U.S. readers only)

When one looks under the potential problem carpet, it is amazing what one finds. Along with the host of laws, regulations and variety of issues that impact business in general, one finds two specific emotional issues, in addition to the regular "quick-sand" issues. Common sense should prevail. More often than not, it doesn't.

Equal Employment Opportunity

I don't intend to rehash The Equal Employment Opportunity (EEO) regulations. However, they are important. Be aware that the data can be found elsewhere in great detail, (State and Federal regulatory offices). It's appropriate for you to gather that information for yourself, because states differ in their approach to the topic. One strong piece of advice: make sure your labor law posters are current, and hanging up where employees can see them in places such as break rooms.

Normally the key words here are "size of your organization" and whether or not you market to, or service, Federal, State, or Local Governmental Agencies. Size is defined by employee numbers, (i.e., over 100 employees) and you're under everyone's jurisdiction. You need to check if and where you are impacted. If you have over 100 employees, you most likely have a manager who stays on top of the issues. Ignorance of the law, as we all know, is no excuse.

Other than the above, there are two major issues of the day. They are the privacy issues, and the Federal Labor Standards Act, FLSA.

I use four sources of information containing well over 1000 pages, to address our needs on these topics. Interestingly enough, attorneys always advise to the letter of the law, as they should. Their objective is, "no risk." I try to stay away from the "legals" as long as I can. Here are the sources I recommend.

Reference Material

- The Fair Labor Standards Act
  Federal Publications Inc.
  1120 20th Street, N.W
  Washington, DC 20036
  About $90 (Published, 1998 and regularly updated)

- US Department of Labor
  Employment Standards Administration
  Wage & Hour Division
  Washington, DC 20210
  Ref. WH Publication #1363, (free for the asking).

- *The Complete Guide to Marketing and the Law*
  Prentice Hall
  Written by Robert J. Posh, Jr.
  Englewood Cliffs, NJ 07632
  ISBN: 0-13-160904-1
  About $65 (Published, 1998, and regularly updated)

- g. Neil Companies
  720 International Parkway
  P.O. Box 450939
  Sunrise, FL 33325
  State & Federal Labor Law posters (About $30 and regularly updated)

> *To show you how sensitive all of this is, it is imperative to say that I am providing this information with the understanding that neither the author (me) nor the publishers are engaged in rendering legal assistance. If assistance is required find yourself a competent professional.*
>
> *The American Bar Association and the Committee of Publishers and Associations say this will get me off the proverbial hook.*

FLSA, What is It?

Simply stated, the "Act" (Fair Labor Standards Act), sets standards for minimum wage, overtime pay, equal pay, the required record keeping, and child labor standards. And, it is not simply stated or understood.

Congress enacted the FLSA as a means for economic recovery from the Great Depression (1938). The act sought to ensure that covered employees were paid a minimum, livable wage.

Within the Act are two classifications, not covered and covered, (exempt or non-exempt). The Act is enforced by the U.S. Department of Labor, Employment Standards Administration, Wage and Hour Division, via scheduled audits, or based on employee complaints.

> *The vast number of employees, my guess is 99.9%, involved in the medium of telemarketing are considered as non-exempt (hourly) by these regulations. Second, the FLSA does not truly reflect the working situation as it exists today in a number of these areas. That is not likely to change.*

Why We Have a Problem

U.S. Senators, and people in Congress have told me that it is easier to enact a new law than to adjust or change a regulation. They are right.

Overall, the FLSA is on target and does what it is supposed to do. It protects the employee from unfair labor practices. As much as I would like to believe that fairness is not an issue, occasionally it is.

However our problem starts with definitions, followed by employer/employee perceptions, followed by good, or not so good, common sense. Let's start with the bad news first.

By brief definition, employees must be paid an hourly wage and all accrued overtime (more than 40 hours weekly) is paid at time-and-one-half.

All performers in our field are considered as clerical, non-administrative, task-oriented, production type people. They are not considered as professionals (doctors, lawyers, school teachers, etc.). Well, I think some of that applies and some of it doesn't. The biggest issue, however, is with outbound telemarketing sales people and customer service staff. That's a very large group of people. The number by some estimates is over five million employees. I think it's more like eight million.

Occasionally, the terms "blue collar," and "white collar," are tossed in the cooking-pot for additional emotion and confusion. The crux of the situation is, hourly is perceived to be less professional than salaried. This perception exists with employee candidates, employees, and employers alike, as well as salaried (exempt) employees who have no overtime expenses attached to their wage programs. No doubt, some management types view these positions positively because they get no overtime, and thus are desirable.

Under the "I want to be treated like them" syndrome, field selling representatives are non-exempt (not hourly). Why? Because they are away from the office, and not because they are considered as professionals. They lose their exemption if they spend more than 20% of their time involved with tasks at the office. In other words, if more than 20% of their time is at the office, they are considered as just another non-exempt employee and must be paid hourly.

There are exemptions for professionals, but mind you, terms like "intellectual," "learned," and "advanced types of knowledge" are used to describe professionals. The word "professional" has nothing to do with how we act, feel, or perform our assignments according to the FLSA.

Everything fits when comparing inside sales people to outside sales people, except nine words: "regularly engaged away from the employer's place of business."

Really, we have no choice. You can title them anyway you want. You can pay them as much as you want. It has no impact. These are hourly positions. And, if over-

49

time is an issue, it's 40 hours divided by their total weekly income. That includes prizes, commissions, bonuses... the works. So don't fight it. Call it salary, but compute the income hourly. You can be sure that these are still professional positions. And if overtime is required, you must pay it.

The real issue FLSA brings to the picture is cost and compliance. For instance, if you hold an offsite training session on the weekend, and it is mandatory, you could very well be in an overtime situation. The 40-hour week could very well be exceeded. Given this new understanding there most likely will be new costs to consider against return on investment.

Compliance, or lack of it, can become interesting as well as expensive. If you have what is considered a willful violation, you're going to be prosecuted in the Criminal Courts, with fines up to $10,000 for each occurrence. On the second time around, you can go to jail! In addition, if this is an employee claim, and it's determined that it is a willful violation, the Feds can go back three years and collect the underpaid compensation. Take heart though, it's only two years if it's just an oversight. And that goes for every employee found to be wronged in your entire company! It gets worse but I don't want to wreck your month. The best advice I can give you is simply to comply.

FLSA Case History -- Cooper Electric

In a recently tested case, (No. 90-5785) filed August 8, 1991, Cooper Electric Supply Co., Richard Cooper individually, and the National Association of Wholesaler Distributors and National Association of Electrical Distributors, agreed in principal to test the FLSA. They lost to the U. S. Department of Labor (USDL) on FLSA litigation. This was an appeal of a case that was lost earlier, on March 5, 1991.

Briefly, Cooper said their employees were exempt from the wage and hour guidelines, because they fit the test of administrative employees, with discretionary decision making capabilities for their exemption. The USDL successfully argued that they were not.

On the appeal, the judge reversed an opinion of the District Court, and further stated that not only will the back pay be paid, but liquidated damages would also be applied. In other words, this cost big dollars, usually the original fine times three.

A large key to this case, and why Cooper lost (in my opinion), was that they stated that the inside sales department's work "was of substantial importance". The USDA argued that these people were production people, as opposed to administrative types, which are occasionally exempted. In other words, non-exempt.

I have two opinions. First, the courts failed to recognize that without this unit's contribution, there would be no Cooper Electric. There was no other sales channel.

Second, and more important, the case should have been argued on the definition of professional, and how limited the current definition is, when compared to the classic definitions (doctors, lawyers, etc.).

The courts take the entire field of career sales and marketing and treat them as if they were routine tasks that anyone can do. As we have found, that's not necessarily the truth. The courts absolutely have no empathy for any other view of the position.

To my knowledge, no company of any importance has beaten the USDL on the FLSA issue(s). These cases are interpreted in black and white, with no empathy involved. The reported fine was negotiated down to $40,000 from some ludicrous amount for this small company. Unless the regulations are adjusted, you can't win. For a brief description of the FLSA regulations, tests, etc., write to the USDA, Employment Standards Administration, Wage & Hour Division, Washington, DC and ask for Publication WH 1363. Carefully read "Outside Sales Activities," page 9 of the booklet.

Monitoring of Service and Taping of Phone Presentations

Even as this is written, this section may go up in smoke if the U.S. Congress has its way. Even if it doesn't, the assault on management and their organizations will most likely continue. The issue is invasion of privacy. Because of the few, we all may suffer.

The objective here is to not allow others to interfere with your ability to manage your department. Second, to convince you that service monitoring has a big payback result, and that it is used as a training function only, and as a normal business practice. These are important words. Don't forget them. Finally, when service monitoring and taping are done properly, your team actually enjoys the process, as opposed to fighting the event. The issue is feedback. Our general discussion first.

In January 1987, Julie S. Crocker (then the Director of State Government Affairs for the DMA) wrote an article for *Telemarketing* Magazine titled *The Legality of Monitoring and Taping Calls*. The department was titled *Telemarketing Corpus Juris.*

Ms. Crocker accurately provided the background. It was the need to reach a high level of proficiency, and maintain that performance on a continuing basis. She noted that the best way to do this was to observe the call by listening to both sides of the conversation. Second, it was important to take notes and coach the employee to perform in the manner desired. Finally, the two methods available for use were monitoring of service and actual taping of the conversations for later use in the education of employees.

Ms. Crocker went on to explain that taping of calls fell under the jurisdiction of the Federal Communications Commission (FCC), and that in 1981, tariffs (rules) permitted taping, but only if an audible tone was heard, as in "beeping". Rules started to change to the degree that if both parties knew the call was being taped, it was okay and no tone or sound was needed.

Throughout all of this the FCC found that the rules were difficult -- if not impossible -- to enforce, and that generally, the rules were unworkable. States have rapidly adopted laws requesting both parties' consent to call recordings, but that appears to apply only to intrastate calls. In addition to all this, there is federal law, referred to as Title III of the Omnibus Crime Control and Safe Streets Act, 1968, that notes legality for call interception, or recording, as long as one (responsible party) has given consent, and/or knows that the call is being recorded.

According to Bob Posch, Jr., *The Complete Guide to Marketing and the Law*, the aforementioned act (Omnibus Crime Act) attempted to address the privacy issue in this fashion. If you are involved in a lawful and proper business activity, and you need to ensure proper behavior and method with reference to your employees conversations with customers, prospects, and suspects, as an "ordinary course of your business", there is no interception, as in "wire tapping", etc. The key is the wording "ordinary course of business". In my opinion, training staff is within the ordinary course of doing business.

He lists several test cases, and the issue was, "Were the employees' rights to reasonable privacy intercepted, by either taping, or service observation?" The answer was, no interception was involved, because the activity and the equipment were utilized in the "ordinary course of doing business", thus, a lawful and proper activity.

Then, in July of 1993, The Monitoring Bill proposed by Senator Paul Simon, (Bill S-948) was offered but was defeated. I am not sure which way this issue will eventually go, but I have sent my letters stating what a disaster this would be if passed. Please review Figure 4.1. *(See next page.)* I believe this letter covers the important points for you to consider. Also, you should keep those letters going to your federal officials.

Ms. Crocker, Mr. Posch, the industry, and I, agree that in managing to excellence these tools are needed, and that without them our collective lives will become difficult. Again, this is your call, but I just don't see how you will be able to manage without these basic tools. Here are rules to consider.

- The vast number of employees involved in the medium of telemarketing are considered as non-exempt (hourly) by these regulations. My guess is 99.9%! Second, the FLSA does not truly reflect the working situation as it exists today in a number of these areas. That is not likely to change. Unannounced service monitoring drives announced service monitoring. Never take formal action of any type based on unannounced monitoring activities.
- Announced service monitoring objectives need to be specific and during a planned period of time, i.e., "John, let's work on your introduction statements today. Here is how they are done, etc., etc. I'll be monitoring between 10:00 AM and 11:00 AM to see how you're doing, and then I'll review the training with you at 11:00 to 11:30 AM. You're scheduled for Tuesday the 15th. Any questions?"
- Completing an announced or planned monitoring session plus the corresponding coaching and feedback loop can drive a management requested taping session. This would allow the rep and the coaching manager to hear the lesson point or coaching issue as it actually occurred. To hear it yourself (the rep) is worth a thousand words.

We suggest having the reps tape themselves, as opposed to you handling the activity. That way any embarrassing situation can be removed, and thus a positive

Figure 4.1

Senator William Bradley
506 Hart Senate Office Building
Washington, DC 20510

Dear Senator Bradley:

I have a great deal of concern about Paul Simon's S-948 "The Monitoring Bill". I'm late in writing, I just didn't think it would go this far. After reading some industry press, DM News, I see there is reason to worry.

I've included my bio and firm history only to establish credentials as an industry expert. Also to note that I have offered to provide background information on the so-called areas of telemarketing and its issues to all of our elected (both Federal and State, New Jersey). I am disappointed that no one has ever sought my input on any issue as it relates to the above subject matter.

As is always the case there are two sides to every issue. I'm afraid Senator Simon does not truly understand the total issue. My position is this.

Yes, there has been some abuse, and the invasion of privacy thing, if truly an issue, can be satisfied to near every one's satisfaction, but not the way S-948 is written. Quality tele-marketing is important to the millions of representatives of this business and the 100,000 plus managers as well. The benefactor is the customer.

It is impossible to coach, council, train, and adjust rep performance from just hearing one side of the communication. For years I have advised my clients with methodology along these lines:

1. As a condition of employment employees must know their conversations can be monitored for educational purposes. (If that is unacceptable to them for any reason this may not be an assignment of interest.)

2. That certain identified phones were never monitored and could be used for private call purposes (reasonable use, of course, and according to company policy).

3. That unannounced monitoring could be used anytime to drive announced monitoring sessions and for no other purpose! And if the call appears to be personal, discontinue immediately, but advise the employee of the availability of the non-monitored phones.

4. Also, on a scheduled or pre-announced basis monitoring with a specific training objective could be and would be used for skills improvement purposes. All involved, the customers, the reps, the company, and the customer benefit from these planned skill improvement sessions.

5. That immediate feedback is given and a follow-up sessions planned to review the progress of the training objective.

Supervisors/management, with the rep have sessions that takes place daily in non-phone environments, feedback coaching is the activity. Field Sales Managers travel with their reps for the same purpose.

I'm fearful that we have run into the "baby and the bath water" situation. This is not a good statute nor will it be a good law.

May I count on your response to vote no? And, if you need help to write legislation that will be good for all concerned, I would be happy to help.

As the Co-Founder of the American Telemarketing Association (ATA) and a believer in self-regulation, I agree we need laws to bring into line the real offenders (a clear definition). The industry, on its own, will do just fine. We don't need anymore mindless business

---

restrictions at this date. With 280,000 businesses discontinuing each year for one reason or another we just don't need to drive another nail in that coffin. It's tough out here in the business world Senator. Let's concentrate on helping businesses ... not hindering them.

Respectfully,

Lee R. Van Vechten

LRV:tlv
Enc: Bio/Fm. History
   DM News Article

training session can be accomplished.

We have two forms that can be used during the hiring process that addresses the issue of headsets, taping, and service monitoring. See Chapter 6, Figure 6.11 and 6.12. If the candidate has an objection to our training methods, and/or preconditions, this is not the job for them.

Closing Comments

You will need to be sensitive on these issues, and maybe even assertive. It really comes down to managing without interference. I find it curious that the proposed and existing laws impact you, but not the government. Check out the fine print on any IRS Form. They monitor and tape at will, and without permission. I will continue to recommend the aforementioned processes, but will tell clients to be very careful.

The ATA and the DMA stay on top of these issues on a day-to-day basis. It will serve you well to review the topic as laws are enacted that may not be supportive to your business mission. You may even wish to be heard. It may be a truism that the squeaky wheel gets the oil.

CHAPTER 5
Management Guidelines

"A Business Guideline for your Telephone Sales Manager."

Setting the Stage for You,
The Inside Sales Manager

It is helpful for the inside sales manager to review what is important for these assignments. The primary task is understanding and managing people. Five topics or groups of people come into play for the successful manager. They are:

- Those whom we manage
- Those who manage us
- Our peers
- Our customers
- Those who assist us, i.e., suppliers, consultants, friends, etc.

The investments for us are the human assets that we work and associate with, that help make things happen. These assignments are different from other individual assignments where the requirement is only to manage one's self. Some examples of those who manage one's self would be the artist, the designer, and the consultant. One should consider that the investment in self to ensure we understand how to work with others always pays a handsome dividend.

All other tasks, learned or needed, tend to support your effectiveness with the above primary tasks. Some of the business buzzwords used by managers are good examples.

- "He is an up-stroker." One who favorably massages relationships equal to or above one's business station or status.
- "She is a down-stroker." One who massages business relationships with subordinates.
- "Political skills," or company politics, refers to the learned skills that address the organization's culture, chemistry, and traditions; as well as the other "players" likes and dislikes, and the effect that they have on one's individual objectives or mission.

We all have heard of managers who either are tired, frustrated, disappointed and even unfulfilled, who say, "That's it! I am going to the Eastern Shore of Maryland and just rake clams in Chesapeake Bay. I'm tired of this rat race. I just want to deal with me." It's only my opinion, but I think that condition is the result of a lack of skill or understanding of the wide range of personalities, and behavior styles of the human resource assets around us. The expression, "No man is an island," says it all.

If you consider your assignment as a "people-understanding" assignment, as opposed to Customer Service, Sales, or Order Entry, you're better than halfway there. The whole psychological profiling world that uses the Myers-Briggs Type Indicators (personality profiling instruments) has a single objective. It's not whether you're introverted or extroverted, sensing or intuitive, thinking or feeling, judgmental or perceptive. It's really a plea for understanding and to be understood. If we feel comfortable with these understandings, we will manage effectively, with confidence, and even enjoy our assignments.

Who Develops A Management Guideline?

The answer is, you should have a lot to do with developing the guideline. If you are to take ownership of the input to the guideline, then the document must work hard for you.

We have developed guidelines for clients over the past 20 years that address specific needs. Many managers for these new assignments are coming from other management disciplines. They want to know what to expect, and how they should adjust or behave in their new environment.

The guidelines are a potpourri of other documents, i.e., job descriptions, company philosophies, mission statements, marketing plans, human resources, codes of ethics. They will often be subjective in nature, with some objectivity interjected.

A Management Guideline is not an end-all document, but a summary of what this assignment is all about. The document is not meant to be carved in granite, but can be changed or adjusted to fit specific needs. It is heavily oriented towards dealing with, and supporting, the human assets around us. I have provided an example for your review. In this case, it has been designed for a proactive selling management assignment. Please review the following multi-page example entitled Telephone Marketing Guidelines.

TELEPHONE MARKETING SALES MANAGEMENT GUIDELINES
FGI0199

I. INTRODUCTION

Telemarketing in a sales management environment is either a success or a failure depending on the management people that are assigned to the unit. Experience reveals that, like a Street Sales Organization, management gets what it asks for, and that is made possible by how you manage your unit.

These points are the keys to your success.

- Hiring and terminations.
- Training, both product, and telephone skills and sales techniques.
- Motivation via compensation, and recognition systems.
- Advancement opportunities for staff and yourself.
- Customer and competitive marketing research.
- Product line ability to support your sales unit's efforts.
- The technology of your profession.

Each item listed above is equally important.

II. KNOWN BENEFITS FROM THE MEDIUM TELEPHONE MARKETING (TM)

- TM is the only selling medium where the Inside Sales Rep (ISR) can be in direct contact with the customer on a highly frequent, economical basis, if required.
- Both the marketplace and the selling organizations are a great deal more comfortable with this selling medium at the end of the century than they were previously.
- Unlike direct mail, catalogs, and other print media, an outstanding opportunity is available for add-on services, enhanced cross selling, or order upgrading.
- TM is unmatched in its lead-time to generate positive cash flow. The turn of the century, with a variety of business revolutions, can use this outstanding benefit.
- Front-end marketing investments and lead times, causing risk, are reduced substantially.
- Double-hit programs, that is, programs of mail and phone combined, increase results dramatically for both mediums with reasonable investments. (Synergistic)
- Product or market testing is in the hundreds of calls or less, not thousands of company contacts. Compared to direct mail, where a

TELEPHONE MARKETING SALES MANAGEMENT GUIDELINES -- *continued*

test is 5,000 mailings, the time needed to learn about anything is short and immediate. It is not measured in months, as in the past. In fact 279 calls will do it.

- Marketing directions may be changed almost instantly, as opposed to taking months or years.
- TM protects erosion of business in a "down economy", and for that matter, in any economy.
- TM enhances the company image if run in a professional sales environment. The reverse is true if it is not operated professionally.
- TM and its sales activity are able to be computer linked for ease of information processing (the database, CTI, etc.).
- TM is a time management asset to sales organizations, allowing multiples of 3 to 5 times the "bang" for the invested marketing dollar. This is because of expanded decision-maker contacts per day.

III. TELEPHONE MARKETING OVERVIEW

Telephone Marketing (TM) is the skill and art of selling to needs. It is the process of:

- Managing the operation;
- Managing the process;
- Managing the people.

Telephone marketing is never a "boiler room" or "bucket shop" operation. It is an ethical selling unit, and any infraction of the ethical guidelines developed should have penalties that are severe -- such as dismissal. The Direct Marketing Association and the American Teleservices Association, both have Codes of Ethics by which all TM units can, and should, abide.

- The TM unit can be a Sales Production Unit. It has a self-generated urgency that most other sales units do not have. The sales reps are hard working, and need a balance of warm, human relations from their management.
- The TM unit is profitable, accountable, and measurable. It has both the fortune, and misfortune to operate continuously under management's eye. Be sensitive to this feature.
- TM has the ability and advantage of being statistically sound. It can forecast sales and expenses with a high degree of accuracy. A plus or minus 5.5% confidence factor is not unusual.
- TM units have the ability to make unbelievable market contacts.

TELEPHONE MARKETING SALES MANAGEMENT GUIDELINES -- *continued*

Three proactive TSRs, working five days a week, eight hours a day, 47 weeks a year, can make 12,000 to 15,000 outbound calls a year, providing 6,000 to 7,500 decision maker contacts. They can do this in a relaxed functional communication facility and neither snow, sleet, rain nor heat of the day will stop their progress. There is only one thing of note that can be detrimental to a TM/TS unit, "A day's effort lost, is a day lost; it can never be recovered."

IV. MANAGEMENT TECHNIQUES

A. *Managing the operation.* This requires that we identify the most promising customers and related prospects, within our Customer Companies. It does not pay to call a "cast of thousands" or "cold call".

- A decision will be made on the options we have for customer segmentation, based on the database information gathered. Our choices are:
  - by potential size (based on employee size, sales, etc.);
  - by current sales, or sales history;
  - by geography;
  - by line of business, size of business;
  - by category (present customers or past customers);
  - by type of offer (new product, special promotion, etc.);
  - by type of call (new, lead follow-up, cross-sell, penetration, etc.).

- You will need to set specific objectives for these calls on an on-going basis, they are:
  - Call-to-close ratios, and presentation-to-close ratios;
  - Number of attempted calls per day (dials) and ratios to the above;
  - Gross and net revenue per day, as well as returns, cancellations, and adjustments tracking.

- Design the sales presentation.
  - We will sell to *needs* rather than use the phone as a mass coverage vehicle. Staff training including new topics, as well as review topics, is important.

- Project Benefits and Cost
  - Benefits/Revenue Per 100 Calls, less cost per 100 calls equals gross operating profit.
  - Marketing expenses may be reduced for our customer mailings. We may not need the quantities once used.

TELEPHONE MARKETING SALES MANAGEMENT GUIDELINES -- *continued*

- Collect data that will tell us:
  - average sale by dollars;
  - how many sales per 100 calls (numbers);
  - how many net sales dollars per day, per representative;
  - how many gross sales dollars per 100 calls (before returns and adjustments);
  - results, when measuring the objectives to a control group, during and after testing.

- Costs: Telemarketing costs should not be bundled, or included in overhead costs for the entire company. They are to be considered as a stand-alone marketing, and/or sales cost, similar to Direct Mail Marketing, Telephone Marketing, or Field Sales expense. All department selling expenses apply, and should be uniquely tracked. What should occur, is what we call assignment of the full burden expenses to the TM cost. Expenses eligible for assignment to the TM unit are:
  - all salary of the unit and allocated salaries of other staff. (Optional: allocation of staff who contribute more than 33% of their time to assist the unit.);
  - bonus;
  - commissions;
  - FICA and company benefits;
  - rent, utilities;
  - phone, fax;
  - postage, express mail;
  - unique promotional support;
  - samples;
  - outside expenses uniquely purchased by or for the unit;
  - equipment, furniture, and fixtures;
  - T & E, Management;
  - contests and awards;
  - internal EDP charges;
  - miscellaneous;
  - all other *direct* expense.

The objective is to have our *Gross Operating Profits/Margins* measured in like fashion to other selling mediums. The objective is to be at least equal to, or better than, other selling media so that we can understand the true contribution.

TELEPHONE MARKETING SALES MANAGEMENT GUIDELINES -- *continued*

B. *Managing the process.* This has as its concern procedural topics. It is a map and plan of the department's activities, and who is accountable for what. It is at this level much of the company's interaction takes place, i.e., sales tickets to the accounting department, who does accounts receivable collections, who approves credit, etc.

- The design of the organization changes like the quarters of a moon. Change is healthy and is required in order to take advantage of market place opportunities. If this is a minimum start-up unit it will consist of:

  - 1 manager;
  - 3 ISRs;
  - 1 supportive fulfillment person.

The manager will review prepared job descriptions for each position to ensure they fit the existing business environment, which in turn ensures employee understanding.

In managing the *process* of the organization, you must remember these jobs are high-tension producers, and mentally strenuous in their nature. A high degree of *stress* is a part of the representatives (ISRs) daily routine. Street sales reps have travel time, lunch breaks, shopping time, autos and socializing with customers to relieve tension and stress. Not so with the ISR. They are selling all the time. And, management personnel are always on the premises. There is no place to hide or let down.

Management must be aware of these factors and manage accordingly.

Confinement is another issue. No matter how large and well appointed the TM physical installation is, the rep is basically confined. Having the ISR at his/her desk continuously causes problems quickly. It's called turnover/burnout, and/or poor results.

Another problem is *operating in the blind*. Information can be scarce. No face-to-face intelligence, no body language to work with is a hidden stress producer.

Because of the above we do not want the ISR involved in anything but selling. No tasks like:

1. telephone number look-ups;
2. mail handling, incoming or outgoing;
3. report tabulation tasks;
4. fulfillment of programs, like brochure X to customer Y;
5. billings, collections;
6. commission statements;

TELEPHONE MARKETING SALES MANAGEMENT GUIDELINES -- *continued*

7. claiming sales against the house, etc.

These tasks, and all other tasks of a similar nature, should be assigned to sales administrative support people. Let your sales staff maintain momentum/pace: Respect your best calling hours.

ISR CONTROL SYSTEM: You need to hold sales staff meetings at least weekly. It is imperative. At sales staff meetings you learn:

1. about the response to company products;
2. marketing intelligence, competitive efforts;
3. new methods to sell product, training adjustments (skills and product);
4. communication relief and release (a pressure and tension reducer);
5. how to give and take feedback from the ISR.

Remember, this is an instant response medium. If necessary, changes can and should be made quickly. Telemarketing sales activity software is desirable and provides big benefits.

Call Reports are necessary, and one should be designed for your staff. (If not already automated.)

Customer Records are for organization and time management. This document should be custom designed as well. The department needs product books with all pertinent competitive information. These must be maintained and posted weekly, if necessary.

The **Physical Facility** must never be in any condition less than outstanding. It must be clean, cheerful, well ventilated, appropriately lit, comfortable, and kept in a high state of maintenance. It must be located in such a manner that distraction to the reps is eliminated, or held to a minimum.

C. *Managing the staff.* The success of the operation, as previously mentioned, will be dependent on how well the staff is managed. The best designed, most successful installation with finest equipment and outstanding sales reps, will go for naught if the people are not well managed. This point cannot be overemphasized. No matter how outstanding the operation or process is, failure can, and most likely will result, if the sales staff is mismanaged. Sales management techniques begin at the top of the company's hierarchy, and filter down through the organization. Although this may

TELEPHONE MARKETING SALES MANAGEMENT GUIDELINES -- *continued*

seem obvious, one does not mistreat the goose that is laying the golden egg. The company must continue to be committed to this staff management function. Remember, you get what you *inspect,* not expect.

D. *Recruiting and selection* This is a mission-critical task, to be sure. A master profile for locating and hiring telephone sales representatives has not been found to date. But, here are common sense guidelines the manager can use:

- ◆ A good voice, easy and pleasant to listen to;
- ◆ Need for income means that the rep can be motivated by money;
- ◆ A reference check that shows good attendance and successful sales experience, plus achiever clues;
- ◆ The ability to organize work, as well as thinking the sales process through to its conclusion.

- Conducting initial interviews by telephone is a must.
  - ◆ It allows you to check "voice personality."
  - ◆ You will not be biased by physical characteristics.
  - ◆ If a newspaper Want Ad is used, have candidates paraphrase the ad, to ensure they understand the assignment offered, and as a check for real interest.

- Conduct your second interview in person.
  - ◆ Use the impact interview technique (See Chapter Six)
  - ◆ Don't be afraid of being mildly argumentative, it is a form of objection testing.
  - ◆ Do not talk about your company first. Have candidates talk about themselves first. Remember, they are the product and their resume is the brochure. The question for you will be, "Do you want to buy?"
  - ◆ Be honest with candidate. Let them know it's a tough job.

- Don't overlook the handicapped as a source of sales talent. Just make sure they can sell.
- Women do as well as men.
- Military background tends to be a plus. (Management training)
- College dropouts, who have at least completed their second year, are excellent candidates. They are motivated to succeed.

TELEPHONE MARKETING SALES MANAGEMENT GUIDELINES --
continued

V. SUPERVISION AND MOTIVATION

A manager's span of control is no more than nine ISRs in this outbound environment. This person should:

- have sales and phone expertise of some sort. (Empathy)
- be an excellent people manager. (Close working relationships.)
- be a leader. (Able to or not afraid to place calls as the reps do.
- be willing to spend a lot of time in training, coaching, and counseling (40% plus).

A. *Motivation of ISRs:* Managing a telemarketing operation is an exercise in recognition. An ISR sales team needs a lot of attention and tender, loving care (TLC). More than other types of sales organizations, this TLC recognition is required to offset the tension and pressure (even boredom) of the job.

- The primary motivation and recognition device you have is an exciting Compensation Plan.
- The second motivational technique is the use of *recognition*. Recognition takes a multitude of forms. Here are a few:
  - Verbal ... "Outstanding production today Mary. You must be eating telephone sales pills. Keep up the good work!!";
  - Letter from the VP of Sales or President, noting outstanding performance (Distribution to other top managers helps.);
  - Sales rep of the week, month, and quarter;
  - Night out on the town; vacations; exciting rewards;
  - Special note or memo paper;
  - Consistently published sales reports for inter- and intra-company recognition;
  - Friendly internal competitive contests;
  - Posting of daily sales results by the ISRs (themselves) on a sales "menu board".

- The third motivational technique is the planned career path, the belief that one can get ahead. A chance to be promoted. And a chance to earn the same recognition that you have, as well as a chance to feel good about one's self is a great motivator.

TELEPHONE MARKETING SALES MANAGEMENT GUIDELINES --
continued

VI. TRAINING THE SALES STAFF

You will find that there are four distinct training areas for your sales staff.

- product knowledge training
- procedures, and order or document processing (operational skills)
- selling skills and telephone techniques training (proficiency in sales software usage), planning call objectives, and customer behavior patterns
- team building

A point to remember is that selling skills used on the telephone are basically the same as the selling skills that a face-to-face sales person possesses. The difference is applying the skills in a blind environment (the telephone).

VII. UNDERSTANDING THE RESOURCE AND FACILITY

The manager must have a thorough working knowledge of the resource. They must know all the parts that make up the whole. Some of these areas are:

- Your phone system, ACD, PBX/switch, computer, software, etc.
- How marketing data may be retrieved from the database
- The details of any sister marketing effort
- The paperwork support area and trails
- All major functions within the division, i.e., what does Customer Service do, mailroom accountability, fulfillment activity, credit, etc.
- Company objectives, Mission and Philosophy
- Competitive awareness (an up-to-date file and related staff training)
- Well read on the topic of telemarketing, selling, customer service, etc.
- Computer and CTI literate

SUMMARY

It is all of the above that contribute to a successful, integrated sales and marketing investment. Finally, it is imperative that what happens in your shop is known by the rest of the senior management team. "Together, as partners" is the motto. As strange as it may seem, in the beginning there is the need to sell the concept internally as well as externally, and to continue to inform and educate all relative staff members, long before they ask.

☎   ☎   ☎

Managing Your Boss

If you have not yet figured this one out, life becomes unnecessarily difficult. The relationship involves mutual dependence, and is not the sole responsibility of the boss. Both should work hard at managing the relationship, and even if the boss doesn't, you should. Chapter Five of this book will go a long way in assisting you to understand the boss's behavior style, i.e., what are the likes and dislikes, and at least give you the opportunity to deal with any situation by being prepared to understand.

It makes a great deal of sense to understand the boss's world. The boss has goals and pressures, as well as strengths and weaknesses. Understanding this allows a fairly decent relationship to develop. The development of that relationship is critical to your success. Try to find answers to the below listed topics or questions. Incidentally, the best source is the boss.

- Personal objectives
- Organizational objectives
- Types of pressure the boss faces, short and long term
- What does the boss do best?
- Does the boss have blind spots, or is he/she short on skills, i.e., computer literacy?
- How does he/she like to relate, to work, to digest information, etc.?
- How does the boss deal with conflict?
- And, in general, turn-off's and turn-on's

I wouldn't say that the objective is to change the boss. It's more to have an understanding. It's not likely the boss will change to suit your management style or behavior. That is not to suggest you will change either, but you should try to adjust.

Remember, there is much to be learned, and skill (along with information) to be transferred. I can remember my first "big-time" manager while employed with Dun & Bradstreet. My impression was that he had the power of God. I was literally frightened to death of this individual. So many times I wanted to disagree with the man, but fearfully did not. Finally, and out of frustration, I said to the gentleman, "Boss, if I don't agree with you, and I think it is important to advise you of that, how do I do that, or don't I? Can you help me out?" Much to my surprise he noted that no one had ever asked him that question before. From that moment forward, we had a great relationship. And, at that point, he became my mentor and the key to my upward mobility while employed by Dun & Bradstreet.

No Surprises

The key to a fine relationship is no surprises. I can't think of a worse catastrophe than being involved with a situation, a problem, or an event, that impacted the boss's position, because you did not keep the boss informed. It is the cardinal sin of all junior managers, and so unnecessary.

Conclusion

This is a people business. Managing a variety of reporting relationships is the primary task. You're as good as your people are, and they are as good as you. We recommend reading, for more depth, a Harvard Business Review reprint, No. 80104, by John J. Gabarro and John P. Kotter, called Managing the Boss. I trust these guidelines will be helpful.

CHAPTER 6
Finding and Hiring Your Staff

Introduction

I am reminded of my second eight weeks of training in the U.S. Army, while "saving the world for democracy during peace time." I must have watched one too many movies featuring John Wayne, and for some reason enlisted, and asked to be assigned to a combat military specialty. Leave it to the Army, they sent me to Fort Sill, Oklahoma, to be a Weather Ballistics Meteorologist for the Artillery branch of that service.

Ft. Sill is also the leading rocket and missile training center in the world. The sign that was posted in front of every entrance to this military reservation read something like, *"You are entering the U.S. Army Artillery Military Reservation, Ft. Sill, Oklahoma. This is the largest artillery and missile training center in the world. Our motto is 'If it doesn't have it up front... it doesn't have it.'"* The motto says it all when you think about staffing, and who we want to put into these front line positions.

It makes absolutely no sense at all to put people into these positions that are not capable, reasonably well educated, great phone personalities, and able to think on their feet. In all cases these people will be communicating with your customers, and that makes them very important. It doesn't matter whether they are internal or external customers. What does matter is that the communication is in a blind environment. In other words, no body language is available to help with the communication process or call objective.

Experts will tell you that we have less than 21 seconds to establish a link between caller and callee. Expressions like, "You only have one chance to make a first impression" are appropriate. Perceptions of who we are, (the company as well as we, personally), are quickly formed by the one being called. What most managers don't understand is that these representatives *are the company*. Not employees of the company, but the company itself.

Given that Figure 1.4, Chapter One, notes that the inside representative is what the customer wants most, how can we not put the very best people into these positions?

Let me share with you a well-known quote that I think fits the situation nicely. The quotation describes the degree of difficulty for a lot, if not all, of these assignments. First let me set the scene.

The following quotation was reported to have been given at a follow-up meeting, immediately after a press conference during the worst days of the Vietnam War. For whatever reason, the original information was misinterpreted, and a SNAFU (a military acronym for a crude expression) occurred. Robert McCloskey's manager, Secretary of State Dean Rusk, advised him to straighten out the situation quickly, and here is how Mr. McCloskey opened the meeting.

"I know that you believe that you understood what you think I said, ... but I am not sure you realize that what you heard is not what I meant."

Robert McCloskey, State Department Spokesperson

In telephone sales, customer service, etc., misunderstandings happen all the time. I would agree that training is a part of the formula, but you must have something to work with first. You're as good as your people. If you put less than the best on your phones, then you and your company will be perceived as less than the best.

NOTES –

A Variety of Staff Needs Will Govern Your Hiring Process

For years I have used a practiced and successful methodology to locate, talk to, and hire inside sales managers and their representatives. A conservative estimate is that I have assisted organizations in their search for over 500 managers, and at least 5,000 representatives, specifically in the proactive sales area. The latest statistic we have is that where my firm participated in the hiring process for management, we missed three times, and we lost only 25% of all the reps during the first 28 months that we measured. Of the 25% that did not continue in the assignment, half were terminated for a variety of reasons, and the other half were promoted or changed assignments of their own volition, or left the company with positive references. I tell you this because that track record speaks for itself, and demonstrates a reasonable methodology that can be used with an excellent payback.

This is not to suggest that different staff positions or assignments can, and will, require adjustment of the methodology. For an example, do you need to hire differently, or use the same method when seeking inbound order entry staff (reactive) as you do when you are after outbound proactive sales people? The answer is no, but nearly the same, with some adjustments.

The difference between part-time and full-time, and even between highly scripted vs. consultive communication styles, will dictate what you will or will not use. Again, this chapter could be a book in its own right. To simplify matters, the more complicated or more difficult the assignment is perceived to be, the more of this method we would recommend that you use. My opinion on job difficulty is listed below, with the more difficult first.

Degree of Difficulty

1. Proactive, outbound, selling business-to-business
2. Proactive, outbound research and lead qualification
3. Customer Service, inbound and outbound
4. Credit and collections, inbound and outbound
5. Tech service, inbound (Answer Center)
6. Order Entry, inbound
7. Anything formally scripted to include outbound business-to-consumer

Not only is this a list denoting degree of difficulty, but as you will see in our compensation chapter, it also impacts types and amounts of compensation. Thus, the more difficult the assignment, the better the reward system.

General Points to Keep in Mind

Job posting is okay, and in my opinion, should be done. However, please remember that an important element of selection is securing the appropriate behavior style. Each of the aforementioned positions seems to function better if staffed with an employee that has a specific behavior style that is suited to the assignment. In general, reactive or inbound assignments work better with amiable or analytical behavior styles, and proactive or outbound work assignments are better with expressive, persuasive, driver behavior styles. For an in-depth review of behavior styles, see *Chapter Eight, Behavior Systems*. Nothing is absolute of course, but the following experience example demonstrates the situation to be avoided.

Over the years many clients have asked me the following questions.

"Why won't my Customer Service people make outbound sales calls during the off-peak time from their regular inbound assignment?"

"We are going to promote staff from our inbound or reactive area, to the outbound staff or project. Will it work?"

And finally, "Our outbound effort is faltering, why?"

The answer, more often than not, is that they have staffed the wrong behavior styles in these positions. Incidentally, the reverse is also true. Proactive or extroverted styles really don't enjoy tons of detail, and are not as service-oriented as "amiables," who like to help, like to listen, etc. Think this one through. It can save you a ton of time and money, and prevent migraine headaches or worse.

The manager/rep relationship carries a lot of weight. Reps are underfoot all the time. There is no place to hide. If there is anything that is annoying, distracting, or not quite right, don't consider or don't hire that candidate. With this in mind, let me take you through a sensitive area. You will need to clear, convince, or even demand of your HR department or senior management that you be permitted to run the process as I am suggesting. Having others hire for you is a death wish.

When we get involved in someone else's domain we are viewed as stepping on their turf. The entire hiring process may be in the hands of your human resource personnel department. These people are specialists, especially in the EEO area, and want to keep it that way. Thus, be sensitive to their accountabilities, and the situation in general. They, of course, can be of great help.

Here is a rule of thumb: The "report to" must be involved in 90% of the hiring task, literally everything but placing the ad. This is one area where delegation of the task doesn't pay. This is a selection, and, if you will, a marriage process. The objective is to find staff that you can personally work with. The relationship between employees and their direct supervisor/managers is a critical part of the success formula.

Next, (and this will be controversial) you do not need a cast of thousands interviewing your candidates. When multiple interviewing takes place, all you are doing is saying, "I really don't know what I am doing. I need someone to share the risk in case this hire misfires."

Understand that once the rep is on the phone, it won't take more than three weeks to know if they will survive in your sales assignment. So don't prolong the agony needlessly. Additionally, you should remember that good people are not in the job market for long. A long, multiple-interview process does not help (especially as it pertains to selling staff). More on this later.

Finally, and I believe this to be the most important point to remember, is that no matter if this is a selling position or not, the candidate, from the time they submit their resume up to the in-person interview, is in a selling mode. Thus, they are selling you on their capabilities for your position. The product presented is themselves. How they present the product (by letter, by phone, or in person), is how they will present themselves to your customers. Forcing them to participate in an "acted-out" situation or "sell me this coffee mug" routine is ludicrous. We can assume they know themselves very well. If they can't present themselves, then how can they work with your objectives/products/call missions?

A brochure usually goes hand-in-hand when selling a product or service. The same thing happens with the hiring routine. The resume/letter is the brochure. The point is, that you would not buy from a sloppy brochure, and the same is true for the resume used by the candidate. Neat, clean, and brief is the rule of thumb. Before we present the step-by-step process, we will review what needs to be addressed right up front: the human resource policies for inside sales departments. The following section takes the format of a White Paper, an in-depth discussion on a specific topic or issue. It might be helpful to present this to your senior executive in order that you may influence your HR policies.

Position Paper On the Topic of Human Resource Policies for Inside Sales Departments

"Is there a difference in policy when applied to the reasonably new environment of telephone selling?"

Inside Sales Departments

Introduction: In my years of consulting experience with a variety of clients, in a variety of businesses, one topic is always open for discussion. "Should we treat these people differently with reference to every day employee policies, or should we insist that one size fits all employees in our company?" Why is there a question in the first place?

Call centers, with a variety of missions and objectives, tend to be staffed with task-defined employees. They are also non-exempt in their FLSA status, which may also be defined as non-professional staff who are paid hourly, and who are eligible for overtime compensation should they work more than 40 hours a week.

Many companies have call centers that satisfy a variety of requirements or missions. The call centers are both inbound (calls coming in) and outbound (calls going out of the company). A few examples:

- Customer Service
- Order Entry
- Reservation Centers
- Customer, Company, employee information providers
- Marketing Research
- Account receivable (collection)
- **Outbound sales**

It's the last category that is so different from all the rest. It's the only category that's not task driven. It requires counselor or consultative selling skills, techniques, and activities. It also requires reps to make discretionary decisions. Hardly ever is this group reacting to a customer inquiry, unless something they have said creates immediate interest. It is this group's responsibility to develop interest, and/or maintain interest as it relates to new business and what is most commonly called account maintenance of existing account structure. Only one other group of employees can be compared to proactive call center sales staff, and that is a field selling organization. In practice and in theory, they are proactive in their call mission behavior styles as well.

All of the aforementioned assignments, except for field sales and inside telephone sales, are task driven. Tasks that are often described as repetitive, and relate heavily to the operations side of the business.

77

Sales jobs tend to have risks attached to them. Management is quick to respond to a non-performing field sales rep. Literally, if they don't make their numbers/objectives as planned, they are released. This is because the selling medium is very expensive. In fact, when comparing all mediums used, field selling is most expensive, and inside sales is next. Productivity is the rule.

In most cases, the company wants sales reps who can keep the customer happy, bring in new business, prevent loss of business, and who also are able to get their fair market share with the account, as it relates to the products and services offered.

The reason to question whether there a difference i.e., sales types vs. all other employee categories, is that we suspect that there is a difference. Many companies are not sure where that difference is. Thus, many organizations lump the selling call center with all other call center activities. And, unfortunately for the company and specifically sales management, the result is one size fits all, in policy and practice.

Human resources, the HR Department, performs valuable services to the company and make no mistake about it. The entire area resembles a minefield, given the employee/employer responsibilities to each other. In addition, government regulations, laws, and preferred employee practices are added to the mix. It's very easy to lose a proverbial foot here, and preventive maintenance is the HR rule of the day. The fear is massive and expensive lawsuits, judgments, and punitive awards, coupled with a damaged company reputation. In one sense, the hard-pressed manager is begging to be allowed to manage without interference. This expression is often used for those who wish to be union free. What is the organization to do?

There is a Solution

In more progressive companies, HR policy and departments are in fact walking away from "one size fits all." They (HR) are responding to their company's needs, by determining what the operating problems are, what will be good for the company and the employee, and providing guidelines that are suitable to meet everyone's needs. Where most companies get into trouble is the employee's expectation level, and equally important, total management training as it relates to the policy, and implementation of that policy. Here is a crude but frequently referred-to case example.

The Facts

A sales employee has gone through six employee performance appraisals over a three year period. The evaluation of this employee was "Acceptable performance."

The supervisor treats the performance appraisal as a task, and one to do quickly. Subjective evaluation vs. objective evaluation appears to be the bulk of the document. Then, the rep starts to miss work, misses sales objectives, develops an attitude problem, and in turn is dismissed after a 30-day notice. The employee takes legal action and wins the case, and is awarded three-times back pay for punitive damages, and the chance to go back and reclaim the assignment, which she/he does.

Given our previous comments, one can see the manager's needs, and employee expectation level, most certainly did not match. Traditionally, what happens here is that the probation periods become longer, and HR steps in to ensure the operating manager is within the defined policy. Which leads us back to the gray area of the policy for sales departments or "one size fits all."

Is HR Policy Different for Field Sales Organizations?

Apparently it is different. Why is there an interest in comparing field and inside sales? The major reason is the thinking "different strokes for different folks". Thus, if our assignment is to sell, and the only difference is the market segment (size of customer/prospect) to be worked, then selling is selling, and never the twain shall meet. Thus, why should we have two HR policies?

I believe we should, and further note that sales managers in the field appear to be able to separate their non-performing sales representatives much easier than their counterparts in the selling call center. Then what or where is the problem?

We suspect that the company, under the tons of regulations and compliance scenarios, sees one scenario that drives this non-compatible thinking. It's the FLSA (Fair Labor Standards Act). The U.S. Department of Labor, Wage and Hour Division enforces this act. This is the entire discussion of who is exempt, and who is not exempt, based on these regulations. Thus, inside sales people are considered as non-exempt, and outside sales people are considered as exempt (no ifs, ands or buts). What is not understood is that Field Sales Representatives lose their exempt status when they spend more than 20% of their time in the office doing clerical or repetitive tasks. They are not exempted because they are considered as professional but because they are away from the office, which makes the regulations impossible to monitor.

The above being said, we have observed that many organizations exempt their inside sales people, as they do their field sales people. This action puts the company at great risk, i.e., fines, awards, even jail, for each occurrence of non-compliance.

HR logic tends to then follow the path of, "If they are not exempted, they (the employees) must be like our other hourly employees, and thus the one size fits all HR policy applies".

Quite frankly, that's wrong, and that is where the real problem lies. We do need H.R. guidelines, but they should, in fact, deal with the issue. The issue is simply this. No matter how skilled you are in your hiring practices, the best condition that exists for successful hiring is 50/50. Organizations who hire sales representatives, either inside or out, and who enjoy a better hiring success ratio, are indeed rare. Following this logic, one needs to remove the non-performers as quickly as one can. One does not need an HR standard to complicate this management operating priority. We need standards that respond quickly to the uniqueness of the assignment.

What Do Others Do?

First, the problem. If inside sales staff, including reps, supervisors and managers are not meeting their sales objectives, which are clearly defined and relate to specific periods of time, then we need to have guidelines to move on them quickly, and to replace them with staff who will meet these goals and objectives. More on this later.

We researched three firms. One was a major car rental firm, one a business-to-business manufacturer (no field sales reps) who is a catalog direct marketer, and one large battery/lighting device manufacturer (one of the big three). They also have Field Sales Reps, and sell to distributors. All asked not to be identified, which in turn suggests the sensitivity of the topic. All companies had 300 or more employees, and 20 plus proactive inside sales representatives. All three had traditional call centers servicing a variety of company needs.

All three have a distinct set of sales, HR guidelines that are similar to, but different from standard HR guidelines. All three deal with the issue of non-performing inside sales reps, supervisors, and managers. All dealt with educating the staff prior to acceptance of the position, insofar as to what the criteria were, and the risk/rewards of the position.

These were some of the policy features in all three situations.

- All were non-exempt, but paid salary computed by the hour. Executive time logs were kept, and all members, exempt and non-exempt, signed in, in one fashion or another.

- All had policies for time-off for non-business events, sickness, etc. No employee was docked if late, tardy, or for leaving early. These situations were considered as management issues, and fed into the frequent performance appraisal programs. The staff knew that abuse of these programs quickly led to non-sales assignments, and/or discharge. This was a staff expectation.

- All treated the first 30 to 90 days as casual employees, in other words, probation. A mismatch would allow removal from the second week on.

- All managers could terminate sales employees within any 30-day period. Assessments occur weekly.

- All supervisors and managers were trained in performance appraisal tasks, policies, coaching, counseling, feedback loops, monitoring, being consistent, etc.

- All reviewed job descriptions frequently, and reps were encouraged to participate in job description maintenance, to ensure performance appraisals would be on the money.

- Because sales reps usually enjoy the opportunity for larger incomes they were constantly reacquainted with these department policy positions which were biased towards performers/achievers. Reasonable risks were a part of the assignment, i.e., no sales, no assignment.

All of the above works well because of management's commitment to monitoring for performance and provide immediate feedback to the staff. Assistance is provided where needed. Thus, performance appraisals were taking place on a daily basis, and no less than weekly.

Conclusion

The sales department and HR responsibilities can take a proactive position in these matters. They don't have to run scared from their respective staffs. Apparently explanation of the department's expectations early on, solves most of the HR perceived problems. Training the management staff to work with their staff covers the remainder of the problem.

Recommendations

Your company should develop a distinct and unique set of HR policies and guidelines that are both fair to the inside sales employee, and to their management team. Keep in mind all employees involved in sales activities may not be able to sell. Thus, the managers and supervisors are empowered to release employees quickly, based on objective data, i.e., sales results and monitoring sessions. When compared to other employees, i.e., operations staff (C/S, reservations, etc.) the policy may appear different, and even aggressive. The sales department's emphasis will be on how we can help you to do it better, and if you can't, you're gone.

Furthermore, that employee expectation levels, as well as employee candidate expectation levels are met from the very first interview, right on through to their day-to-day performance. They know and understand that, "that's the way it is". No surprises, and knowing this, is very similar to being an athlete. If you can't play the game, you're off the team.

* Author's note: The above White Paper is used frequently with clients who perceive that they need a review/change in HR policy as it relates to inside sales departments.

The Job Descriptions

Occasionally, we really go to extremes with job descriptions. We either get carried away, or one doesn't exist at all. And more often than not, these documents are out-dated. Job descriptions need to be living documents. What they don't need to be, is a policy handout. Leave that for the "Employee Operation & Policy Handbook." That's the manual that covers vacations, holidays, benefits, etc. The job description describes the job.

Curiously enough, we often confuse for whom the job description is written. It's not written for the job classification and compensation people. Granted they use the document for their purposes, and that's another reason to keep it updated. It is written to eliminate any confusion as to what the job entails. All other purposes are secondary.

I would agree that it also has another purpose. If the job is accurately described in the first place, it prevents employee misunderstandings should they occur later on. Not truly understanding what the job is all about can result in terminations, resignations, broken promises/dreams, turnover, etc. Also, if you have a document that clearly describes the job, it can be used as the foundation for performance appraisals, and if needed, the documentation for corrective action, recognition, and/or separations. It is an important document.

Job descriptions are briefly written, in a communicative style, easy to understand, and are receipted. By that I mean, signed by the applicant/employee. The signature denotes an agreement that they understand what the position entails. There is room for a feedback loop here as in asking the employee to tell you what they think the job entails.

Job descriptions answer the following seven points of interest.

1. What is a brief description of the job?
2. What are the general objectives?
3. Who does the employee directly report to?
4. What are the specific accountabilities?
5. A general description of a typical day or workweek.
6. Other secondary, but important duties or concepts (or both).
7. Where additional information may be found on this assignment.

Topics like experience and education requirements are really a function of your selection process, and don't need to be in the description. Compensation specifics are found in the compensation plan. Please review Figure 6.1 for the job description(s) we use when working with our clients. The example given is specifically designed for a proactive, outbound, inside sales representative. However, it can be used for Customer Service reps, inbound sales reps, part-time employees, etc., with slight adjustments. I have also provided examples of a Sales Support Staff, and a Manager/Supervisor job description, (See Figures 6.1, 6.2 and 6.3 for your examples).

82

Figure 6.1

JOB DESCRIPTION INSIDE SALES REPRESENTATIVE
NON-EXEMPT

I.   This position is a proactive selling assignment. Your objectives will be to call prospects and customers for the below reasons:

   • To establish or reestablish the vendor/customer relationship by calling active or inactive accounts.
   • To determine product and service needs for both new and ongoing accounts.
   • To introduce and upgrade new products to these accounts, via needs satisfaction routines.
   • To entrench our position with these accounts, by maintaining the relationship that will serve the needs of both the customer and our company, by using our products and services.

II. The overall objective is to sell/market the assigned product lines at a targeted cost of sales, on a national basis, through this central selling resource in your territory.

III. This position reports to the Inside Sales Manager

IV. This position has the accountability to maintain department records on a daily basis. This data, numerical in nature, will provide self-management guidelines and records for the department's management evaluation purposes. The data collected measures the day's effort, both by amount of effort, and results of the effort.
   The current record keeping devices are:
   • The Daily Call Report, and the Customer Call Diary (the record of the effort).
   • The Customer Account permanent file (the history/database)
   • The Customer Call Card (the sales activity record)

   Records and data are primarily maintained in the departmental database, along with some hand-prepared documents.

Figure 6.1 (continued)

V.   Duties/Training: from time-to-time, service and sales monitoring/taping of calls will occur for training purposes, but only on a pre-announced basis.

- Be available for training as it relates to telemarketing sales skills and techniques, and product knowledge.
- Wearing a headset is mandatory, and is both for your health and well being and rep productivity.

VI.   This position will endeavor to make a consistent effort, using the telephone. Effort is defined by calling objectives.

- Attempted calls per day   60
- Completed presentations per day   30
- Sales units per day   4
- Average dollar volume per sale/per day   TBD*

*To be determined. Goals, by dollars and numbers, will be set daily, weekly, and monthly by your Manager and yourself.

VII.   This position also will have a testing concept as its mission. Sales and marketing information (by service/product, by section of geography, by ISR) is important to the success of this unit.

         The objective, simply stated, is to market nationally, from a central location, the assigned product lines, at a reasonable cost of sales. More importantly, it is to provide a value-added service to our clients.

VIII.   Neither the above, nor the compensation plan should be construed as a contract for employment. Specific compensation arrangements are listed in your "Comp-Plan".

Acknowledged

_____   _____
Manager   Inside Sales Rep

                                             _____
- Copy to ISR, Copy to File   Date

Figure 6.2

Job Description Sales/Service Administrator
Inside Sales Department

Creation date: (Current date)

Review date: Six to Nine Months

Title: Sales/Service Administrator, Exempt, Non-task

Description: This position fills a specific need, but can and should have two other organizational objectives.

I. Primary Objective: Support of the inside sales manager/ISR sales staff and coordinating service requirement activities for customers and prospects.

II. Secondary Objective: Support the "SERVICE" call programs for the department.

III. Third Objective: This is a training position that eventually leads to an Inside Selling assignment (career path).

Duties and Qualifications:
1. Keyboard skills (accuracy is preferred over speed)
   - Simple word processing skills
   - Reasonable math/statistical/numerical/reporting/presentation skills
   - Ability to handle and enjoy working for a department, as opposed to one supervisor/manager/representative
   - Good proactive phone personality
   - Organizational skills for self and others
   - A desire to career path into Inside Selling Assignments.

2. Are generally the same as in entry level inside sales, however, no sales experience is required. That will be provided by "on-the-job-training."
3. Use discretionary, self-managing activities to guide your daily performance. Therefore, this is a non-task assignment. You are considered as departmental support staff.
4. Compensation and recognition systems are available from your compensation plan.

Figure 6.3

Job Description Manager, Inside Sales

Creation Date: On Approval

Review Date: Six to nine months, then yearly on employment anniversary

Job Title: Manager, Inside Sales, an exempt position

Calling Card Title: Inside Sales Manager

Position Reports to: Vice President, Sales

Accountability: This position has full accountability for the net sales and call objectives set by Management. These accountabilities and objectives, after the initial six months of operation, are to be reviewed by Management, keeping in mind the overall profit and growth targets set for your department.

These objectives will then become the active and measurable budgets, goals, and targets that determine the gross operating profits/margins for this Inside Sales Department. Upon the settling down of these start-up activities, this data will control all other operating budgets. As for example:

- Compensation input for ISRs, supervisors, and support staff
- Marketing investments for and by the department
- Staffing recommendations, including both existing, as well as expansion opportunities
- Phone/telecommunications; software, EDP needs
- Postage, Express Mail, UPS, samples, etc.
- And, other selling expense categories that are tracked to this unit, and considered as a direct expense.
- Shared overhead expense with other departments is a negotiated item.

Compensation: The compensation plan for this position is set and approved by Management (after approval via standard Corporate practices). Compensation is a combination of base salary and rewards, commensurate with experience and performance. Bonuses are available monthly, quarterly and end of year. Additional compensation details are described in the current Manager's Compensation Plan.

**IMPORTANT**: The manager must be employed by the company at the end of any bonus period in order to be eligible for payment of the award(s) for the period covered by the specific bonus.

Responsibilities:

- Staffing, hiring, and terminations, as described by current company personnel policies. Discretionary decision making is a part of this assignment.
- Training of staff, new, and exiting
- Ethics of the Department and maintenance of the Company's marketplace position. (Reputation)
- The overall adequacy of the phone systems, software, and hardware as it relates to the Inside Sales department.
- Net sales of the department/group
- Expenses of the department/group
- Inter and intra department harmonious relationships on a favorable basis, and the same for all communications.
- Persistent search for marketing intelligence as it relates to company products and the competition, as well as improved marketing techniques and tactics for this department.
- Maintenance of competitive marketplace information, and dissemination of this information to the sales organization and the company.
- Continual review of ISR compensation plans to insure their effectiveness, i.e., motivational and relational to other corporate units.
- Cancellation/returns, controls, and objectives
- Selling only quality business contracts and services as opposed to "Maybe" business.
- Recommendation of tools necessary to support the inside selling resource, i.e., promotional tools or intra-marketing department support (brochures, letters, etc.)
- Handling of specific major accounts already in existence (as required)
- Providing accurate counsel and guidance on all marketing activities to Senior Management, including Marketing Management. Also loyal and dedicated support to all marketing/sales programs for the entire company.
- Maintenance of all reports and records of the department, and their interpretation to both Senior Management and representatives.
- Providing adequate selling support recommendations for the department. Specifically, as these activities relate to Customer Service activities and Administrative support.

Figure 6.3 (continued)

- Publication of results and achievements of the department on a timely basis, i.e., weekly, monthly, etc., to all who have a need to know.
- Attend sales meetings and all other meetings
- Specific attention to a coordinated relationship with Customer Service/Credit, Field Sales, distribution, order entry, collections, etc.
- Establishing the department's mission, and insuring that it agrees with the company's overall mission statement and inside sales philosophy.

This position __does not have responsibility for__:

- Collection of bad debts: Credit will be approved by the Credit Department or Credit Policy. Collection activities are via the accounts receivable department.
- Support of other company activities unless sales, service or marketing oriented. Available selling time is a scarce commodity. Other telemarketing activities may be managed by the manager, i.e., service bureau support, outsourcing, etc.

This position is to be <u>informally</u> reviewed by the Management three months after start; <u>formally</u>, six months after start, and reviewed as quickly as year-end results are available. Management base pay increases are recommended, but not automatic after these reviews. See compensation policy. ___This description is not to be construed as an employment contract.___

_____   _____

Signature   Date

————o————

FGI0199BK

My final advice is use date codes at bottom of forms, job descriptions, etc., i.e., GE021499MGT. (Translation: General Electric February 14, 1999 Management.) This makes sure you are using the latest form. Also note, the caveat in the final statement. It is **not** an employment contract!

Hiring the Manager

Even at this writing, there is no such thing as an abundance of experienced telemarketing, telesales management people in the marketplace. There are only a few specialized search agencies that service the business community's need in this area. Neither association, the ATA nor the DMA, list more than 2,500 company names of what I would call true telemarketing management people, in their membership directories. So where do these folks come from, and how do you find them?

This isn't going to make anyone happy, but other than by networking, I don't know, and have not spent a lot of time worrying about the problem. However, there are some excellent opportunities to meet these people at industry shows, where these types are in abundance as attendees. To name a few examples of the day:

- The DMA National Conference, as well as their Business to Business Direct Marketing and DMB annual meetings. Also their Telephone Marketing Council annual meeting.
- Target Marketing Conference Corporation, NCOF, National Catalog Operations Forum (Annual)
- The ATA, (American Teleservices Association), has both regional meetings and two annual events, the National Fall Convention, and the Spring Conference, Washington, D.C.
- ICSA, (International Customer Service Association), has regional Chapter meetings and an annual convention (same as the ATA).

And of course, several magazines and papers have both "I am available", and position wanted-ad's. Some of those are:

- TeleProfessional Magazine, Waterloo, IA
- C@ll Center Solutions Magazine, (formerly Telemarketing®)Norwalk, CT
- JATA, Journal of the American Teleservices Association, North Hollywood, CA
- DM NEWS, New York, NY
- Direct, Stamford, CT
- Target Marketing, Philadelphia, PA
- Call Center Magazine, New York, NY

(For details on contacting these publications, associations and conferences, please see Chapter 14.)

But, like I said, I don't worry. I use the good old Sunday newspaper and get all the candidates that I need. I've never failed in over 20 years (close, but never shut out).

The two main points to consider are, do you want to develop your own manager, or do you want to hire experience, or hire similar experience? By similar experience I mean, not all managers are created equal. Business-to-consumer managers can have a difficult transition when moving to a business-to-business applications. An inbound manager may have difficulty with an outbound position. Service bureau type mangers are considered project based, or operational type management. Can they commit or adjust to your application? I worry about the applicability of similar experience candidates, and would interview carefully, and with caution.

Similar telemarketing experience is important. However, similar product experience is not as important as one might think. It's nice to have, but it's not the highest priority.

If you hire a non-experienced telemarketing manager, you will need to commit to training or networking for their education. The reward has immediate pay back.

Many telemarketing managers are promoted from within existing departments, and generally, we like to see that happen. They may not have general management skills, seem very young for the responsibility, but they have experience. They usually are fast learners, and eager to advance.

Again, I think the Sunday papers (Wednesday in Canada) will do the trick nicely for you.

Hiring the TSR, ISR, CSR

Remember, pay attention to behavior types. Proactive assignments should have either an expressive persuasive, or a driver behavior style (a controlled driver, of course). Reactive positions work best with amiable and analytical types.

Experienced customer service staff is easier to find. Similar career fields work well with reference to finding staff that will match these reactive assignments. However, finding proactive staff is difficult. Again, someone who is used to scripted call objectives for a business-to consumer-application does not necessarily make a good proactive sales rep, especially where consultive or counselor sales techniques are required. The reason is that the script did the selling, not the rep.

Myths

Here are myths that need to be watched. [True or False?]

- *Field sales people work well in an inside selling (proactive) environment.*
  False -- In general, it depends on how long they have been in field sales. Over five years, and it's risky. The number of calls per day and the Field Sales freedom issues may be too hard to overcome.

    While I am on the topic, do not let the call center become a dumping ground for other departments, no matter what they do, or who they are. This would be a big mistake. If they meet the job description requirements and can meet your objectives in three weeks, maybe.

- *All confirmed TSR, ISR, CSR interview appointments show-up as scheduled.*
  False -- The group in total has a 25% no-show rate. One out of four just disappear into the big employment interviewing crack in the sky, and no matter what you do, that's the way it will be. I always schedule five people for four interview slots. I usually end-up with four completed interviews, and an occasional juggling of my time slots/schedule now and then. Three to four in-person interviews should get you one good candidate.

- *It makes a lot of sense to hire the handicapped. They make good employees.*
  True -- Up to a point. However, what really makes sense is if they can sell. That's why you want them. Being handicapped has nothing to do with employee skills, or finding sales people, customer service people, etc. Their sales skill package does.

- *Women make better sales people than men.*
  True -- To a degree. I personally am inclined to think so, but the truth is that these positions lend themselves to the female candidates. Why? No travel, and for the most part 9-to-5 type jobs. Literally, more women apply for these positions and are accepted (for all the obvious reasons) about 65% of the time.

91

- *You can't sell highly technical products over the telephone, and big-ticketed items can't be sold either.*

  False, and **False** -- How about an entire building in downtown Manhattan. Or, a $30,000 IBM mainframe software application to an IBM customer? The truth is, you can, and it has been done. (I've done it!)

- *Product knowledge is more important than sales skills and techniques.*

  False.-- Both are important, but it's the other way around. I can teach product knowledge and applications, or find out where that information is, but when it comes to teaching sales skills, I am not certain that you can teach everyone to sell.

How Many Do You Hire?

In a start-up situation there is a real risk in starting with one person. There is nothing to compare to. The question becomes, "What is good, or not so good?"

Thinking of hiring a pair? Well, the "buddy system" seems to take hold, and the situation is not much better than having only one rep.

But, if you hire three reps, you're automatically in a competitive situation, and that is healthy. Of course, the size of your customer file, or numbers of inbound calls per day has a lot to do with the number of people you need to hire.

Contrary to popular belief, outbound reps can not work thousands of accounts per year unless it's a campaign mission or a reorder call objective. That is, one call, an announcement and keep moving to the next call. However, account maintenance missions very rarely have more than 500 accounts, and most likely have 325 to 350 accounts. Thus, 1,200 accounts will keep three ISRs profitably busy, all year long.

Thinking of CSRs, or reactive staff, and how many to hire, will depend on the amount of inbound traffic, abandon call rates, busy hours, etc., when you consider your staffing levels. We would recommend any call center management seminar for the best answers to these questions. Technology (ACD's, software, etc.) will have more of an impact for these departments, than in your proactive departments.

However, four specific issues come to mind.

1. Product knowledge or product knowledge routines are as important as phone skills and techniques. (The reverse of proactive assignments)
2. Part-time staff will round out your full-time staff, and can be used to impact customer service levels and abandon call rates, especially during busy hours.
3. The inbound manager/supervisor to rep ratio is no worse than 1 to 15, and has a better dividend at 1 to 12. The outbound manager ratio is no worse than 1 to 9. The span of rep control, and helping them to be all they can be is the issue.
4. Amiable behavior styled reps work best for reactive assignments.

Staff Profiles and Survey Data

I commissioned Schlenker Research Associates of Morganville, NJ, to perform a multi-client, primary research project that identified telemarketing uses and growth patterns. Schlenker interviewed 707 company operations (employee staffed), and 64 telemarketing service agencies. From time-to-time I will refer to data gathered, to give you hard facts, as opposed to my experience and opinion. I believe the information gathered is still reasonably valid and meaningful, with reference to hiring criteria. Besides, I do not know of any other current report that has this specificity.

Most Important Hiring Criteria

Topic	Outbound %	Inbound %
Communication Skills	37%	35%
Verbal Skills	16%	17%
Sales Skills	12%	9%
Assertive, Confident Manner	11%	10%
Product Knowledge	6%	9%
Good Voice	5%	5%
Telemarketing Experience	3%	2%
Grammar	3%	4%
Prior Sales Experience	2%	2%
Keyboard Experience	0%	1%
Other	3%	3%
Not Stated	2%	3%
	100%	100%

Education Requirements for New Reps

Topic	Outbound %	Inbound %
High School Graduate	35%	43%
Some High School	5%	5%
College Graduate	17%	15%
Unimportant	23%	18%
Not Stated	5%	4%
	100%	100%

Hiring From Within or Outside the Company

Topic	Outbound %	Inbound %
Within Company	17%	23%
Outside Company	48%	30%
Both	34%	44%
Don't Know/Not Stated	1%	3%
	100%	100%

Female vs. Male

Topic	Outbound %	Inbound %
Females Only	32%	32%
More Females than Males	36%	40%
Male Only	7%	5%
More Males than Females	13%	12%
Equal	10%	9%
Not Stated	2%	2%
	100%	100%

Length of Service

Topic	Median
Outbound Staff	28 Months
Inbound Staff	38 Months

The most critical problem that telemarketing managers of all types faced, was the personnel issue, according to the *Telemarketing Intelligence* study. The issues are maintaining morale, the enthusiasm of the staff, and managing what is called burnout.

Burnout is caused by the working environment. It just does not happen. I am reminded of Peggy Lee's ballad, "Is that all there is?" Burnout is a management topic that needs to be continually addressed. Just remember this: burnout is a symptom of a problem, not the problem itself.

The Hiring Process

Please review the entire hiring process first, and then we can go step-by-step. (See Figure 6.4) Please remember, if they are to report to you, you'll do 90% of the hiring task.

Interviewing Aids and Forms

While we are on this topic, it pays to be highly organized in your hiring process, which in turn allows consistency and leads to a higher ratio of successful hires. We are recommending that in addition to the resume, letter or other candidate generated documents, you always have the in-person candidate fill out your standard application form, twenty-minutes prior to the in-person interview. As you will later see, this becomes a form of rehearsal for the on-site interview. Also, there are two more forms that you will find helpful for the interview. (1) The Candidate Evaluation Form (CEF, Fig. 6.5), (2) The Appointment Tracker (AT, Fig. 6.6).

The CEF Form is used twice. Once for the telephone interview, and if the candidate is successful, for the in-person interview (Figure 6.5). The benefit of this form is to have interviewing consistency for your part of the interview, and it insures that you speak as little as possible, thus making you a good listener. When reviewing the CEF, note it is topic based. (Reason: Guides open-ended questions.)

Example: Income last year, W-2. The telephone interview question would be, "Would you discuss with me how you earned your income last year? as opposed to, "How much money did you make last year?". Or you may ask, "I am curious, why are you changing assignments?" or, "Tell me why did you leave your last assignment?" Your questions need to be open-ended. In other words they must be answered with more than a few words, staying away from yes and no answers. The reason is that you can access the candidate's phone personality in this manner. That's difficult to do with yes or no answers.

For the telephone interview, you will be judging the phone personality, along with some modest qualification questions. Detailed interviewing is left for the in-person phase. Note, that on the bottom of the CEF there's a subjective measurement system, i.e., how intelligent do you think the candidate sounds, on a scale of 1 to 10. Examples of qualification questions could be, "Our position is inside, no travel, income up to $25,000 and starts on September 3rd. Do you have any problems with any of these points?" Or, "It looks like you'll have a 30 mile one-way commute. Will that be a problem for you?"

All of these questions may be changed to suit your needs. Just make them topical in format, use open-ended questions as often as possible, and try to stay conversational.

We also attach importance to remembering the position ad, and being able to briefly describe it. This gives you a clue as to specific interest of the candidate. We also

---

Figure 6.4

Hiring Personnel with Inside Selling Capabilities

Guidelines

1. Sunday newspaper ad requires mailing of resume or letter only (e-mail and fax-ing are also acceptable); no phone calls are to be accepted. Advise reception staff of this request.

2. Scan and select resumes to call.

Phone Interview

3. Call within five (5) days of receiving first resume; determine phone personality, along with reasonable qualification routine.

[ ] Judge Voice   [ ] Mannerisms   [ ] Continuity   [ ] Brief
[ ] Clarity   [ ] Enthusiasm   [ ] Compensation   [ ] Interest

     Assuming interest, confirm that this is an inside sales assignment, and the start date. The candidate can not miss your training dates! Set the in-person appointment if compliant.

In-Person Interview

4. Set one-hour impact interviews, one right after another (arriving 15 to 20 minutes early to fill out your job application, a rehearsal).

5. Cover these open-ended areas:
     [ ] 5 years of employment history
     [ ] Any unemployment during the same period
     [ ] Set objectives
     [ ] How they relax
     [ ] Topic they wish to discuss that may impact the interview

6. Tell them about the job

7. Free-style

8. Explain notification process

9. Rank candidates 1 to 10, immediately

10. (Optional) Get a second opinion, but don't drag out this process.

11. Make job offer, quickly.

12. Get Employment Agreement and Understanding statements signed upon acceptance.

can add clues and prompts to ourselves on this form, i.e., our phone number in use for this task, and who they should contact if they need to adjust their onsite appointment. The reverse side is for notes, and the rest of the form is self-explanatory.

The second form (AT) is a scheduling form entitled, "Appointment Tracker" (Figure 6.6). Because we recommend phone interviewing be continuous, or calling the candidate all at one specific time, a schedule or appointment tracking form is helpful.

The Thirteen Steps

1. The Job Placement Ad

Now that you have gotten this far in the Chapter, I will assume that you have seen the typical ads that are placed in your local newspapers. Often they are five or six lines in length, listed with other similar positions, both part-time and full-time, with an offer to make lots of money, and for evening hours. They are not very exciting, and I can assure you, it's most likely a business-to-consumer application. More often than not, it is the last job opportunity to be reviewed by an applicant, if it is reviewed at all.

Management tends to look at the ad as an expense as opposed to an investment. Keeping costs down are the marching orders of the day for many companies. When this happens, less than exciting inferences are being made by the company, and to the prospective employee.

Ad Perceptions
1. The smaller the ad, the less important the job/assignment must be.
2. These are not skilled or professional jobs, so the company doesn't want to make any more of an investment than is absolutely required.
3. "A telemarketing job? Maybe, I'll check it out until a real job comes along."
4. "Not for me. That's beneath me, I have an education."

It's prudent to remember that these people are the folks who talk to our prospects and customers. Many activities start and stop with these contacts. They are your company, the organization. No one knows how many people, or opportunities, are literally driven away by company representatives who should not be on the phones. It is wise to put your best foot forward with all these positions. The position wanted-ad is the first step.

Figure 6.5

CANDIDATE EVALUATION FORM

Supervisor   TSR

Dates called to interview on phone _____

Candidate Name	Our phone #	
Telephone #	Planned interview date	Time
Address	Directions given	Yes No
City State Zip	Candidate contact name	
Resume attached	(Candidate must come 20 mins. early to fill out	
	employment application for in-person interview)	

PHONE INTERVIEW

Remembered Ad-wanted?	Can they describe?	
Income last W-2 year	What part base?	%
Commission $ %	Value of other compensation	
Currently employed?	Reason for leaving:	
Years of selling experience	Manager or Line Sales Rep	
Telephone Sales experience, Years		
Have you put together budgets? Sales	Expense	
Do you have training experience in sales?	Other? What?	
Ever hire and or fire?		
Business to business? %	Business to consumer? %	

IMPACT INTERVIEW
(Use for both phone and in-person interviews)

Note: This is a perception of the voice personality over the phone and perceived impact in-person

	POOR				AVERAGE			EXCELLENT		
	1	2	3	4	5	6	7	8	9	10
Intelligence										
Voice Quality										
Sales Skills										
Communicates Clearly										
Appearance*										
Overall impact										
Ask, rank yourself										
On assertiveness										

*In-person only

First interviewer _____   Second interviewer _____

Recommend for in-person interview?

99

(Reverse side for comments)

Figure 6.5 continued

COMMENTS

WHAT I LIKE: **WHAT CONCERNS ME:**

1. _____   _____

2. _____   _____

3. _____   _____

4. _____   _____

5. _____   _____

6. _____   _____

7. _____   _____

8. _____   _____

9. _____   _____

10. _____   _____

BE CONCERNED WITH THE "PHONE PERSONALITY"

ADDITIONAL COMMENTS

_____

_____

_____

_____

_____

_____

_____

_____

First, Some Do's and Don'ts

- The Ad should be two columns wide, and about 5" in height. Certainly larger is better than smaller. (See Figures 6.7; 6.8; 6.9)
- Place ads based on job function areas, not the medium, i.e., "Telemarketing". If it is Sales, the selling section; if it is customer service, place under Customer Service.
- Border or display your ad to attract attention
- Always identify your Company -- no blind-ads, please. It makes applicants nervous.
- Place ad in Sunday papers, one time; Wednesday is best in Canada
- Review with your EEO specialist, and stand your ground. Compliance, yes, change in format no.
- Accept no phone calls from your ad. Force a reply by letter, or resume, or both. Notify the receptionist that an ad has been placed, and to comply with this instruction.
- Post your position(s) internally before ad hits the paper, no surprises.
- Keep in mind, you're trying to catch attention, not drive response away, so use only modest selection wording.
- Do not place ad to close to exciting holidays, i.e., Easter, Christmas, etc.

Figure 6.6

TELEMARKETING APPOINTMENT TRACKER
ACE COMPANY

Phone number to be used _____

Contact Name _____

TIME	DAY	CANDIDATE NAME	DIRECTIONS
8 AM - 9 AM			Take Rt. 33, Exit to Wilson Rd. We are on the left #123, 2nd Floor, ask for _____
9:00 - 10:00		10:30	
11:00 - 12:00			
		LUNCH	
1:30 - 2:30			
2:30 - 3:30		2:45	
3:30 - 4:30			
4:30- 5:30			

Instructions to Candidate:

Please arrive 15 to 20 minutes in advance of your appointment to complete our employment application.

Additional Details for Interviewer

Fill in the day, date, and clear directions on how to get to your location. The 10:30 am and the 2:45 pm slots are for "no-show" replacement candidates (1 out of 4 will not show-up for this appointment). Also, select a contact name for candidates to call if their plans change. Finally, make the phone number available, with extension to be used for these occasional calls.

REVIEW SCHEDULE WITH CANDIDATE TO INSURE COMPLETE UNDERSTANDING FOR THE IN-PERSON VISIT.

Figure 6.7

POSITION WANT AD

Example 1

INSIDE SALES MANAGER (OR SUPERVISOR)

THE VAN VECHTEN GROUP, a 25-year leader in telemarketing publications, consulting, and seminar presentations, is seeking a candidate whose management/supervisory background will support our proactive marketing effort.

The (new/expansion) position will report to the V.P. of Sales. A full training package is offered. Travel is minimal. Full company benefits, including a 401K program are provided. We are in a growth environment, and this position offers career potential. Telephone sales, business-to-business sales management experience is desired, but not the final criteria.

Our compensation plans are based on contribution against objective. For consideration please e-mail, fax or send letter of interest and resume (no phone calls, please) to:

F.G.I.
51 Hampton Drive, Suite 1
Freehold, NJ 07728-3148
www.thevanvechtengp.com
Fax: (732) xxx-xxxx

Attn: H.R. Director (ISD)

An equal opportunity employer

PLACEMENT AD INSTRUCTIONS

- Sunday paper, display ad, or bordered section
- Two columns wide
- 3 to 5 inches high
- Use company name and address
  Attn: H.R. Director (ISD)

Figure 6.8

POSITION WANT AD

Example II

INSIDE SALES REPRESENTATIVE

THE VAN VECHTEN GROUP, a 25 year leader in the management education, publication, and consulting field, is seeking sales candidates for its inside sales department. We are in the information and training business, and are known worldwide for our products and services.

You will be telemarketing (inside selling) a variety of information and training products to our valuable customer base. We use counselor and consultative selling techniques. A full training program will be provided. No travel, regular business hours, and company benefits are a part of this career package.

Our compensation plans are open-ended and offer base, plus commission-with bonus for achievers.*

To be considered as a candidate, please e-mail, fax or send letter/resume (no phone calls, please) to:

F.G.I.
51 Hampton Drive
Freehold, NJ 07728-3148
www.fgi.com
Fax: (732) xxx-xxxx

Attn: H.R. Director (ISD)

An equal opportunity employer

(*)If a qualifier is needed, an income range may be used, i.e., "Our rep ranges from $32,000 to $38,000 yearly."

PLACEMENT AD INSTRUCTIONS

- Sunday paper, display ad, or bordered section
- Two columns wide
- 3 to 5 inches high
- Use company name and address
  Attn: H.R. Director (ISD)

Figure 6.9

POSITION WANT AD
"THE NET"
Example III

INSIDE SALES REPRESENTATIVES

Serious about a career change? Business-to-business telephone sales may be the answer. We need three AE's (account executives) today!

Qualified individuals who have an aptitude and attitude and are interested in sales training, no travel, standard business hours, and starting income that will meet your needs, should send resume or letter of interest to:

F.G.I.
51 Hampton Drive
Freehold, NJ 07728-3148

Attn: H.R. Director (ISD)

An equal opportunity employer

PLACEMENT AD INSTRUCTIONS
- Sunday paper, display ad, or bordered section
- Two columns wide
- 3 to 5 inches high
- Use company name and address
  Attn: H.R. Director (ISD)

2. The Resume: Scanning and Selecting

Your position wanted-ads are in the Sunday paper. Using our examples for ads, we specifically state, "NO phone calls, please!" There are two reasons for this instruction:

1. Can the candidate follow simple instructions?
2. Random calls into your office do not allow you to be fully prepared for the interview process. We like to batch this work for comparative purposes, and in fact we get better at interviewing on each consecutive call.

Despite our best efforts, lo and behold, on Monday morning the phone rings, and it's the "eager-beaver" candidate. It just never fails. We politely instruct the can-

105

didate to mail, fax, or even e-mail their job interest letter and/or resume to be considered for the position. By the way, handwritten letters and resumes are okay as long as they are neat.

Normally, by Wednesday the first mailed resume hits your desk. From that date, we advise you to mark your calendar five-to-seven working days ahead. That is when you will start your outbound phone interview process. Don't second-guess when all the resumes will be in. Second-guessing does nothing but lead to procrastination. The go-getters will get their response in, and that is who we are after.

The next activity may surprise you. The resume review is initially to look for reasons not to interview, as opposed to studying each document. It makes sense to weed out those resumes in the no-interest category. Here are a few reasons that there might be no interest:

- Not neat
- misspellings
- a mass mailing (one resume fits all situations)
- no cover letter
- not signed
- their stated objectives are totally different from the position offered
- lack of achievement clues
- chronologically incomplete
- higher salary expectations than we can afford
- printed on odd-shaped paper
- more than four pages (counting the cover letter)
- picture of candidate included
- wording on the introduction letter suggesting, "here is a chance of a lifetime." (See Figure 6.10 Introduction letter)
- Ink stampings, i.e., "Highly Explosive, etc.".

When you stop and think about it, the resume and introduction letter are the candidate's advertising brochure. It needs to attract your attention. It needs to respond to the situation that exists – their document is mixed with others, and must attract your attention the correct way. The product is the candidate. All that really needs to happen is to create enough curiosity for the reader to make the first call. Interviewers scan resumes and I am sure we all know that. Time is the issue. The candidate doesn't know that, and occasionally makes the mistake of sending volumes of information that bores everyone to death. Brief is better.

We also need to remember that conversations on the telephone are brief events. The condition and length of the resume is a clue as to how they will perform on the phone with your call objectives.

My experience is that fully 60% of all resumes submitted will end up in the no-interest pile. On the next review, you will disregard even more resumes. Statistically, it works something like this:

- 100 resumes received
- 60 disregarded, quickly
- 5 more dropped on second review
- 18 lost for one reason or another
- 35 called for the first phone interview
- 17 in-person appointments made
- 4 candidates were no-shows
- 13 interviewed, and 3 hired

It's a grueling task. No wonder managers hate the hiring task.

3. The Telephone Interview

To review, the objective of the phone interview it is to judge the following, "Do we have a rep that sounds like they can do the job?" The direct report manager makes these outbound interview calls.

1. Make the first call during your business day, to work, or at home. If at work, start the conversation like this, "Russ Betts? Russ, I have your resume for Ace Companies job opening in front of me. Is this a good time to talk?" Please remember, all of the previous discussion applies. We have part of this topic in the preceding forms and aids discussion. In that we are in a sightless environment, it's how the candidate sounds that is critical. This is a subjective evaluation at best. However, if they don't sound right, for whatever reason, I wouldn't interview them in-person, no matter what their other qualifications were.

2. If only a home number is listed, still call during your business day. If you run into an answering machine, use the above introduction, and tell them to call you tomorrow with some specificity, i.e., between 9:00 am and 12:00 pm. Batch this task, i.e., call all your candidates today, for phone interviews tomorrow. By doing so you will save tons of time.

4. The In-Person Interview

Assuming you are reasonably impressed with the phone interview you will have invited them to come for an in-person, impact interview. It should be one hour in length, with an extra 20 minutes at the start for them to fill out your employment application, per your appointment tracker.

Figure 6.10

🎆🎆🎆🎆🎆🎆🎆🎆🎆🎆🎆

🎆 HIGHLY EXPLOSIVE!! 🎆

🎆🎆🎆🎆🎆🎆🎆🎆🎆🎆

JOSEPH RICHARDSON, JR.
7329 Burko Ave.
Freehold, NJ 07728
(732) 555-1212

WATCH OUT!!   November 1, 20XX

Gentlemen:

My substantial experience in sales may be very *valuable* to you. This is what I can offer you to help build your profit.

    -The ability to manage sales, build key accounts personally and to grasp the essential elements in your business.

    -Experience in developing substantial sales through better customer relations.

                                   WATCH OUT!!

    -Intelligence and the capacity to learn.

My resume is enclosed in great confidence and I will appre-ciate your consider-ation. May I come and talk to you?

                               Very truly yours,

NOT SIGNED!

                               Joseph Richardson, Jr.

Enclosure

Remember, the person conducting the interview needs to be the direct report manager. These interviews are also called impact interviews. The reason is, that if the impact is unfavorable for any reason, do not consider that candidate. All candidates should be interviewed the same day if at all possible, and one right after the other, for comparative purposes. The interview is in four parts, but to the candidate it will appear to be in three parts. Prepare an outline for yourself on how the interview will go. Secure an appropriate interview room. Give a list or schedule of interviews to the receptionist. Provide pads, pencils, and company propaganda for the applicant to read or take with them.

5. The Introduction

Explain how this interview process will work, and get the candidate to relax. For example, "Thanks for coming to see us, I trust the commute wasn't too bad. Please try to relax. I've provided material for you to take notes, if you so desire, and I'll give you additional material about our company for your review, at the end of the interview. This will not take more than an hour. Is there anything you need before we start? Good. The interview will be divided into three parts. In the first part, you will be telling me about yourself, and your employment experiences. In the second part, I'll tell you all you need to know about our company, and this position. The final part will allow us to talk about anything not covered in the first two parts of the interview. Okay?"

6. The Five Interview Questions

"I am going to ask you five questions, all at one time. You may answer them in any order you wish. If you would like to write the questions down, please feel free to do so. Please flavor the answers with what you want me to know that will favorably impact our meeting today.

Question # 1. From today, and going back five years, talk to me about your employment experiences.

Question # 2. Did you have any unemployment in that same period of time? If so, talk to me about that.

Question # 3. Tell me about the business and personal objectives that you have set for yourself, and how you are doing with these objectives.

Question # 4. Tell me how you relax, relieve stress, and deal with pressure or tension.

Question # 5. Here is your chance to tell me about anything that you think would favorably impact this interview today. It can be anything that you want me to know and have not mentioned previously."

It makes sense to review the questions for the applicant. Don't help in any way with the questions or definitions of the questions, once the interview has started. Tell the person when to start. Your job is to be a good listener. If during their response something in unclear to you, ask for clarification, then tell them to continue. This section should take no longer than 20 minutes of the interview hour.

No doubt you have noticed their dress, appearance, grooming, and anything else that provides an impact. Take notes on good characteristics, and well as poor impact items.

In essence they are talking about a product they know very well and should be very comfortable with – *themselves*. Your entire review is to determine, "Did they understand, respond, and execute in a reasonable fashion?" If they did, that's likely how it will go when they call your customers and prospects. Being brief is important. Most telephone conversations are less then 3.5 minutes in length. Also, judge the same elements that you were judging in the telephone interview, voice, clarity, language, enthusiasm, sentence continuity, volume, rate of speech, inflection, tone, and personality.

As the interview proceeds, fill in the in-person section of your CEF, the same one you used for the phone interview. This is a confirmation exercise. Here is where you can check off general appearance. Again, this is a sales presentation of the product, the candidate.

7. Tell them about your company

After they have finished, it's your turn. Start with "On a scale of 1 to 10, how assertive are you, considering 10 is obnoxious". Mark the CEF. Again, whether you agree with the candidate is the question. Mark CEF again.

Then use your position job description, and outline the position. Topic examples for your outline are:

* typical day	* number of calls, etc.
* who is on the other end of the phone	* number of accounts
* starting time	* how measured
* compensation	* holidays
* benefits	* training

Ask if there are any questions, while giving them your material. We have just used another 20 minutes of your one-hour interview, and are entering the final phase.

8. Free-Style

I save this part for questions about the resume, my sales pitch, if I am strongly interested, and any clarification. This is also the place to ask if they are interested in the position, and to explain the rest of the process.

9. Explain Notification Process

"We will call you one way or the other, within 24 hours. Our start-date is the 27th. If you don't have any more question, thanks for coming, and good luck."

10. Rank Candidates 1 to 10, Immediately

After the candidate leaves, immediately score your evaluation form on a 1 to 10 basis, (with 10 the highest), and go to your next interview. Remember, it's a subjective score. The first candidate sets the median. All others are equal to, better than, or worse, than the initial score.

11. Second Opinion

If you're to use a multiple interviewer method do it quickly. Our recommendation is that it is not necessary, because you are not making an 18-month decision but, in a worst case scenario, a two-month decision. Second opinions tend to drag out the process and lose good candidates. You will be able to know whether you're successful or not well within a two-month period.

12. Make the Job Offer, Quickly.

Call within 24 hours and offer the job, or consult with the job applicant.

13. Employment Agreements and Understanding Statements

If the candidate is offered the job, ask if they have any objections to signing your two agreements. These agreements are a condition of their employment. (See Figure 6.11 and 6.12)

Hiring Summary

If one were to stop and think about the most important element in using the telephone successfully in a business environment, it's the people. All else comes after that. I say this emphatically.

Finding staff is difficult. It is a task that never ends, and is a sensitive asset that erodes easily.

Show me a highly successful group, and I'll show you people who can make the best of anything or everything. Good people can successfully service or sell in a poorly supported environment. Not-so-good people won't survive in the best environment. Trust me on this one.

Figure 6.11

EMPLOYMENT AGREEMENT

As a condition of employment with our company, the employee agrees that he/she will:

1) Not take materials or documents (either originals or copies) pertaining to this operation out of the offices of our company, without the prior consent of his/her office manager.

2) Will not seek to associate for a like purpose with this company's clients, active prospects, or competitors, in a role comparable to the one performed as an employee of this company, for a period of six months after separation of his/her employment with this company, for whatever cause or reason.

F.G.I. & Affiliated Publishing Companies, Inc.
Freehold, NJ 07728-3148

Agreed:_____   By: _____
      Employee representative   Management representative

Date: _____   Title: _____

                                                   Date: _____

Please note: This agreement is not to be construed as an employment contract.

Original to file
Copy to employee

FGI021599AGRE

Figure 6.12

UNDERSTANDING STATEMENT

PLEASE READ AND SIGN THE FOLLOWING INDICATING YOUR UNDERSTANDING AND AGREEMENT.

I understand that my telephone sales conversations are eligible to be monitored and/or recorded by my employer. I further understand that if the calls are recorded it is for training purposes only, and the exercise review or tape will be erased as soon as the training has been completed. With my permission, the recording may be kept and cataloged for the department's sales training library.

Finally, I understand that the monitoring and occasional recording of my sales calls, as well as the use of headsets, are conditions for my employment.

Signed: _____
                Employee

Date: _____

Noted: _____
     Manager

Date: _____

Original to file
Copy to TSR

FGI0199

NOTES –

CHAPTER 7
Compensation Reward and Recognition Systems

Introduction

My guess is that at least two billion words have been written on the topics of compensation plans and recognition systems and what they can and can not do for you, and for the company. Let me add another 10,000 words to the topic and relate the topic to business-to-business telephone sales.

Because this group feels it is different than all other groups, and they are, and confusion exists as to what telemarketing really is and does, the entire compensation topic, as it relates to the variety of positions that exist in telemarketing, is a muddy issue at best.

A major problem stems from the history of the medium, as well as perceptions about what these people do in respect to their value in the organization. Some interesting examples of that thinking are:

- For the longest period of time the people who performed these tasks were called communicators. Do we see big "comp" plans here? No, because the perception is that it is a task, anyone can do it, especially part-timers.

- Scripted business-to-consumer programs (presentations that are read or highly structured) were often the order of the day. Anyone can dial and read a script, right? It is just another task and another lower-paying job. There is a lot of turnover and staff is easy to replace.

- These are campaign programs, like calls made to sell glue for the glue gun, or it's time to reorder your computer ribbons, or "have I got a deal for you" type calls. They are seen as not too difficult. It means lots of calls, a production environment, another task type assignment, and surely less-than-exciting compensation arrangements.

- Inbound calls that take an order, means simply, if you can hear, you can do the job. Well, I am not so sure we aren't missing something here as well.

- Customer Service is a reactive skill, right? Well, you do need to know a lot about products or services. Maybe it is a little better paying position, but still task driven. "It's fairly easy to get these folks and we don't need to pay an arm and leg." Well, maybe, but are we missing something here as well? I think so.

- The complexity of the product, as well as average order, impacts rep compensation, right? Well, sometimes it does.

- The telephone is an inexpensive selling tool. Not really, in fact, second in expense only to field selling expenses.

- Extra incentive is always a motivator. Well, yes and no. It depends on how you do it and with whom.

The point you ask? The entire topic of compensation and recognition – which includes, the why, when, how, and the people – is not simple or easily understood. It's also a topic that can quickly give you an ulcer. In this business there appears to be a contradiction in terms. Management's perception vs. the employee's perception of the same assignment is often quite different, and therein lies the rub.

To start we need to revisit our simple definition of telemarketing when used as a sales channel.

Definition

> *Telemarketing is the intensive use of the telephone in a business environment.*

That covers a lot of functions, e.g. sales (inbound and outbound), customer service, market research, customer relations, answer centers, call centers, and anything else where the phone is an integral and intensive part of the specific business function.

Second, what we do after we have described the medium, is literally, what we do. It is order entry, and servicing the customer after the transaction, or proactive selling. Compensation is impacted by the degree of difficulty, economics, revenue, and expense of the sales function, and the designed job risk, i.e., no performance, no job.

Compensation programs translate into the degree of difficulty or how easy it is to satisfy the call objective and how business missions are impacted. Basically, "Is it worth it?" Finally, if you are selling, you're a sales person not a telemarketer. Field sales people aren't called "automarketers."

Recognition Systems

As in other job assignments, not all positions need extra incentive in order to obtain the extra effort. The question one needs to ask is, "Why do I want to recognize the representative, and what will the activity do for our organization if I do?" A second question is, can this activity be measured? You need to know the answer in order to evaluate the worth of the recognition system you wish to use, and to validate the system.

There are a couple of buzzword phrases that I always keep in mind when I am addressing these topics. They are:

- If you can't track or prove the result, don't compensate for it.
- For every recognition activity there is an opposite and equal result or activity. That's not unlike Newton's Third Law of Motion.
- Not all people enjoy all recognition systems.
- Motivation tactics used to foster better or stronger performance can be impacted by a recognition system, if the employee agrees to, and understands the system.
- Recognition systems that are not understood by the employees impacted are **worthless** and don't impact stronger performance.
- Individual behavior styles, staff value systems, training, and management all impact the success of recognition systems. When one thinks about the topic in-depth, one quickly understands that performance appraisals are in fact recognition systems with specific objectives. They answer the question, "How am I doing?" They do so with a formal feedback loop as a part of the process. By the way, no feedback adds to possible system failure.

We won't spend a lot of time on the topic of performance evaluations, other than to say employees want to know how they are doing, and how they can perform better. For better than average performance they generally enjoy recognition, which in turn feeds their self-motivating process. Here are a few examples:

- Employee of the Month (with the best parking spot and a lot of company press about the award).
- Cash rewards for cost saving suggestions.
- One's name at the top of a published performance list showing outstanding achievement (proactive reps only).
- Promotions
- Work-leader assignments
- Assigned as the "Product Knowledge" source in the department
- A raise, a prize, a trip, or even merchandise
- A recognition article in the Company newsletter

- A letter from the boss, and a pat on the back
- Special recognition stationery, or a unique workstation
- Special award plaques
- Compensation plan (risk/reward)

NOTES –

Compensation Logic

Before one designs a plan, there are three other topics that need to be addressed. They are: (1) compensation philosophy for the entire organization, i.e., "If we sell $50,000,000 it's worth $35,000." (2) the degree of difficulty, with reference to your inbound/outbound tasks, and the specific complexity of the call objectives (3) finally, the comparative value of the assignment if it is successfully completed, or objectives are exceeded, compared to other sales type assignments. Let's look at examples of all three.

(1) Compensation Philosophy - At General Foods (White Plains, NY), in their food service division, incentive systems, (as in sales commissions or bonuses), are frowned upon and non-existent throughout the division, however, merit increases are available based on the division's performance.

(2) The degree of difficulty and/or job risk, as it relates to the reason for the call, i.e., call objective. Thus, the inbound order entry task is perceived to be less difficult than the outbound account maintenance specialist with new business responsibilities. These are different skill levels, and in turn require different compensation arrangements.

(3) What would you pay a rep who could turn $300,000 of existing business into $411,000? That assignment might have a value of, $32,500, for example. Of course, your financial math would apply. Once value is decided, comp plans are much easier to design. Also impacting this question is the geographic section of the country, and what others are paying. Please be advised that the geographic section of the country has a marginal impact on proactive, inside sales positions.

In general, reactive calls coming into your facility are salaried, non-exempt positions, with wages computed by the hour. Recognition systems, more often than not are for the unit/department, and are based on the total departmental objective. Rewards are often bonus in nature. Proactive slots nearly always have individual rep incentive systems applied. These positions are non-exempt as well. FLSA issues are important considerations for you to think about when planning or designing compensation or recognition systems. Review this with your HR people. The systems are often commission and bonus driven.

Again, why this topic is confusing, is that most compensation data confuses, or does not adjust for, the various telemarketing/telesales functions, or degrees of difficulty. There are six major functions that impact difficult and less difficult categories. (Figure 7.1)

120

(Figure 7.1)

> ## SIX BASIC FUNCTIONS OR TASKS
> 1. Outbound
> 2. Inbound
> 3. Business-to-business
> 4. Business-to-consumer
> 5. Employee-staffed (on-site)
> 6. Service bureau-staffed or outsourced (off-site)

The most difficult assignments are numbers 1 and 3, handled by 5 or 6, and the least difficult assignment are numbers 2 and 4, handled by 5 or 6. You may have any combination of tasks with the above. For example, business-to-business (3 plus 2), inbound or (2 plus 4 with 6) business-to-consumer, handled by a service bureau, which is telemarketing for hire. **All require different compensation plans and or recognition systems.**

Other points to remember are, anything with job-associated risk will pay more, as will complicated call objectives on an outbound multiple call basis. Complexity of product, and product margin value will dictate higher or lower compensation systems. Believe it or not, the section of the country issue only impacts reactive positions where the name of the game is expense contribution, not top-line contribution.

How do you answer the occasional objection from other functional disciplines, as in warehouse staff? "Why don't we get extra incentives? If we pick the wrong product, or ship to an incorrect address, the customer might not reorder. Our job is important too." The answer to that is, "You get paid to pick and ship correctly. That's the task, that's the requirement, and that's the job. Yes, you are important, but if you screw-up enough, you lose that job, but, direct contact with our customers and prospects pays more for exceptional performance, over and above what might be considered as operational performance". The clue here is customer contact is not a 100% task position.

The above situation has another face, and it's called a union shop. The nature of union contracts, i.e., Communication Workers of America (CWA), does not lend itself to individual recognition systems for achievers. In theory, what you do for one, you must do for all, and the unique individual purpose may be defeated. Therefore, group recognition is the only way to go, if at all in this situation. By the way, big time sales achievers in this environment leave anyway.

Past and Current Compensation Practices

If you think about how direct mail came of age, you will understand the evolution of the telemarketing medium. Simply stated, business-to-consumer applications came first, followed by business-to-business applications. The universe of contact possibilities is vastly different, i.e., 260 million people, compared to 10 million businesses. The cost per contact is an issue for both mail and phone.

Thus, cost per contact has driven compensation practices for telephone sales people since the 1950s. Well, there is nothing wrong with that, however, a postage stamp does not suffer from boredom, stress, pressure, or tension. Sales reps do.

Right up to the 70s, these positions were perceived to be temporary in nature, or fill-in slots until something else happened. The result was low pay hourly positions for everyone involved. These positions, for the most part, were not considered as real jobs or perceived valuable by the employee or the employer.

Current Comp Practices

Since the 1980s several influences have impacted compensation. Most important is the recognition that a customer is a perishable commodity, and that they are not unlimited. Second, the expense in acquiring new business is dramatic. Finally, with the Malcom Baldridge National Quality Award, and associations like the American Teleservices Association (ATA), The Direct Marketing Association's Telephone Council (DMA/TC) and the International Customer Service Association (ISCA), we understand that the customer is king, and that customer quality treatment is important. How we staff to meet the needs of our customers, talk to our prospects, and sell to both, often means the success or failure of our own business activity. In summary, we need to put our best, highly trained, deeply devoted people on the phone, servicing and selling our marketplace. That is where compensation programs come in.

The oil and gas crisis of 1975 literally forced the business-to-business sales segment to use the telephones more intensively, with and for its customers. They simply could not afford to service and sell all of their customer and prospect bases, considering the expense of operating field sales organizations. Thus, telemarketing assignments were upgraded to meet the current need. In turn, compensation levels were impacted, and in this case favorably.

If you now consider the nature of these assignments as no travel and reasonable growth opportunities, these jobs became particularly attractive to the professional women in the work force. Today (and I would forecast in the future as well), easily 65% of telemarketing positions are filled with professional women, both managers and reps.

These telemarketing organizations or units are now considered as a highly desirable element in the scheme of business, and its corresponding objectives. They are efficient, productive, highly trained, and 100% managed. For those who are just starting, they are considered as a self-liquidating investment expense. Often the return on any investment pays off well within the first year, with the average being six months, when a solid marketing plan is in place. Compensation is a predictable expense and can easily be weighed against the return. All of the above has helped with levels of compensation and a more professional approach to the entire topic.

NOTES –

Schemes for Motivation/Compensation -- Negative and Positive

Unfortunately, the majority of compensation plans are developed by people who either do not understand the topic, are crazy, or just plain lazy. I apologize for being blunt, but that's what I see when I am asked to help design a working plan to replace an existing plan.

In one way, it's how the plan designer views the assignment. If it is viewed as how to pay as little as possible, we are in deep trouble before we even get started. If we view the assignment as how we can motivate and compensate for reasonable or outstanding performance, we are in better shape.

Negative and Positive Plan Motivators

Over the years a variety of methodologies were in vogue for field sales organizations. These plans were often borrowed, and installed for the inside sales organizations. They fall into two general categories. They are positive or negative motivating plans. Let's look at each.

Negative Plans can cause negative motivation. Where we find management that feels commissions, bonuses, and incentives are a necessary evil, we also find plans that in one way or another are telling the plan participant, "We don't trust you," or, "You take all the risk, pay us first, and if there is anything left over, you can have a little." Often there is a failure to recognize that products and services do not sell themselves. They are sold via one vehicle or another, to one degree or another. Here are examples of negative motivation. I don't recommend their use.

- Fear motivation: Do the job that we have described and you get a chance to keep it.
- The first $20,000 in sales or $10,000 in margin has no reward. All contribution over the objective is at 1%. This is what we call a Company greed motivator.
- Your first $250,000 in sales is worth 2% commission, the next $250,000 is worth 1%, and everything over $500,000 is capped, with no commission. This is just plain insane.

Statements like, "Underages are carried forward, and you need to make them up before commission is paid", or "Windfall sales over $20,000 will not fit under your plan, and are to be negotiated," etc., are negative motivators. There is an implied message here, and it's not favorable, nor is it motivating.

Positive Motivators will drive a successful program. Remember, the objective of the above plans is to reach an objective, but you don't need the aforementioned negatives. We refer to these plans as risk/reward plans. The risk is the amount of extra incentive that can be earned, and the reward is the base salary. Depending on the job function itself, e.g., customer service, selling, order entry, etc., the degree of risk will change, as you will later see. The impression we want to instill when writing these plans is, you are in control of your income and your destiny, not the company. This is an exciting concept for the player. In other words, the more you achieve the more you are rewarded, the less you achieve, the less you get.

These comp plans (RISK/reward) can even drive away the non-achiever and that's good too.

Another positive plan feature for management is that it can deal with the age-old problem of, "Well, I don't need any more commission this year, so I am going to let up a little." The reps can not afford to come to that conclusion, if you design your plans properly.

It's not a well-known fact, but compensation plans can become boring. They occasionally are taken for granted, or the rep loses interest, i.e., "What will be, will be." In this case, the plan neither motivates nor demotivates. It is advisable to have plan mechanics that allow rewards to be paid for a variety of behaviors, including the super achievers. We call these *compensation legs*. The legs address all staff, but tend to emphasize and address the top 25% of your staff, the super achievers. Super achievers will go where the money is. It's not unlike the joke, "Where does an 800 lb. guerrilla sleep? Anywhere it wants!"

Other Design Considerations

- Reps must know how their plan works, and how to work the plan. If they don't understand the mechanics, they will not be motivated to use the plan to reach their compensation objectives. We recommend creating a model, then compare to three months of real sales production. You can apply last year's results, for the same period of time. Run the plan by the reps so that you achieve the "aha!" syndrome. The result should be, "I see how it works! Okay, I can do this," after they work through the exercise.

- Keep in mind, compensation plans are forms of recognition. Reps like to own the reputation of being highly compensated. In fact, it's not unusual with this behavior style, for reps to show other reps their commission check. They want to be recognized.

- Pay out on the plan should be frequent, at least monthly. The truth of the matter is if you could pay out daily with cash, you would have a highly motivated, proactive sales staff.

- Payouts for reactive staffs can be quarterly, without a problem. In fact, it is advised.

Compensation Plan Parity

This topic can, and often does, become an issue within your company. The question becomes, with reference to other disciplines within your organization, "What, and how much should these people earn?"

The question also becomes sticky when compared to field sales reps, as well as distributor, and/or manufacturer's reps that are under a contract or agreement with your organization.

Finally, if you are in Memphis, TN, you need to know the correlation to the Silicon Valley in California, or Chicago, or New York City, as it relates to exciting compensation programs locally.

There are a variety of sources of information available from associations, industry publications, and search agencies. However, caution is the word of the day. These organizations tend to lump all the data from all the disciplines, the functions, the assignments, and the companies (and their locations) together. The published data is then some sort of an industry average, and is very suspect. I believe you need more specificity than they provide. So what is a manager to do?

Develop a Profit and Loss Model, and adjust (if necessary) to all of the above gathered data. A brief example of the model you want to use follows. It is driven by the expense or cost of sales data (COS).

Compensation Model Logic

You can use margins or top-line dollars for your P & L model. Which you use will depend on how much you know about your business. I will show both models. Let us assume you are a business-to-business cataloger, specializing in office supplies, with a Gross Margin Contribution (GMC) of 45%. You have set an objective of 35% gain in sales revenue for your inside sales department, with assigned account structure for the compensation year. Each rep has 425 active accounts to work, having an average sales volume of $5,000 yearly, at 45% margin. The formula or computation might look something like this:

1. Current performance: 425 accounts x $5,000 average performance x 45% Gross Margin Contribution (GMC) = existing GMC

    425 x $5,000 x .45 = $956,250 GMC

2. Planned future performance (Net sales and margin): 425 active accounts x $5,000 average production = existing sales volume, x 35% gain objective = Incremental Sales Volume Gain, x 45% = Incremental Margin Gain (IMG)

    425 x $5,000 = $2,125,000

    $2,125,000 x .35 = $743,750 (ISVG)

    $743,750 x .45 = $334,687 IMG

3. Existing sales volume plus incremental sales volume, equals planned sales volume objective

    $2,125,000 + $743,750 = $2,868,750

4. Incremental margin objective plus existing margin objective, equals planned gross margin objective

    $334,687 + $956,250 = $1,290,937

Kind of exciting, isn't it? The question now becomes, would you pay $40,000 total compensation (base and incentive) for these results? I think you might. That's a 3.1% cost of compensation on gross margin. Not bad at all. Of course, you would apply G & A, and all other direct expenses including FICA. But, on the surface, this makes sense, and you now have the basis of starting to develop a comp plan to make your objectives happen.

- Please remember that new business applications are more expensive. More calls, more cost. But don't lose sight of the lifetime value of the customer when deciding if it is worthwhile.
- If the productivity can not be measured, extra incentive is hard to apply, thus:
  1. Appointment setting, up-grades, cross-selling, dials, minutes on the phone, and net sales can be measured against previous results, and can be incentivized.
  2. Creating a warm and fuzzy feeling can not be incentivized.

Selling Your Plan to Management

We run a series of management seminars in New Jersey called *TELEMAR-KETING BLACK BELT*, for inside sales management. There are three, 3-day seminars in the series. *Black Belt I* spends one-half day on Compensation Plan Design. Without fail the attendees exclaim, "My manager should be here!"

Selling the upper management can be a challenge. We suggest you learn the language of management before you take on this challenge. Here are some pointers that will help. Profit center management is motivated by expenses, profits, and revenues, whether they are for profit, non-profit, or revenue-neutral organizations.

- Management always thinks about budgets in percentages first, then in hard numbers. (For example: "We are talking about a more than 23% profit improvement, amounting to over $100,000.")

- Management is often concerned, even fearful about disturbing existing compensation practices. "If it ain't broken, don't fix it". It's called fear of the unknown.

- Management often perceives the TSRs' job as a simple one, "So why such a complicated compensation plan?".

- Even worse, the effort may be perceived as an expense. This concern will be exhibited when the results are unable to be clearly tracked for their true incremental value, i.e. lead qualification routines. Given these inclinations and preconceptions, it's important to prepare justification, evidence, and proof of a compensation plan's worth *before* approaching upper management for approval. Specifically:

(1) Collect case examples of organizations that reduced their sales expenses, and enhanced revenue, by using the telephone medium as a sales channel.

(2) Know the necessary numbers, i.e., profit percentage your company is seeking, margin contributions, etc.

(3) Know your existing sales expenses, and the percentages when compared to net revenue production.

(4) Prepare a model compensation program with plenty of what-ifs, i.e., strikes, bad weather, etc.

(5) Offer to test the compensation plan against the previous year's actual sales results for the reps and sales management team.

(6) Compare your sales costs to field sales costs by percentages of contribution (e.g., $20 million in sales at a 9% sales cost and 4% contribution for field sales, versus $2 million in sales at 8.2% sales cost and 23% contribution for inside sales).

(7) Compare new accounts, or reactivated account results, to the results of other marketing methods, i.e., field sales, direct mail, trade shows, etc.

(8) Get management involved. "I need your advice, Boss. If we could reduce our overall compensation percentage inside our cost of sales, when compared to revenue, and at the same time increase top-line production, while enhancing our bottom line by 30%, by simply adjusting our compensation plans, would management be interested?".

(9) Test to prove plan effectiveness. You can try one or two reps, on the plan for 6 months, as opposed to the entire department for one year. Also, use *control groups*, i.e., A vs. B, with and without inside sales.

Testing can help, both in plan design and justification to management. Because of the large volume of calls that can be made in a short time period, statistically sound samples can be developed, often in periods as short as four months. In that time, testing a subset of your people, you should be able to determine how a given compensation plan will produce and pay out for both the organization, and the plan participant. Objective results are always better than subjective promises.

Over the past twenty-five years, based on well over 305 inside sales units, I have personally demonstrated that these types of compensation plans, with fixed and variable expense concepts, can be used to motivate performance. In other words, as soon as base salary, FICA, and insurance contributions (which are fixed expenses) have been covered, then only the variable compensation expense (commissions) would apply, when goals are surpassed. This drives down your cost of sales percentages, and that is what these assignments are all about.

In practice, the variable expenses, as a percentage of increase, over fixed costs, turns out to be very small. In mathematical terms, the more the TSR sells, the more the cost of sales (as a percentage of sales) will drop. This can be pointed out to management in many ways, including graphically, and it can help change an entrenched opinion about compensating the inside sales staff, from no interest, to a very positive position.

In summary, sell your compensation plan. Nobody else will do it for you.

Start-up Comp Plans

The question for new units or new staff is, "Should we have a plan that adjusts to actual data, once the numbers stabilize, and/or once we believe the new rep can make the grade?" The answer is yes. It is not a bad idea, but not always necessary. It is your call.

If you should decide to use a start-up plan for either category, the plans should be very simple. Some points to consider:

- A duration of 60 to 90 days
- Have increased production schedules in that period, as in increasing step quota.
- Establish quotas that can be reached. As experience is gained, quotas can be increased.
- If the rep or the unit is successful, in your opinion, apply the actual results to the standard plan, and as you will later see, you can go on from there.

Example:

Let's assume that at full production an experienced, proactive sales rep could close 6 units of sale (on average) a day, valued at $200 each, 5 days a week, for 12 weeks. For our new person the plan will address the lack of experience, and increase monthly.

Period	*Average Daily Production*	*Fixed Reward*
1st month	(3 units @ $150 = $450)	$150
2nd month	(4.5 units @ $175=$788)	$175
3rd month	(6 units @ $200=$1,200)	*Standard Plan

* Apply results of the start-up plan (net revenue sold) to the standard plan. In the third month, the pay out is per your standard comp plan. To determine current commission rate, treat the results as if they were on the standard plan from day one.

The same logic applies to an entirely new department. Just multiply the numbers by the number of reps, with the above quotas. You can, if you choose, count the manager as one-half of a rep. Thus, 4 reps and one manager are 4.5 times the above numbers, divided by 4 (reps).

Case Example

1.65 Million to 8.25 Million in 30 Months

Good compensation planning radically improved the sales and profits of Advanced Management Research, Inc., New York, an education company selling seminar registrations to businesses. The company marketed through direct mail (20 million pieces yearly), and had no field sales organization. They began proactive telemarketing with a staff of seven. Here's what happened:

Initially, the new inside sales unit was viewed as an organizational pariah. The average order was $324. The starting compensation for TSRs was $12,000 annually, with 3% commission on all sales over a $12,000 per month quota. All underages were carried forward, and TSRs lost their jobs if under quota three months in a row. TSRs were, for the most part, rejects from other industries, or out-of-work New York actors.

Fixed bonuses of $1,000 to $3,000 were awarded on net sales over $120,000 per year. Average income was $16,000. Top income was $32,000. The cost-of-sales, fully burdened (i.e., including rent, utilities, overhead, etc.), was 43% of net revenue sold. Combined sales volume for the four TSRs, two managers, and one fulfillment person was $1.65 million.

Dissatisfied with these results, AMR's president hired me as their new vice president of sales. I took action immediately by terminating all non-sales personnel, essentially the entire management team, retrained a fulfillment person, and fired two non-producing proactive selling reps. We then added 52 TSRs and 5 managers over the next 18 months.

We redesigned the compensation packages, and developed professional sales programs similar to those presented in this chapter. As the basis for the redesign, I used 50% of planned compensation for the base, for both managers and TSRs (90% base for support staff). The remainder of compensation was to be earned by reaching assigned sales objectives, with open-ended compensation rewards for exceeding objectives.

We then changed the call objectives, concentrating on consultative selling techniques and the benefits of business education and the AMR service, no more *"Do you need any seminars today?"* Here were the results we achieved at the end of 30 months:

- Direct mail revenue was unchanged, $17,000,000
- The average sale rose from $324 to $465
- Telemarketing revenues increased from $1.65 million to $8.25 million in 30 months
- Cost-of-sales dropped from 43% to 26.8%, and the company paid dividends to its stockholders for the first time in its 16-year history. They also paid cash for everything they purchased.

The results for existing telemarketing staff compensation were just as dramatic. Average income moved from $16,000 to $28,500. Top TSR incomes went from $32,000 to more than $60,000. The two top management incomes went from $40,000 to $129,000. Don't forget that the cost of sales percentage dropped dramatically. Turnover rate shrunk to 25% over the same 30-month period! Terminations and resignations amounted to 13% and promotions or new positions amounted to 12%.

The credibility this selling operation achieved producing these results was impressive. From the Chairman of the Board on down, upper management perceived this unprecedented success to be attributable to the new compensation plan, plus having career sales management personnel.

It took courage for the Chairman of the Board to install this compensation plan at AMR, but he clearly recognized it was the most effective way to achieve the organization's objectives. They increased top-line revenue, lowered selling costs, and achieved profitable operations. The plan ignored the old concept of paying an exact amount for a specified job. Instead, we chose to reward contribution that was directly related to achieving objectives now, both on an individual basis, as well as departmental basis. Literally, the more you sold, the more you earned. We both smiled all the way to the bank.

Compensation Plans by Function or Mission

Enough theory and general commentary. It will now be helpful to look at the actual plans that are designed to perform and motivate, based on the department's mission. Please remember, that if results can not be tracked, based on recorded effort, these plans are not recommended. Second, I am not a proponent of discretionary awards. We find this method to be dependent on the feelings of the awarding manager, and the whole event is more subjective than objective. The compensation plans we will review are an award system for an outbound selling program, but they will also work with a variety of other missions, i.e., account maintenance, new business programs, campaign programs, appointment setting, etc. With appointment setting programs, you can use either dollars sold, or appointments set and completed. If you prefer margin as opposed to sales objectives, that's fine as well.

Base Salary & Commission Plan for the Proactive Rep

In our example of the risk/reward plan, the risk part (commission, bonus, etc.) represents 33% of planned income, and salary represents 66%. We prefer 50/50 risks reward plans wherever possible. 50/50 type plans tend to attract sales types and often pay out more. The reason is that there is more risk. The designer should never have plans any worse than 75% salary, 25% risk, because they lose their motivational ability after that.

Now, let me input a three-month example to show you how this works. Again, you may want to have a copy of Figure 7.2 in front of you for this review.

EXERCISE

Net Sales by month	Payout & Commission %	Eligible for bonus @ 2%, of amount	Total Award
1. $30,000	All in Level #1 @ 2.5% $750	Yes $11,000/$220	$ 970
2. $30,000	$20M Level #1 @ 2.5% $10M Level #2 @ 4.5% $500 and $450	Yes $11,000/$220	$1,170
3. $30,000	All in Level #2 @ 4.5%	Yes $11,000/$220	$1,350

Please remember that the proactive reps enjoy individual compensation mechanics. In this case, the rep's yearly quota was $230,000, and monthly quota was (straight-line) $19,000. If your business has any seasonal highs and lows, you should adjust quotas to fit your specific situation. Determine your quota by determining what percentage of your total existing business comes in for each month (January (6%),

February (9%), etc.). Then take 6% of $230,000, i.e., $13,800. That would be your accountability objective for January. Assigning monthly quotas in this fashion is fair, and more reflective of actual (forecasted) results, as opposed to a straight-line basis, all months being equal.

Reactive (Inbound) Sales Rep Plans

Customers who call you (800 toll free) to place their order are often calling the Inside Sales Department. In some direct marketing applications, that represents 90% of all business written. When they call, we may wish to motivate the reps to up-grade the sale, e.g., quantity price breaks, or, not to sell off the bottom, an expression used to describe the lowest price or minimum order quantity initially offered, or, to sell intrinsic value product, i.e., glue for the glue gun. We can't do much more than that otherwise, we take the risk of increasing the abandoned call rate or customer service level. However, doing just that has substantial rewards. Please review this simplified budgeting example.

EXERCISE

- Revenue normally coming in over the phone $10,000,000
- Average product price increase for
  new budget year 5%   <u>500,000</u>
          Subtotal: $10,500,000
- Budget 5% increase for the enhanced order,
  inbound program   <u>525,000</u>
          New Budget: $11,025,000

Figure 7.2   **INSIDE SALES REPRESENTATIVE (ISR), PROACTIVE COMPENSATION PLAN:**
EFFECTIVE (T.B.D.) NON-EXEMPT

THIS COMPENSATION PLAN ADDRESSES:
  A) BASE SALARY, $20,000
  B) MERIT INCREASE TO BASE SALARY, AN OPTION
  C) MONTHLY COMMISSIONS
  D) MONTHLY ACCOUNTABILITY BONUSES

A) **BASE SALARY** WILL BE DETERMINED BY THE INSIDE SALES MANAGER AND SENIOR MANAGEMENT PER COMPANY POLICY. BASE SALARY WILL BE REVIEWED ONCE A YEAR. IT MAY BE REVIEWED ON A CALENDAR YEAR BASIS OR EMPLOYMENT ANNIVERSARY BASIS, THE BASIS WILL BE DECIDED ON ACCEPTANCE OF EMPLOYMENT. THERE IS NO PERCEIVED ADVANTAGE TO EITHER METHODOLOGY.

B) *MERIT INCREASES TO BASE SALARY* WILL BE AWARDED FOR CONTINUED AND SUSTAINED HIGH PERFORMANCE. THE AWARD IS AN OPTIONAL ADJUSTMENT TO BASE SALARY. A MERIT REVIEW WILL BE HELD WITH ANY SALES PERSON WHO EXCEEDS THEIR ACCOUNTABILITY FOR THE YEAR BY 10%. AN INCREASE IN BASE PAY MAY BE GRANTED OF UP TO 10% OF THE AMOUNT SOLD OVER ACCOUNTABILITY (110% IS THE BENCH-MARK). THE MAXIMUM THAT MAY BE EARNED SHALL NOT BE MORE THAN 10% OF EXISTING BASE PAY. ACTUAL AMOUNTS WILL BE DETERMINED BY THE INSIDE SALES MANAGER, PER COMPANY POLICY.

EXAMPLES

ISR ACCOUNT- ABILITY	NET SALES	GAIN OVER ACCOUNT- ABILITY	10% BENCHMARK	GAIN OVER BENCHMARK	10% OF GAIN CAP AVAILABLE FOR SALARY FROM OLD BASE INCREASE (10%)	BASE INCREASE
$230,000	$270,000	$40,000	$23,000	$17,000*	$17,000*	$2,000	$1,700
$230,000	$235,000	$ 5,000	$23,000	- 0 -	- 0 -	- 0 -	- 0 -

*SALARY INCREASES AWARDED WILL RESULT IN AN INCREASED SELLING OBJECTIVE FOR THE FOLLOWING YEAR BY A CORRESPONDING % INCREASE TO ISR'S SALES RESULTS FROM THE YEAR JUST COMPLETED.

C) **COMMISSIONS ARE PAYABLE MONTHLY**. THE SCHEDULE OF COMMISSION RATES HAS FOUR LEVELS. ISR'S CAN PASS THROUGH EACH LEVEL BY SELLING PRODUCTS TO THEIR CUSTOMERS IN THEIR TERRITORIES. THESE STEP-THROUGH LEVELS WILL REWARD PRODUCTIVITY BY ALLOWING EACH PERSON TO COMMAND AN INCREASING COMMISSION RATE AT HIS/HER OWN ACHIEVEMENT PACE.

COMMISSIONS ARE BASED ON INVOICED AMOUNTS AND NET OF CANCELLATION AND ADJUSTMENTS.

- ISR/COMP 1 -

FGI0199

136

Figure 7.2 (CONT)

ISR COMPENSATION PLAN (CONTINUED)

EACH ASCENDING LEVEL IS EARNED BY INDIVIDUAL SALES PERFORMANCE AND RELATES SOLELY TO THAT REPRESENTATIVES ACHIEVEMENTS. EVERY ISR CAN ADD TO THEIR COMMISSION AT THE HIGHEST PERCENTAGE RATE BY SELLING INTO THE CURRENT COMPENSATION YEAR. BUSINESS SOLD BUT NOT INVOICED AT THE END OF THE COMPENSATION YEAR FOR THE FOLLOWING YEAR WILL BE COMMISSIONED AT THE FIRST STEP LEVEL. THESE FOUR LEVELS AND CORRESPONDING COMMISSION RATES ARE AS FOLLOWS:

NET SERVICES SOLD

STEP LEVEL	NET SALES OF SERVICES	% COMMISSION RATE	COMMISSION	CUMULATIVE COMMISSION	CUMULATIVE SALES
FIRST	$ 50,000	2.5%	$1,250	$ 1,250	$ 50,000
NEXT	$ 80,000	4.5%	$3,600	$ 4,850	$130,000
NEXT	$100,000	5.5%	$5,500	$10,350	$230,000
OVER	$230,000	7.0%	INFINITY	INFINITY	

D) ACCOUNTABILITY BONUS IS AWARDED TO EACH INSIDE SALES PERSON WHO EXCEEDS THEIR ASSIGNED MONTHLY ACCOUNTABILITY.

- EVERY SALES PERSON WILL BE ASSIGNED A MONTHLY NET ACCOUNTABILITY.
- CANCELLED SALES, OR ADJUSTMENTS NO MATTER FOR WHAT REASON, ARE SUBTRACTED FROM THE TOTAL AND ONLY THE NET AMOUNTS ARE ELIGIBLE FOR COMMISSION.
- IF THE ACCOUNTABILITY IS EXCEEDED, A 2% COMMISSION BONUS WILL BE PAID ON ALL NET SALES OVER ACCOUNTABILITY.
- ALL SALES THAT ARE AUTHORIZED, INVOICED, AND SHIPPED IN A MONTH WILL COUNT TOWARDS THIS ACCOUNTABILITY.

ACCOUNTABILITY BONUS EXAMPLE

ISR REP	* ASSIGNED ACCOUNTABILITY	*NET SALES FOR THE MONTH, GRAND TOTAL	AMOUNT ELIGIBLE FOR BONUS	BONUS %	BONUS AMOUNT
"A"	$19,000	$36,000	+$17,000	2%	$340
"B"	19,000	38,500	+ 19,500	2%	$390
"C"	19,000	18,000	MISSED	2%	- 0 -

*USUALLY 1/12 OF TOTAL YEAR (OR REFLECTIVE OF ACTUAL MONTHLY % OF THE YEAR'S TOTAL)

- ISR/COMP 2 -

FGI0199

Figure 7.2 (Cont)

ISR COMPENSATION PLAN

E) **ADDITIONS TO SALES STAFF** STARTING AFTER ORIGINAL START, ALWAYS START-UP AT THE BEGINNING OF THE COMMISSION PLAN, I.E., LOWEST STEP COMMISSION. AT THE END OF THE COMPENSATION YEAR, THE PLAN REVERTS TO THE LOWEST COMMISSION ON THE SAME OR ADVANCED SCALE.

F) **MANAGEMENT RESERVES THE RIGHT TO DISCONTINUE THE ACCOUNTABILITY BONUS ENHANCEMENT** FOR THE ISR. IF NUMBERS OF ORDERS/SALES AND DOLLARS IN CANCELLATION/ADJUSTMENTS EXCEED 10% FOR THE MONTH, ACTION MAY BE REQUIRED. COMPANY WISHES TO ENCOURAGE ONLY SOLID BUSINESS.

LOGIC FOR INCENTIVE COMPENSATION PLANS

• EVERY ISR STARTS EVEN, NO PREDETERMINED PREJUDICE.

• ISR SETS OWN PACE ON COMMISSION GROWTH, NO ARTIFICIAL WAITING PERIOD.

• THE MORE THE ISR SELLS, THE HIGHER COMMISSION AND BONUS HE/SHE WILL RECEIVE.

• NO INCENTIVES IN THIS PLAN TO HOLD BUSINESS OUT OF THE MONTH. STRONG REWARDS FOR ENHANCING THE MONTH.

• PLAN ENCOURAGES QUICK START FOR NEW ISR REPRESENTATIVES, LOW DOLLAR REQUIREMENT BETWEEN STEP 1 AND STEP II.

• PLAN MOTIVATES DAILY (COMMISSION ON THE VERY FIRST DOLLAR INVOICED); MONTHLY VIA (ACCOUNTABILITY BONUS); YEARLY, WITH THE INCREASING STEP COMMISSION PLAN PROVIDING MORE COMMISSION DOLLARS, BASED ON MORE EFFORT, AND A FEATURE THAT ALLOWS THE ISR TO DETERMINE YEARLY BASE INCREASE. A TRULY EXCITING ASSIGNMENT, AND COMPENSATION PLAN.

(THIS COMPENSATION PLAN IS **NOT** TO BE CONSTRUED AS A CONTRACT OF EMPLOYMENT.)

_____
MANAGER

_____
INSIDE SALES REP

- ISR/COMP 3 -

FGI0199

Assuming we have ten inbound ISRs on the program for the year, we can design a comp plan that has a fixed bonus reward system for reaching targeted quarterly objectives. If the department makes their objective all reps will win the award. That's how they enjoy their recognition, by department. The mechanics (straight-line basis) would look like this.

Total Objective:		**$11,025,000**
Quarterly Target (divided by 4)		$ 2,756,250
Payout by Quarter, Per ISR for reaching Objective:		
First Quarter	$150	
Second Quarter	$200	
Third Quarter	$250	
Fourth Quarter	$300	
Subtotal		$ 900
End of the Year		$ 100
Total Available:		$1,000
Ten ISRs x $1,000 =		$10,000 planned compensation

The question becomes, would you pay $10,000 to the department to get an additional $525,000? I think so. Notice that nothing needs to be tracked. They either make it, or they don't. It is a super program. There are some caveats to the program that are the same as those for the manager's program. Please review that program's fine points, which follows shortly.

Support Staff Motivation Plans

As hard as it is to believe, the current trend is to establish plans for all support staff who also have contact with the customer, as well as those who help the rep stay on the phones, by handling non-selling tasks. It's called team building, and often these positions are career path assignments. From this group comes your expansion or replacement reps. Everyone now is working towards departmental goals for obvious reasons. The rules that apply to the manager also apply to the support staff. In other words, if the manager makes the quarterly award, so does the support staff, including the reactive sales staff previously mentioned.

A simple way to compensate support and fulfillment people is through a fixed bonus arrangement, with bonuses paid quarterly, and increased quarterly, throughout the year. This kind of a plan can be very curious to people not used to anything other than straight salary or hourly wages. If they have the following traits however, the chances are good that they will respond and can be pulled together as a team:

139

- They can be motivated by recognition and more dollars.
- They show potential for working with others.
- They are interested in moving up to a more advanced selling assignment.

As with the two plans described previously, the following plan was designed for one of our client companies. Again, don't pay too much attention to the numbers. You can fill in your own amounts depending on your type of business, your location, and the economic environment.

This compensation plan addresses: base salary, merit increases to base salary, and bonus.

A) Base Salary. Base is determined by the inside sales manager, per company policy. It is reviewed annually, either on a calendar year or employment anniversary basis, as decided upon, on acceptance of employment.

B) Merit Increases to Base Salary. Merit increases to base salaries are awarded for continued and sustained high performance. Actual amounts are determined by the inside sales manager, per company policy.

C) Bonus. Bonuses are earned whenever the entire telemarketing department meets its quarterly objectives, for example:

Base: *$18,000*

If the unit meets sales objectives:

Bonus:

First Quarter:	$125
Second Quarter:	150
Third Quarter:	175
Fourth Quarter:	200
Bonus Total:	$650

The logic behind this plan is as follows:

- Every sales support person starts even, no predetermined prejudice.
- Sales support people enjoy bonus growth based on the success of the telesales department, with no artificial waiting period.
- Sales support people will earn a quarterly bonus if the sales unit meets its revenue goals.
- No complicated tracking system is required for the pay-out.

Management Risk/Reward Plans

These plan mechanics also fit a number of other motivational situations. The mechanics not only work for managers, but the following listed areas as well. Only the amounts are different, the logic is the same. A few examples are as follows:

- Inbound Sales, Order Entry, Technical, and Tech Service Sales, which are all reactive environments
- Customer Service applications
- Support Staff applications (on previous page)

Also, notice that in the previous proactive plan (Figure 7.2), as well as these plans, intensity and momentum are built into the plan mechanics. The device used is the increasing step reward programs, i.e., more today than yesterday, but not as much as tomorrow!! This plan feature prevents slacking-off for both reps and managers. The reader should ignore the compensation and sales revenue numbers themselves, and just digest the concept. See Figure 7.3.

Figure 7.3

COMPENSATION PLAN
MANAGER (EXEMPT)

THIS COMPENSATION PLAN ADDRESSES:

1. MONTHLY QUOTA
2. QUARTERLY QUOTA
3. YEARLY QUOTA
4. EXCEEDING BUDGET OBJECTIVES

In order for the Manager of Inside Sales to qualify for any bonus, they must achieve 100% of their total budget objective and be an employee at the end of the period represented. The plan is not to be construed as a contract for employment.

Cumulative Dollar Values:	Each Month	Available per Quarter	Available per Year
• Base for this position is			$37,000
• A bonus is paid each month for achieving the projected net sales objective for the month. If a monthly objective is missed, bonus may not be recovered.	$250@	$750@	$ 3,000
• A bonus is paid each quarter for achieving the quarterly sales objective. In any quarter where sales exceed the objective the over- age may be carried forward into the sub- sequent quarter to assist with that quarter's objective. (A positive plan feature)		1st $1,750 2nd $2,250 3rd $2,750 4th $3,250	$10,000

Note: If the objective is missed for any quarter, that quarter's bonus can be recaptured if the deficit is neutralized with overages obtained from the existing quarter. However, that current quarter must have its objective complete in order to exercise this feature.

• Sub-total planned compensation:	$50,000

• Year-end bonuses will be paid if the margin/sales objectives are exceeded. The bonus is payable in the first quarter of the following year (or fiscal year) and after reconciliation of the unit's sales and margin contributions.

Margin (by 2%)	$ 4,000
Net sales (by 10%)	$ 2,000
	$56,000

FGI00199

142

The manager's plan exhibit works well with start-up situations, and has four *legs*: base, monthly rewards, quarterly rewards, and yearly revenue and margin awards for exceeding objectives.

The second year plan should pay attention to exceeding sales objectives by moving from a fixed to an open-ended feature. Thus, the plan is not capped. It does not have an artificial boundary that restricts compensation. Please remember that once the original target is exceeded, all fixed expenses plus planned contribution have been covered. Exceeding objectives only drives your cost-of-sales percentage down.

Finally, this plan takes into consideration events that the manager can not control, i.e., Desert Storm, a warm winter, product failure, etc. The manager may miss two monthly rewards, but "smack" the third month, and make the quarter, or, "blow" the first quarter, but have an outstanding second quarter. That allows recouping bonus loses. The objective is to get the job done, not penalize the manager for an event out of their control. However, if two quarters are missed in a row, there may be another problem.

Here is an exercise to ensure understanding. Assume straight-line mechanics on a $24,000,000 objective.

Exercise

Input Data (Net)

Yearly Sales Objective		$24,000,000
Quarterly Sales Objective		$ 6,000,000
Monthly Sales Objective	$ 2,000,000	

50/50 Risk/Reward

Compensation plan pay out objective for the manager is:	$ 65,000
Base (50% of total, i.e. $60,000)	30,000
• First Quarter Bonus (5% of total)	3,000
• Second Quarter Bonus (10% of total)	6,000
• Third Quarter Bonus (15% of total)	9,000
• Fourth Quarter Bonus (20% of total)	12,000
Total Plan Pay out:	$ 60,000
Monthly Award, @ $250 each month	3,000
End of Year (10% over 20 million dollars)*	2,000
Grand Total Available:	$ 65,000

*Paid following year

Results Example

(Budget, $2 Million in Sales, Monthly)

($Millions) Sales/Month	Quarter	Yes or No Monthly Award	Yes or No Quarterly Award
Jan. 2.5	1st	Yes	
Feb. 1.7	1st	No	
Mar. 2.0	1st	Yes	
Total: 6.2			Yes
Apr. 2.0	2nd	Yes	
May 2.0	2nd	Yes	
Jun. 1.7	2nd	No	
Total: 5.7			No
Jul. 2.0	3rd	Yes	
Aug. 2.0	3rd	Yes	
Sept. 2.4	3rd	Yes	
Total: 6.4			*Yes

*Feature kicks-in. Yes, 3rd Quarter was made. Yes, there was enough overage to pick up the deficit in the 2nd Quarter. Yes, there is enough overage ($100,000) to help with the 4th Quarter's objective. Is this neat? Yes!

By the end of 1990, compensation levels were becoming quite exciting. Industry experts were reporting that the rate of growth of management compensation was close to 15% yearly. Assume that 1990 is a benchmark. By the end of 1995 the growth percentage was pushing 50% yearly.

Alternative Methods of Compensation: Contests

Most sales departments have contests of one type or another, although the reasoning behind them isn't generally well understood. Here are the basic justifications for sales contests:

- Contests, by definition, suggests competition. It is a well-established fact that salespeople like to compete for recognition and money (another form of recognition).
- Organizations can get a second effort through a well-designed contest, with clear objectives for both the sales representatives and the company.
- Contests can temporarily eradicate, if not neutralize, the negative impact of boredom, pressure and tension.

There are negative sides to contests. They can be run too often and sales units can become addicted to them. Sales people may hold back production, called *sandbagging*, if a contest is anticipated. The way to control these problems are to announce "sprint" (short duration) contests, only on the day the contest starts. Also, start them on Tuesday as opposed to Monday, and stay away from the first of the month. Another problem may be that the same players win every contest. The solution is to have two contests, one for the achievers and one for everyone else. You will get better production out of both groups.

Further, a contest should have a budget, and a reward that's worth shooting for. Forget the Stetson hat or passes to the movies. Offer the sales staff what they think is interesting. Ask them to tell you what is worth the additional effort.

Here are some examples of "sprint" or short-term contest designs:

Example 1 — The "Balloon" Contest. This contest was run in an organization that wanted to add service contracts to product sales. The specific objective was to generate 200 new service contracts at $250 each.

To qualify to break a balloon at the end of the day, the rep had first of all, to maintain daily production objectives. After four service contracts were sold, each contract thereafter was worth two throws at the balloons. After 15 contracts were sold, three throws were won for each contract sold.

The game was played at the end of each day. The balloons, stuffed with slips of paper indicating a bonus value from $.50 to $100, were pinned to dart board-like material, and reps were allowed to throw the number of darts they had won during the day at the balloon display. Value slips were distributed in the balloons as follows:

BALLOONS	AMOUNT
1	$100.00
4	50.00
10	20.00
24	10.00
5	1.00
10	.50
54 Balloons	$750.00

With $250 budgeted for replacement balloons, the total budget for this contest was $1,000. The contest provided a lot of fun, some excitement, and the required competition. It ran for one week and then was discontinued. If service contracts were subsequently cancelled, the awards were charged back against regular commissions. Notice, dart-throwing skills are not required. No one knows where the awards are.

With contests like this, it's important to keep careful payout records and to post blurbs as to who won what. Cash awards should be paid immediately with the typical deductions worked out later.

Example 2 — The "Wheel of Fortune" Contest. This contest is similar to the "Balloon" contest, except that a 36-inch Wheel of Fortune is rented, and each "win" gets a spin of the wheel. Awards can be dollar values, trips, tickets to special events, etc., secured to the wheel in place of the graphic, dice numbers.

Long-term Contests are possible, but they can be a problem. The primary difficulty is the short attention span of the people you're trying to motivate. Contests running a month or more in duration can and usually do, suffer a significant decline in interest. The option to terminate the contest at any time should be left to the manager's discretion, as well as posted on contest material, bulletins, etc.

I have found that the only reason to run a long-term contest is to distract the unit from another distracting event. Sounds like double-talk I am sure, but let me explain. I once had to move a unit from 42nd & 5th Avenue, NYC, to 68th Street and Avenue of the Americas, from poor facilities to the Riveria, if you will. Well, that's all the group could think about. Sales production was near non-existent. The solution was a two-month contest based on stock ownership, in other words, a theme contest with counterfeit "stock" in our make-believe company. Stock listings from the *Wall Street Journal, Barrons,* etc., were hanging on every wall to support the theme. Here is how it worked:

- 100 shares of Stock were issued, par value of one-cent to each player.
- As quota objectives were met, both individually, and by department, splits and options were issued.
- The price of the stock would rise and fall daily, depending on the pace of the department's daily effort, and the budgeted objectives.
- At the close of the theme contest, stocks were traded for merchandise of equal value, or cash at 75% value, or combinations of both.

It worked nicely and was a lot of fun. This contest required a lot of hype, daily bulletins, skits, anything to maintain the attention span, in order for it to work.

Other Resources for Contest Ideas

"Motivating with Sales Contests: The Complete Guide to Motivating Your Telephone Professionals with Contests That Produce Record-Breaking Results. Including 79 Contests You Can Run Right Now," by David L. Worman. Paperback, 252 pages, $29.00

"Telephone Sales Management and Motivation Made Easy, With 50 Sales Contests You Can Use Immediately," by Valerie Sloane and Theresa Arvizo Jackson. Paperback, 161 pages, $19.95

Both are available directly from the publisher: Business By Phone, Inc., (402)895-9399, or 800-326-7721. Or order online at www. businessbyphone.com.

Closing Thought

Compensation plans by themselves are not the total answer to organizational success. Recognition, feedback, training, or a thank you now and again, are also important. Keep these thoughts in mind when designing and installing compensation plans.

- Find ways to pay for results, not ways of not paying
- Frequent changes in comp plans give the impression that you don't know what you're doing, or that you are trying to "stick it" to the performers. A three-month introduction period is advised before starting the plan.
- Educate the staff intensively on how to beat your plan. When your department figures out how to beat your plan, you will both be smiling. Beating the budget and your compensation plan is what compensation programs are designed to do.

Chapter 8
Understanding Sales Staff Motivations

Manager and Rep Behavior Styles

Introduction

This is one of those topics where some information can be dangerous, because the topic has not been studied in-depth, as it relates to professional telephone assignments. I am neither a behavioral scientist nor an industrial psychologist, but I have gathered enough experience and information over the past twenty-five years to suggest that I know some things that can be helpful to you.

Some Background: In 1971, I was a Regional Sales Manager with Dun & Bradstreet's Marketing Services Division. The Division decided to spend some of its training dollars on the corporate staff and twelve regional sales managers. The topics chosen were, "Interpersonal Relationships", and "How to Hire a Winning Sales Staff." This week-long event changed my business life and management style for the better, forever.

As a part of the pre-session prep work, I was asked to complete several written profiling instruments, and also to have others do the same for me. The reference point was, "Please think about the subject and answer the questions accordingly." My boss, two peers, two subordinates, and one person outside of my business, and I completed identical research questionnaires. Each had 250 questions that looked like this:

149. Which would be of more interest to the subject?
a. Reading a good book on the creation of the universe.
b. Hospital volunteer's service
c. Flying a jet fighter
d. Making difficult decisions on Company direction

I was being evaluated by others on my perceived behavior, and comparing the results to my beliefs about my own behavior. Equally interesting was that, out of twelve sales managers, ten were close to being profiled identically. Finally, the entire premise suggested that it became easier to manage people based on my new understandings, because I now clearly understood how they saw me and responded to my management behavior style. It's appropriate to note that others often see us differently than we see ourselves.

We also learned that behavior is learned, based on our lifetime of experiences. That's different from personality traits that we inherit. Personality is in our genes. Behavior can be somewhat adjusted based on learning. Personality basically does not adjust.

We also learned that operating outside of our defined behavior style for lengthy periods of time caused us discomfort, and stress. Continued doses of sustained stress can cause or show itself physically, as migraine headaches, strokes, heart attacks, etc. Trying to behave like others, or in a way you think will help your cause can be devastating to you as well. You are who you are, and that is okay.

At this particular session I was digesting five aspirins, every two hours, to deal with constant, reoccurring migraines. My parents thought I had a brain tumor, my doctor thought I was allergic to something catastrophic, as in breathing oxygen. As it turned out I was operating in a foreign behavior style for the better part of six months. That caused the stress, and in turn created the migraines. When I understood why and what to do about it, I nearly kissed the instructor on the forehead. The result was that I have not had a return of the migraines since that training event.

Time passed, and I now have learned that certain behavior styles show up frequently in certain type of jobs and that when there are performance problems, seven out of ten times it's a behavior style mismatch for that particular assignment causing much of the grief.

My question became "Can this knowledge be used in the hiring process" i.e., behavior style selection. The answer was a resounding "yes." Not only did it make sense, but I found out that the entire topic could be used as an advanced training skill for proactive, outbound sales reps as well. The topic turns into understanding how, and in what time frame four behavior styles like to buy and/or make purchases. It turns out to be that this is reliable data, as opposed to smoke and mirrors.

How Can We Use Behavior Style Information to Our Advantage

We can use this in at least three specific ways. Think of the topic as finding the round peg for the round hole. The topics are:

- Match your assignment with a tested behavior style that is considered appropriate for the task.
- Be prepared to adjust accounts and/or assignments if we have a behavior style conflict
- Teach our staff to recognize customer, prospect, inquirers, and suspect behavior styles and respond accordingly.

This topic even helps the organization get along favorably with itself, as well as with others. We can predict how others behave. When colleagues understand each other, you will find that this helps with the unit's motivational and mental health. Before I show you how to use this tool, I need to explain what it is.

The Behavior Style Grid

Please see Figure 8.1. You may wish to copy this page to help guide you through the discussion. Important point(s) to remember:

- There are no incorrect behavior styles.
- You may want a variety of behavior styles in your unit to handle a variety of variable assignments and customers.
- The best teams have a variety of behavior styles housed within the team.
- We, as players, can act in other behavior styles for brief periods of time without serious consequence to ourselves. As long as we know it's best to return to our regular behavior style for job performance, then we have comfort as opposed to stress.
- We are not good predictors of our own style — others are. It's how they view us that defines the style.

Figure 8.1

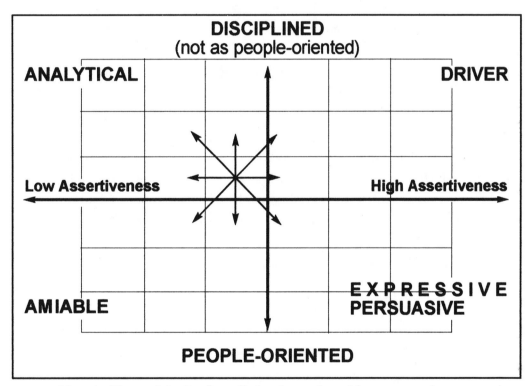

Note in Figure 8.1, the four distinctive styles, driver, expressive-persuasive, amiable, and analytical. The vertical grid divides styles that are more people-oriented, as opposed to less people-oriented. Using myself as an example, I must be around people. I don't like being alone or doing anything unless it's with others. I could even say, "I enjoy me best when I am with you." That as opposed to an extreme opposite example of a not-so-people-oriented type, such as in the movie *Network*, (MGM-United Artists, 1976) staring Faye Dunaway and William Holden. Faye destroyed broadcasting careers at the drop of a hat, with no concern for the people affected, in order to further her own driving objectives.

The horizontal axis shows more assertive vs. less assertive behavior. We live in a world that suggests that the assertive will inherit the world, not the meek. Of course, it's not true, but many of us would like to be more assertive, and some of us are. The example here is that inside sales reps in North Carolina don't relish calling prospects or customers in New York City, because New Yorkers are perceived as being very assertive.

The remainder of the exhibit shows degrees of behavior, with nine variations in each style. It's helpful to note that we can perform without stress in the next contiguous block for brief periods of time. Thus, in the X'd example, our subject is an analytical for the most part, but this person can exhibit all other behaviors to a minor degree, without stress, for brief periods of time (as in hours, days, but not likely weeks or months).

Now please review the abbreviated likes and dislikes, plus the summary on each behavior style listed in Figures 8.2 and 8.3. As a drill to test your understanding, the television and movie series Star Trek had four major characters, each with a distinctive behavior style. See if you can identify them. The characters were:

1. Captain Kirk (the leader)   3. Bones (the doctor)
2. Spock (second in command)   4. Scotty (chief engineer)

The questions might be, would Spock make a good outbound sales rep? I don't think so. A Tech Rep, yes. Would Bones make a good Customer Service Rep? Yes. Would Scotty, no. Would Scotty do well as our New York sales rep? I think so. Would Captain Kirk make a fine proactive, account maintenance sales rep. I think so.

Answers: 1. Expressive-Persuasive 2. Analytical 3. Amiable 4. Driver

Figure 8.2

EXPRESSIVE PERSUASIVE

Does Like	*Doesn't Like*	*Summary*
• Approval and Compliments	• Routine	Enjoy being social; like to persuade, enjoy life and generally are enthusiastic. Ego is super important. They enjoy symbols of success. They listen, and do it. They enjoy a pat on the back, immediate recognition. Urgency relates to "next week for sure, but not today!"
• To be at the Top of the List	• The Administrative Details	
• People	• Tasks	
• Enthusiasm and Spontaneity	• Disapproval	
• To Exaggerate a Little	• Long Term Projects	
• To Select Data They Like and Disregard the Rest	• Slow and Easy Wins the Race	
• To be Trusting of Others	• Being Alone	
• Groups That Give Them Prestige	• Long and Drawn-Out Explanations	
• Ego Symbols in their Office Setting	• Details	

Driver

Does Like	*Doesn't Like*	*Summary*
• Self-Starters	• Status Quo	These folks must overcome all obstacles, tend to have little patience and are known to be impulsive. They want to complete tasks and have tasks completed as of yesterday. No excuses, only results. Delay is a bad omen. Only "now, today!!"
• Competition	• Lazy or Laid Back Anything	
• Difficult Challenges	• Routine, Boredom, Boring	
• Achievement	• Relaxing	
• To be the Center of Activity	• Beating Around the Bush	
• Control	• Lack of Urgency	
• Fast Pace	• Slow Moving Pace	
• Productivity		
• Pressure		

Figure 8.3

AMIABLE

Does Like	*Doesn't Like*	*Summary*
• Appreciation of Self	• Pressure	Enjoys relating to others, likes to be supportive, possessive; definitely enjoys peer attention, procrastinate on time (as in never), are concerned with "What do you really want?"
• Security	• Deadlines	
• To Belong, Help Others	• Conflict	
• Their Things	• An Argument	
• Being a Softy	• Lack of Assurance	
• Asking Lots of Questions	• Accountability	
• Listening	• Change, Change, Change	
• Slow and Easy Wins the Race		

ANALYTICAL

Does Like	*Doesn't Like*	*Summary*
• Established Routines	• Conflict	Very logical and exact/precise; enjoy and want facts/details; like activity/action; believe it or not, avoid troublesome situations. These people look at time in 30-day segments, i.e., "Get it done next month."
• To be Correct, Right	• Data Voids	
• Absence of Conflict	• Non-Logical Situations	
• The Facts, Logic, Charts, Graphs, Proof	• "BS'ers"	
• Competitive Bios (Comparison)	• Non-Detailed Type Salespeople	
• Data (A Crutch)		
• Procedure, Preferably Established		
• Productivity		
• Pressure		

Additional Understanding of Styles

Certain professions and assignments are housed in functions and attract specific behavior styles. Entire basic industries will attract similar styles as well. Let's look at some examples.

Amiables

- Customer Service/Human Resources
- Retail Clerks
- President Jimmy Carter/George Bush
- Education/Teachers
- Health Care providers
- Salvation Army
- Social Services

Analyticals

- Finance, Accounting, Marketing Management
- Purchasing, Buyers
- Specialty Doctors
- Senator John Glenn
- Engineering and Scientific
- Economist, Chess Players

Drivers

- Fast Track "Employees"
- Entrepreneurs/Bill Gates
- General George Patton, Adolph Hitler
- Leaders on the Move!!
- Paratroopers (Military)
- General Montgomery/ Margaret Thatcher/ Richard Nixon

Expressive/Persuasives

- Proactive Sales staffs
- President Ronald Reagan
- Sales leaders
- President Bill Clinton

Keep in mind, there is no wrong behavior style, i.e., amiables can be expressive-persuasive for a brief period of time, etc.

Now I think you have a reasonable answer as to why customer service reps don't like proactive selling, and often don't want to have anything to do with selling. It is a motivational issue, for sure, however it's a management issue as well.

The Customer Behavior Styles

Although this may not be a human resource topic for hiring, it is a topic for matching the behavior styles of reps and customers. I just don't think that librarians want to be serviced by hard-core drivers, or that assigning expressives as Tech Sales reps makes sense. Analyticals would be better for the tech rep position.

Believe me, behavior styles are being utilized more and more, and are worth considering for the selection of staff, and matching staff to their environment in telephone sales, resulting in a positive motivational situation. Many proactive selling assignments are staffed (60% +) with expressive persuasives, and they do quite well.

Value Systems of You And Your Staff, And How They Impact Motivation

What Motivates You?

That could very well be the question of the hour. We do know that along with behavior styles (and there are clues here), personal value systems can motivate or demotivate you, depending on if they are addressed positively or negatively. The same is true when your values are tread upon by others. When demotivation happens, caused by someone who has offended your values, it's almost like stepping on a land mine. It does a lot of damage.

If honesty were one of your top values, and you found out or perceived that your manager was less than honest with you or others, would you be motivated to work for them? Probably not. Leave the assignment, be skeptical, etc.? Probably so.

If family security was your top value, would you be highly motivated if your company dropped all of their health benefit programs. Or, with a different twist on the same value, if a prize was awarded for achievement, would you be more motivated by a trip to an Atlantic City Casino or Disneyland? We think, in this case, Disneyland, because family security is the motivator, i.e., taking care of loved ones.

And, if I had an exciting life as one of my top values, I could be motivated to perform intensively by a trip to Las Vegas, and/or white-water rafting.

I have provided the reader with a list of words and/or noun and adjective phrases that helps to describe a person's terminal values. Once the values are in the open, you have an opportunity to motivate, or be motivated by others. Values, unlike personality, do change because of life's events. Marriage, or buying a home can change one's values.

The list provided (courtesy of ORA, Dr. Scott Golden, Mt. Laurel, NJ) should be considered as one's individual values. If you and/or each member of your staff would number and prioritize these phrases in each list (see Figure 8.4) you will have clues as to what is important in your or your staff's life. Thus, you will find what motivates the person taking the test, making the results a management tool.

Value System Summary

Not all people are motivated in the same way, and it makes a lot of sense to understand individual values for individual motivation techniques. This is not a selection tool, it's a management understanding device. The informal test on the following material is to think of an important decision you have made in the last year, and relate it to the top five terminal values in each list. You should be able to see why and how that decision was impacted or influenced by your value system.

Figure 8.4

THE VAN VECHTEN GROUP's VALUE SURVEY

MANAGER/SUPERVISOR [ ]		*CSR* [ ] *TSR* [ ]	
Number the adjective most important to you	**RANK**	Number the word or noun phrase most important to you	**RANK**
AMBITIOUS		A COMFORTABLE LIFE	
hardworking and aspiring	_____	a prosperous life	_____
BROAD-MINDED		EQUALITY	
open-minded	_____	brotherhood and equal opportunity for all	_____
CAPABLE		AN EXCITING LIFE	
competent; effective	_____	a stimulating, active life	_____
CLEAN		FAMILY SECURITY	
neat and tidy	_____	taking care of loved ones	_____
COURAGEOUS		FREEDOM	
standing up for your beliefs	_____	independence & free choice	_____
FORGIVING		HEALTH	
willing to pardon others	_____	physical & mental well-being	_____
HELPFUL		INNER HARMONY	
working for the welfare of others	_____	freedom from inner conflict	_____
HONEST		MATURE LOVE	
sincere and truthful	_____	sexual & spiritual intimacy	_____
IMAGINATIVE		NATIONAL SECURITY	
daring and creative	_____	protection from attack	_____
INDEPENDENT		PLEASURE	
self-reliant; self-sufficient	_____	an enjoyable, leisurely life	_____
INTELLECTUAL		SALVATION	
intelligent and reflective	_____	saved; eternal life	_____
LOGICAL		SELF-RESPECT	
consistent; rational	_____	self-esteem	_____
LOVING		A SENSE OF ACCOMPLISHMENT	
affectionate and tender	_____	a lasting contribution	_____
LOYAL		SOCIAL RECOGNITION	
faithful to friends or the group	_____	respect and admiration	_____
OBEDIENT		TRUE FRIENDSHIP	
dutiful; respectful	_____	close companionship	_____
POLITE		WISDOM	
courteous and well-mannered	_____	a mature understanding of life	_____
RESPONSIBLE		A WORLD AT PEACE	
dependable and reliable	_____	a world free of war & conflict	_____
SELF-CONTROLLED		A WORLD OF BEAUTY	
restrained; self-disciplined	_____	beauty of nature and the arts	_____

Staff Motivation

Introduction: Probably the most frequently asked question by managers who have responsibility for phone sales personnel are, "How can we motivate our staff." This topic of motivation is important enough to cover in-depth with an additional book. The topic is confusing, and in general, not very well understood.

Webster's New World Dictionary (College Edition) has three brief listings worth review.

- Motivate – to provide with, or affect as, a motive(s); incite or impel.
- Motive – some inner drive, impulse, intention, etc., that causes a person to do something or act in a certain way; incentive goal.
- Motivational Research – a systematic and scientific analysis of the forces influencing people so as to control the making of their decision: applied in advertising, marketing, selling, etc.

I am not eager to take the topic to an academic discussion, however, *when a problem exists, more often than not, it is conveniently described as a motivational problem.* I am not sure I agree that motivation is the problem, but I do agree that when there is a problem, it needs to be identified, a solution applied, measured for the effect, and adjusted to accomplish the desired result.

The old school of thought was:

- If you have a job that has a reasonably clear description, why can't an employee come to work, do the assignment, for reasonably remuneration.
- Why must they be motivated to work well or better? That's the job.
- You really can't motivate another person, they motivate themselves.

Because the answers to the above are vague, and the term motivation is a convenient word to cover a number of evils, so to speak, the search for an answer branches out to other topics. Usually it's to determine cause or blame.

Thus, the following: "It's a *(fill in the blank)* thing?" Try these on for size. Work ethic -- Union -- Values -- Culture -- Training -- Unfair -- Poor self-perception -- Moral -- Dead-end -- Stuck -- Boring -- Tension -- Pressure -- Management -- Location -- Compensation -- Recognition -- Empathy -- Responsibility -- Peer -- etc.

Lack of motivation has many perceived causes. When the above terms come into play, they are the symptoms of the problem, and for the most part are not the problem itself.

An example: A manufacturer in Madison, Wisconsin noticed a drop in sales productivity, increased absenteeism, and an increase of requests for inter-department transfers. Was the problem motivation and morale? Not exactly. These were only the symptoms of the problem.

Seven months prior to the attempted solution, the Department Director was promoted and left this Division for another. The management slot was not filled or replaced. The two sales supervisors assumed the duties of the Director, along with their other duties. The supervisors' previous duties were heavily oriented to proactive investments in staff (monitoring, coaching, counseling, training, "parenting", etc.). Time requirement demands for the new adjusted position literally put a stop to the proactive investments in the staff. Four months later, the problem started to manifest itself. Seven months later it was a raging fire.

How did I identify the problem, and later the solution? I simply asked 18 people for their comments, input, and recommendations. Guess what? They told me how to correct the problem, which in turn restored morale and "motivation".

As General George Patton said (after reviewing troops in Africa who were beaten badly by the Germans in a major battle), "A blind man could see what the problem was!" I, as well, knew immediately what the problem was. But, in order to effect the solution to the problem, the unit needed to take ownership of both the problem and the solution. And that's what happened. The solution, by the way, was that the managers went back to staff investments noted above, and the problem went away.

Summary — When the unit is working well, we say that motivation and moral are in good shape. And of course, the opposite is true as well.

The reader should remember that perceived motivation and morale problems are symptoms of something that is affecting your work environment. Therefore, the first activity is to identify the real problems, then obtain both data, and proposed solutions from your staff, and finally take action and correct the problem.

Different Strokes for Different Folks

Not all telephone staff enjoys exactly the same motivational methods or tactics. Behavior styles and value systems will impact the method you select. For example, proactive, outbound selling staff enjoys seeing regularly published lists (i.e., weekly) that report performance. Achievers enjoy being at the top of the list of their peers, and, quite frankly are motivated to stay there. On the other hand, reactive staff enjoys departmental recognition as opposed to individual recognition. Lists showing individual performance, posted for all to see, are considered as potentially embarrassing, and do not motivate. In fact they de-motivate. Interesting, isn't it? The reason is random distribution of calls, or lack of control vs. outbound calling, and lots of control as to what happens.

The result that you want to accomplish is to provide a comfortable working environment, by function. Train on everything, let the group take ownership of the program, recognize performance (the feedback loop), and get out of the way.

The Maryland Study

Here is another perspective. The University of Maryland conducted a massive study (1981/1982) on what motivates people to do excellent work. A cross section of that study measured "blue collar" (the worker) response, to "white collar" (administrative staff/ management) response. Ten reasonable topics were arranged in alphabetical order and the two groups arranged the topics by perceived importance. Here are the results, and I think they are fascinating. This may help you understand why we have problems in the first place.

WHAT EMPLOYEES SAY	WHAT EMPLOYERS SAY
1. Appreciation	1. Wages
2. Participation in daily operations & future planning	2. Job Security
3. Sympathy for personal problems	3. Promotions
4. Job Security	4. Working Conditions
5. Wages	5. Interesting Work
6. Interesting Work	6. Employer Loyalty
7. Promotions	7. Tactful Discipline
8. Employer Loyalty	8. Appreciation
9. Working Conditions	9. Sympathy for personal problems
10. Tactful Discipline	10. Participation in daily operations and future planning

Quite a difference wouldn't you say? Please remember that this is a blue-collar vs. white-collar study, not a specific trek through telemarketing or telephone sales. However, it is a review of a group of people, and suggests that management of this group could have problems motivating staff, given their perceptions. The result, if not investigated, would be demotivating as opposed to motivating.

After I saw the above, I commented, "I told you so". I then developed an intense curiosity along the same topic. What about proactive or reactive telephone sales reps or customer service staff? It was time to do some research.

In October 1989, and again in June 1990, I ran primary research projects via mail, and also called the non-respondents on the identical topics. Some accidental bias was introduced because the list used was the paid subscription base to *The Van Vechten Report*. That base was 85% business-to-business, with 90% of that being outbound. However, it was statistically sound (confidence factor plus or minus 6.5%) and I am sure highly applicable to this universe. Incidentally, the impact of this research is also evidence that compensation planning is quite important.

WHAT MANAGERS THINK MOTIVATES TSRs (*The Van Vechten Report*, June 1990)	WHAT TSRs REPORTED MOTIVATED THEM (The *Van Vechten Report*, October, 1989)
1. Compensation	1. Compensation
2. Appreciation/recognition	2. Working Conditions
3. Working Conditions	3. Interesting Work
4. Interesting Work	4. Appreciation/recognition
5. Promotions	5. Job Security
6. Company loyalty to employee	6. Promotions
7. Involvement, future planning	7. Involvement, future planning
8. Job Security	8. Company loyalty to employee
9. Tactful discipline	9. Tactful discipline
10. Sympathy for personal problems	10. Sympathy for personal problems

I must say, and with some pride, for the most part inside sales management thinks like their staff does, and the reason for that is simple. There is an excellent chance that three years ago they were the people performing in these very same rep positions.

A few points you may want to remember as it relates to motivation. It's not unlike Newton's 3rd Law of Motion, for every action there is an opposite and equal reaction. Often any change to the work environment causes the reaction, which in turn impacts motivation. Symptoms of perceived motivational problems are just that, problems that need to be identified, and then, and only then, can you begin your search for the solution.

Author's note: Although the research studies appear to have some age attached to them, the information discovered is holding up quite well. Check surveys as late as 1996 were conducted with individual classes of the Black Belt Telesales Management Seminar and the results were nearly identical.

Chapter Nine
Telephone Skills & Training Techniques

Introduction

While on a training assignment for the senior training manager at Union Carbide headquarters in New Jersey, I became duly impressed by their commitment to training, as well as the department's resources and trappings. I specifically noted the uniquely designed departmental stationery that let their company and the world know that Union Carbide was committed to training excellence. At the bottom of each sheet of their stationery or company printed training product, was this simple, but effective quote:

"An investment in knowledge pays the best interest."
-- Benjamin Franklin

That says it all and quite frankly I wish I had said that first. Since Ben's witticisms are now public domain, I too have adopted the quotation as a small banner of our stated beliefs.

The topic of training as a chapter can be massive. It is for that reason this topic is dealt with in two chapters. Chapter Ten covers the workbook itself. I suspect the following material is large enough for a dedicated book, on a stand-alone basis. In a twenty-five year period, and almost by default ("The clients made us do it.") we have conducted skill sessions for well over 10,000 representatives, and more than 5,000 managers, all intensely involved in telemarketing, and more specifically, telephone selling, in one way or another. I've gone through five revisions of our 149-page workbook, and quite frankly it will need yet another revision in the very near future.

I think it's important to note that training per se was not what I envisioned as an important part of our business. However, I literally was forced to develop programs for our clients because of the void that apparently existed. More aptly put, the programs available just were inadequate. Not until the mid-eighties did strong useable material start to appear, and even then the programs tended not to respond to the medium's needs. It was like promotional baseball cap apparel, i.e., one size fits all.

The First Appearance of Quality Training Material

Training program assistance started to appear as needs became more clearly identified after 1985. Managers went on a search for product, and either constructed their own programs, or sought assistance from specialists in the area. Training material vendors such as *The Telephone "Doctor"*, the registered trademark of Nancy Friedman, and the many fine books and tapes such as *Phone Power* and *Power Talking*, by George Walther, Art Sobczak's *Telephone Selling Report*, published by Business by Phone, Inc., as well as our own programs, *The TSR and CSR Hotlines*, attempted to fill the void. All the aforementioned publications were, and still are considered as premium and/or premier products. For a brief period of time, industry magazines like *TeleProfessional* and *Telemarketing* (now *C@ll Center Solutions*) also featured training articles. Both industry magazines now cover more topics relating to CTI (Computer Telephony Integration) and other technology, than they do human resource issues. And last, but not least, your local area phone companies or carriers have been in and out of the training game for years, as a part of their bundled services with "cookie cutter programs."

I am floored when I see the $99 seminar or $6,000 audio/video training device promoted as the end-all answer to your training problems or opportunities. Paraphrasing Benjamin Franklin, "Knowledge pays the best interest," I note that training is not a one-day seminar or even a four-day seminar. It's not an audiotape on "handling objections" or "how to control your rate of speech." It's not reading this book, or viewing a six-hour video, or all of the other varieties of material now being published. **Training is a commitment and it should be continuous.**

Three Major Categories for Your Program

Organizations tend to do a reasonable job with two categories, and not so good a job on the third. The three categories are:

- Product Knowledge
- Operational Requirements
- Telephone Skills and Techniques.

It is this last category that usually gets the short end of the stick. I am not suggesting this happens intentionally, but for the most part it's not perceived to be anywhere near as important to companies as training on the products, or how to enter an order. If your staff is talking to your customers, your prospects, even your suspects, it is highly appropriate to train them at great length initially, and after that continuously, on phone techniques. CTI (computer telephony technology) helps, but is not the end-all solution. It is a tool to help, that's all CTI is.

This chapter will spend only modest time on product training, and very little on operational training, other than to say these elements are a part of your training program. We will spend 90% of this chapter's space on telephone sales, negotiation skills, and phone communications techniques, for anyone and everyone talking to your customers about anything.

Please review and/or think about the below listed classroom training exercises. They are mind challenging and will get you to think. The two statements are from one of our standard three-and-one-half day (onsite) training skills program.

Answer True or False to these questions.

a) Business conducts its business with other businesses or consumers. T or F

b) Business conducts its business with people. T or F

c) People conduct business with other people. T or F

(Answers: C is true and A and B are false.)

Select the correct answer for the following statement:

When customers and prospects are speaking with representatives of your company on the telephone, they believe they are talking to:

a) The order entry rep   d) The tech rep

b) The customer service rep   e) The administrative staff

c) The sales rep   f) The Company itself

(Answer: "F". The Company itself.)

This requires a ton of initial training, as well as continuous, ongoing training. The issue is, *people do business with other people, and these representatives **are** the company, your company*. Customers quickly draw conclusions as to who you are, based on how the rep handles the call, in literally the first 14 seconds.

Anyone who thinks a one-day seminar or an occasional tip on how to perform on the phone is a solution to either short or long term training requirements, is naive. Performance on or over the telephone is not our most natural behavior. Literally, (with reference to communication styles and techniques) all other times we behave like common, ordinary people. It's this fact that for the most part is the cause of skill erosion. We continually revert back to our regular communication methods and styles. In other words, without reinforcement, retraining, managing the process, reps revert to everyday behavior. Techniques training should be a big deal and ongoing.

Operational Training Requirements

All training topics are important. Some of your training topics can be visited once or twice, and the lesson is learned or completed. As an example, once all the features of your phone system are learned, practiced, and performed with confidence, you can reasonably be assured that it's a completed task. All of the issues of voice mail, conference calls, transfers, when to use the mute/hold features, ACD functions, CTI applications, and all of the other capabilities of your phone system, once learned, should not need to be revisited again.

The same is true with organizational software, i.e., prompted or un-prompted order entry screens, sales activity management software, inventory scans, electronic mail, auto-fax and dialing, word processing, quote generation, etc., are also tasks that once learned will only need to be revisited now and again for updates, upgrades, or changes in procedure.

Other systems, procedures, and methods are tasks, and again, once learned, you're basically home free. Most likely it will be a fixed amount of time to learn these. The more you plan and organize these training sessions, the less time you will need to spend on these skills, and the related training events. Time is money, and if we can resist the temptation to put these new folks on the phones before they are trained, the more productive they will be. You will be in pretty good shape by being patient. Needless to say, if they don't know how to transfer a call, don't let them make or take a sales call.

Train, Stop, Train (Rules-of-thumb)
First Rule of Thumb

If your staff will be operating in a reactive environment (calls coming into your center), complete just enough task training to get them on the phones for a brief period of time. Then, evaluate the trainee, and complete your task training. This is because not all of your trainees will fit, or enjoy your phone assignment. I have seen reps complete six weeks of training for the Drawing Board (an office forms supply catalog company in Texas), and then leave after three days on the assignment. They just didn't like the job. I would recommend dividing the assignment into basic skill sets, i.e., first initial training, then "on the phones", then finish your telephone process and skill sets programs. Structuring your start-up training program with this methodology can save money, time, and lessen your trainee dropout risk. Specific training agendas and recommendations follow later in this chapter.

Second Rule of Thumb

If your staff is operating in a proactive environment, that is to say, calls that are outbound in nature (other than traditional follow-up), it is critical that all operational training, i.e., phone system, keyboarding, and software, be thoroughly understood before actual phone time is launched. Why? We call it "phonophobia", fear of

171

the telephone. I am reminded of the circus performer that manages to twirl clay plates on tall, thin, wooden rods. The entire act is one of timing and balance. It doesn't take much to break a bunch of plates. The same is true of any selling presentation. If the rep is unsure of any operational element, i.e., software, the phone system, the product, etc., then the rep is unable to concentrate on the outbound call objectives. It's appropriate to say, never lose sight of your call objective, but that's tough to do if you don't know how to transfer a call.

Not unlike our first rule of thumb, we recommend getting staff on the phones midway through the training program with a simple set of call objectives, ones that don't need a lot of product knowledge. Examples of simplified call objectives (the reason for the call) could be to confirm an address, update a record of information, or seek out and confirm the decision-maker's name. But, we should not make initial hard-core selling calls or have complicated call objectives. This brief test allows an evaluation of the trainee, and gives the candidate an opportunity to check the temperature of the telemarketing application and/or position that they are working. It also allows you to do the same. For new staff, it protects your training investment. If they don't like it so far, cut and run, that goes for both you, and the new rep.

Product Knowledge

PRATO'S 80/20 RULE WHEN APPLIED TO TRAINING

With reference to product training, inside reps have the opportunity to have a wealth of devices or sources to get to the product data they may need. Prato's 80/20 Rule appears to come into play with reference to product knowledge. 80% of your product knowledge questions will be directed towards 20% of your product line. Thus, 20% of your questions will occasionally relate to 80% of your product line. It's easier to instruct new reps to seek answers from support devices as they relate to a unique question, than to teach them about 10,000 SKUs of product. In many organizations it's possible to have computer support (as in prompts) with reference to product knowledge. In fact there are software packages that deal with this issue (FAQs). Secondly, three-ring notebooks, product brochures, and the like can be organized for efficient use. The key to success for product knowledge understanding is the organization of the source material and knowing where to find it, and quickly. That in itself, is a training topic. Training to the most frequently asked question (FAQs) is the answer, not training on each and every product you sell.

New Rep Skills Training -- Nine Elements

It does not matter if the new rep has had previous or similar phone experience with reference to your inbound or outbound positions as it relates to your initial training. No one I know has suffered from too much telephone skills training, myself included.

When you think about the amount of new information that must be digested by your new people, and applied to a three and one-half minute phone call (average time for an outbound call), or six and one-half minutes on an inbound call for a reactive sales rep, the challenge is just mind-boggling. And, given that employees say they understand but really don't, your training must be continuous.

Nine Training Elements

Your overall training programs for new proactive sales reps should have nine major components or segments. They are:

1. Introduction and assimilation into your company call center
2. Product knowledge (the 20% of the product for 80% of the questions)
3. Operations techniques (phones, hardware, software, routines, and good business practices)
4. Telephone communication techniques ☎
5. Telephone negotiating and sales skills ☎
6. Customer Service Skills ☎
7. Understanding customer behavior styles ☎
8. Design and execution of the call objective ☎
9. Planned calls in a live environment ☎

The last six (denoted by ☎ above) change somewhat, based on inbound or outbound assignments or missions. We already have briefly discussed operations and product knowledge training. Before reviewing the last six topics, we need to understand how scripts, or call guides, fit into your training program.

All About Scripts

I must admit that I am not a fan of scripting. Not many business-to-business sales pros like scripting, nor do their customers. That's because so often the scripts sound as if they are being read. Second, you need a real pro to create a script. Most scriptwriters have never been in the sales field, let alone sold anything on the telephone. They tend to write scripts like they write, not like people speak. However, there is a definite application for scripting. First, understand these three definitions, and don't be confused by semantics.

1. *Formal Scripting*: Verbatim, word for word

2. *Informal Scripting*: Written but not verbatim; reps' own words (within reason) like the suggested model and directed to follow the call guide (also known as a Script Guide).

3. *Call Objective Guideline*: The use of counselor or consultive selling methodology. It is the art of needs determination via planned probing techniques. It is also using good listening skills, and making tactical decisions on the fly as you proceed with the call, using a road map (the call objective guideline).

With the above in mind, if the call is a business-to-consumer call, and the call objective is not complicated, *formal scripting* (or something very close to it) is the way to go.

Business-to-Consumer Outbound Example
(Formally Scripted)

- (After the introduction)
- Mr. Van Vechten? How are you? Good.
- New Jersey Power & Light is offering its subscribers substantial savings over the warm summer months if you will consider not using your air conditioner seven minutes a day during the peak energy load periods. Is this savings benefit something you would be curious about? Yes ___ No ___ (if yes proceed, if no, discontinue the call, thank the customer for their time).
- Good, let me send you an information package for your review, and may I call you next week to determine your degree of interest? Good, let me confirm your address. Thanks.

☎ End of call ☎

With the above, we want the call completed exactly as scripted. The training involved is simply to (a) make the script sound natural; (b) be prepared to answer two or three standard questions with standard answers; c) move to the next call. The rep doesn't need to think much about the process, just dial for call completions. The activity is brief, complete and productive, and most importantly, sounds as if it's spoken, even though it is completely scripted.

With an *informally scripted* call, we can introduce more complexity to the call objective, but not a lot. We want the same message presented, but we also want the rep to go with the flow. Thus, we are asking the rep to listen, and quickly think the process through. In other words, we have presented the rep with a script guideline. Let's look at what changes might occur to the previous example. Assume if you will, we now want to close on the concept (save money), and all that we needed was an agreement to put an electronic control device on the household air conditioner. The introduction and interest generating statement would pretty much stay the same, the close (agreement) would adjust and more free-style communication would occur. It usually means more of a dual (the rep and the target) conversation, as opposed to one sided from the rep.

Business-to-Consumer Outbound Example
(Informally Scripted)

- (After interest generating statement)
- "Good, I'm going to send you our information package to review, but on the surface, it looks like we could save you $10.00 to $12.00 a month over the next four-month period. If my math is right, you would be saving around $40.00 on your electric bill, and that makes sense to me, how about for you and your family? (This is the close)
  Yes _____ No _____ (if no, ask, "I'm curious, why not?" Wait for the answer and respond if possible, see Answers to Objections for your response. (If yes, continue ...)
- "If I could get one of our people out there, say in 10 days to make the modification, would that be okay? (Wait for the answer) Good, I'm going to have one of our schedule people call next week for an appointment. What's the best time to reach you? Good, by the way enjoy your savings, and don't hesitate to call our Customer Service folks if you have any questions about this program. OK? Good, and thanks for your time today."
  ☎ End of call ☎

The call objective was to have the target accept the appointment call, and it was completed with a neighbor-type conversation. The additional training required would be practice (role-play), and to provide a list of suggested *answers to objections*.

The use of a *call objective guideline* is required with business-to-business outbound calls. No printed text aid or formal scripting is desired. On the other hand we do want brief, intelligent, productive, natural sounding calls, and it makes sense to plan how we want the calls to proceed. That can be accomplished with informal notes or an all-purpose call planning guideline. Please review Figure 9.1, *The Call Objective Guideline*.

It's true, the calls can go all over the "back lot" if we don't control the event. These calls are more than go with the flow. Controlling the event (impacted by excellent probing sequences) causes this instruction to be very important. Stay on your call objective, don't lose sight of your call objective is the order of the day. The call objective is the reason for the call and what we want to have happen during the call. The call sounds conversational, but is, and should be, very structured and premeditated.

Figure 9.1 -- The Call Objective Guideline
PLANNING THE CALL
"The Worksheet"

❑ Outbound ❑ Inbound   *Call Objective Worksheet*

Reason for these calls   **Product Topics**

1. _____   1. _____

2. _____   2. _____

3. _____   3. _____

Lead-in Statement: _____

_____

_____

Generating Interest: _____

_____

_____

Anticipated Needs (your view)   **Real Needs (their view)**

1. _____   1. _____

2. _____   2. _____

3. _____   3. _____

Motivation to buy: ❑ Greed   ❑ Need   ❑ Fear
Anticipated stalls: ❑ Price   ❑ Don't Need Now ❑ Other, Note

Call Results: _____

_____

_____

What I need to do: _____
Did I post call to cards/computer?_____
Follow-up call on _____

Guideline Explanation

Let me have a brief discussion with you on Figure 9.1, and its components, the Call Objective Guideline (COG).

- This planning vehicle is for categories of calls, not each and every call, i.e., lead qualification, product introduction, determine degree of penetration, etc.
- If the COG is designed, approved, and frequently reviewed (even posted at the workstation), the chance of having effective calls or completed calls is 100% enhanced when compared to any previous methodology.
- If the target being called attempts to change the call objective, i.e., "By the way, I need a credit on my last order.", we are tactically reminded by the guide to get back to the COG as soon as we can. After all, that was the reason for the call.
- To accomplish the overall objective, e.g., sell something. We may need more than one call to make that event happen and more than one COG for call planning purposes to satisfy the overall objective. Remember, an outbound call is an interruption to the callee. Long calls for the most part, are not appreciated and should be avoided.
- The most difficult part of an outbound call for most reps is what happens after you say, "Hello." Thus, a crisp lead-in statement followed by an interest generator allows the caller to complete the initial portion of the call objective, which is permission to continue the call. Therefore, the only part of the COG that is informally scripted is the lead-in and the interest generator. After that, it requires nothing more than call objective preparation, which anticipates the flow of the call. The forced, "thinking it through," activity, i.e., probing questions to use, or answers to anticipated objections, keeps the event conversational and productive.

Call objective planning is particularly helpful in two distinct areas.

1. The COG helps new sales staff members learn quickly how to make the call, and make it the right way. When coaching occurs, both managers and reps are working with objectivity as opposed to subjectivity. This is because there is substance to a planned call objective.
2. New product introductions are made easier, as are planned market penetrations. Why? The staff can get together and adjust the call objective based on call testing (about 50 completes). Because the call was formally planned and tested, there are few variables to consider. Variables often are the death of well-intentioned calls or calling programs.

The form itself is self-explanatory but here are some helpful guidelines:

- **Objectives for the call.** No more than three, topics are listed and prioritized. Remember that brief calls are better. More than one call to complete a call objective is also acceptable.
- **Product or service topics for this call.** Nothing more than the call objective, title, or subject, or the actual product or service, i.e., ZIP Drive (a product), office cleaning (a service).
- **Lead-in and Interest Generation Statements.** Help to gain attention in the first 14 seconds, which in turn allows you to continue for the next three minutes. They are often informally scripted.
- **Anticipated needs.** Are what we think will be interesting to the target via our plan.
- **Real needs.** Are either an agreement to the anticipated needs, or something the target has introduced that will also work for the rep, and assist with COG satisfaction.
- **Good points to close on.** Are either of the two points learned above and so noted and utilized.
- **Motivation to buy.** Which tactic will work best for this situation, i.e., fear, need, or greed motivators.
- **The choice of motivators.** Fear, need, or greed and suggested points to emphasize, i.e., "Which saves you money," is a greed motivator.
- **Objections and suggested answers.** May be on a separate guide, but at least cause to consider for the call preparation.) If price comes up, how will I respond?
- **Results and action steps.** Post-call activity, plus notes for future efforts.

To see how we completed a typical Call Objective Guideline form, see Figure 9.2 as your example. It's appropriate to note that new reps will use the device more than your experienced reps. Experienced reps usually plan the call in their minds. Second, when training is required for new call objectives the COG document is helpful for planning and the related training task, feedback or exercise. Both your new and experienced reps will benefit from this tangible, planning device.

Summary COG

Selling presentations should not be, "Go with the flow events." Call planning, and implementation of these plans are what separates the sales hacks from the selling professionals.

Figure 9.2 -- The Call Objective Guideline
PLANNING THE CALL
"The Worksheet"

☑ Outbound   ☐ Inbound   *Call Objective Worksheet*

Reason for these calls   **Product Topics**

1. Determine Decision Maker   1. Workhorse Flashlight
2. Use Pdt. Now?   2. Plain Utility (w/logo) Lghts.
3. How Much?   3. _____

Lead-in Statement: You may remember we talked earlier last month and I promised you I would call with new product ideas.

Generating Interest: I have two new products that can generate 115% gross margin if we can determine that they fit in your total pdt. mix. (Ask for time + start probe sequence)

Anticipated Needs (your view)   **Real Needs (their view)**

1. Samples   1. _____
2. Referrals   2. _____
3. _____   3. _____

                    ✓ (Excellent ROI)
Motivation to buy: ☑ Greed   ☐ Need   ☐ Fear
Anticipated stalls: ☐ Price   ☐ Don't Need Now ☑ Other, Note
                                        Competitive Agreements

Call Results: Good! Right guy; wants sample + current user list.

_____

What I need to do: _____ Above
Did I post call to cards/computer? _____ Yes
Follow-up call on _____ 10/2/20XX

Techniques Training is Usually the First Training Program Element

An example: The academic argument between those who script presentations and those who don't, to me, is boring. As we have previously discussed, there is a time and place for everything, including the variety of scripting methods. No matter how strongly you feel about the aforementioned, I want to draw your specific attention to a technique for all call center communication applications no matter if it's scripted or not.

Inflection for Success, the First Technique to Master

Remembering that reps and their targeted calls are always in a blind environment (they can't see the customer's/prospect's body language), how we inflect our voices, can and does, create near visual understandings and definite perceptions. Here is an example to further your understanding. Use directional arrows to train representatives as to the specific way we want the inflection to occur (up, down, or level with the planned dialog).

The Wrong Way

(Call Introduction)

1. **Rep**:   Jim Atkins, please. ↗

   Ace Co.:   Speaking.

2. **Rep**:   Jim, I'm Tanya, your account rep with Union Pen. ↗ The reason for my call is to see how your supply of BIC® "Click-Stics" is holding up. We have a special promotion this week that will give you 25% more free product, if you order before the end of the month.

   Ace Co.   No thanks, we have plenty of pens left.

... etc., ... etc., ... etc.

The Explanation

First of all, there are several call elements that are wrong, poor, or represent just plain bad technique. Inflection first. Let's dissect the call:

1.   **Rep:**   Jim Atkins, please? (Inflection was upward and in question form) . ↗

vs.

    Rep: Jim Atkins, please. (Inflection is downward; using an assumptive and confident format. ↘

2.   **Rep:**   Jim, I'm Tanya, your account rep with Union Pen, etc. ↗

vs.

    Rep: Jim, it's Tanya Husk your account management representative with Union Promotional Products. You may remember your company ordered, etc. ↘

(In a matter-of-fact tone or format.)

Why Practice Inflecting Downward?

Again, the inflection is downward in order to create target confidence and a strong, perceived rep image. Plus, real people have both a first and a last name. Always use your last name in your call introduction, even if it is to a regular customer!

182

When inflection is upward, the suggestion to the ear is, "not sure, I don't know myself, or uncertainty." Thus, if it sounds like you don't know who you are, and who their company is, or who your company is, or even if the product truly was ordered before, then, "Why are you calling me?"

Poor or incorrect inflection is a dead give-away that this is a dreaded, waste-of-time, telemarketing call, as opposed to an account rep/customer communication, or service situation update call.

The only time one inflects upward is when one is startled, i.e., "You have not received your order yet?" ↗

While we are looking at this example, you should know that announcements don't work either. The rep must determine if a need exists before making an offer. Thus, "seeing if you are out of pens yet," is a very narrow opportunity. That format will get you a yes or no answer, with limited ability to go forward with the call if the answer is no. In this case the offer, an announcement, was made before an understanding or need was obtained. This call would have been more productive if the need was determined first.

> **Rep:** "Jim, I need your help this morning. ↘ Just how are you using the promotional pens you ordered from me last March?" ↘ (Wait for the answer to the open-ended question.)

The first person who talks now, will lose the opportunity to win the call objective, that is *sell more*, or *sell a different product*. Also, all probing questions are still inflected downward. ↘ By doing so you are guaranteed an answer.

Technique Summary: Inflection upward, downward, or level, is a training issue. It is a technique skill that constantly erodes. Service monitoring is the only method available to determine if the need for a training reinforcement is required. Please remember that many of these skills do not come naturally. We use them for the most part, when performing in our assignments, not necessarily in our everyday lives. Also note, we commented on three other techniques in this discussion. They were (1) first and last name, (2) wait for the answer (3) announcements. All three techniques are eligible for stand-alone instruction, role-play, and re-enforcement exercises.

Selling and Negotiating Techniques:

The Second Training Element

As I noted previously, phone communication techniques training is usually good for six hours of presentation time, or one full day. Time may be extended if the group size is over eight representatives. The reason is simple; exercise time, and additional participant comments and questions can extend your training session.

The second major element, selling skills and techniques, when applied to the phone, is about one-half to three-quarters of a day. The final piece, designing call objectives and understanding customer behavior styles is usually one-quarter to one-third of a day of your classroom time. Here is an example of sales and negotiating skills training.

How To Determine Who the Real Decision Maker Is

Having someone to take your call and/or talk to you about your product or service, and their corresponding needs, may not get you a piece of business. In most of the monitoring sessions I have done for client companies, the item that turned out to be a massive waste of time was the rep presenting (selling) to someone who could not make a buying decision. Worse yet, the rep didn't know that this was the case.

As a standard operating procedure, reps should review and confirm how decisions are made on any given product or service, by simply asking an open-ended probing question. Example:

> **Rep**: "Adam, in addition to yourself, who else will make the decision on the V-Belt 9000?"

If you can train your rep to do the above on practically every call, plus wait for the answer, their call-to-close performance statistic should be enhanced by at least 45%. Remember, it's just not features and benefits followed by objections and closing techniques. It's all the sales skills and techniques as they relate to this sightless format that assist a successful call objective.

Don't forget, each of your lessons or instruction topics then has to be demonstrated and practiced, via a talk through, role-play, or rehearsal. You need to be comfortable that the skills and techniques have been transferred, truly understood, and are able to be used.

Please understand that both communication techniques and phone selling skills material only provides you with a foundation to build upon. However, good selling foundations equal a solid skill base. It's after the base knowledge is understood that creative selling techniques are possible. When excellent sales performance is the result, it's not unlike an Academy Award actor. You don't know they are acting, you believe that they are the people they portray.

Pulling It All Together

This section of your training takes all the elements, techniques, and sales skills, and states, "You now have a complete tool box. Everything you need to be successful on the phone is in the toolbox. Now here is a call objective. It's a new product introduction, e.g., binding systems to customers who have purchased automatic staplers. The call is to an existing customer. Tell me how to plan the call, etc." This exercise is the chance for you to provide reinforcement and feedback. It also is an opportunity to evaluate the rep. Again, it is a potential keep, or not keep decision.

Monitoring: You Just Can't Do Enough of It

I am often asked, "How much time should be spent on the supervisory task of monitoring?" My response is, "As much as you can, but at least a minimum of 35% of your department's calling day."

With reference to training topics and ongoing programs, the major pitfall of these programs, if they even exist, is you don't really know what topics are needed. Unless you are consistently monitoring, you just will not know. The practice of monitoring, and the corresponding feedback to the reps, is a very large part of the training and management process. Reps continually express two concerns with their management team.

- "You don't know what I do."
- "You don't help me when or where I need help."

It's a sight to behold when one visits a proactive sales department that monitors on a regular or planned basis and sees or hears the reps asking their management:

- "Did you hear that last call? It went like clockwork."
- "I wish you heard my last call. After I gave my standard answer... etc."
- "I am not sure I could have done anything more on that last call. Were you monitoring by any chance?"
- "I need you to monitor my next call. Are you free at 2:30?"

All of these statements are comments on the partnership that should exist between the manager and the reps. As corny as it sounds, it's not unlike a parent and child routine. When push comes to shove, reps enjoy the monitoring and feedback process.

Recognition, help, and experience sharing are required parts of the overall management training and motivation process. Ongoing training is heavily linked to management monitoring programs. A poorly administered monitoring program is the forerunner of a disaster. Finally, monitoring should be a planned process, and an important part of the training structure for both your new and ongoing programs.

Setting-up A Monitoring Program

First things first. You need permission to monitor, and that is secured on the first day of their employment, or right after offering the position. (See Agreement, Figure 6.12).

Next, we recommend a monitoring write-up that becomes a handout or a part of your training workbook material. It all boils down to rep expectation levels, i.e., "What can I expect, why, and how often?" Once they know and understand the process, the task, etc., you're in the effective training business. Also remember that monitoring activity helps with performance appraisals, and is of great assistance in proving worthiness of the candidate.

Your first rule of thumb is that monitoring can and should occur on a frequent and random basis. I am reminded of the chemical strip you use in pools and spas to determine if you need to add chemicals. It is monitoring, and it's done frequently. Second, unannounced monitoring drives announced monitoring protocols. Then, if needed, a taping session. By the way, properly released tapes, with permission granted by the rep, make excellent training tools for newer performers. Remember that you are doing these activities at least 35% of your time, at a bare bones minimum, and training examples are abundant.

Most managers try to monitor the entire call, which can be a mistake. You only need to do that when in a random monitoring mode. In this mode, you are able to identify opportunities or topics that may require a refresher skills or techniques presentation for the entire department, or to make the decision to specifically monitor a single rep's performance, for a unique skill adjustment.

More likely than not, you will find a topic that relates to a rep's performance, as opposed to the entire department's performance. It's then that a coaching session is appropriate, followed by an appointment (announced monitoring session), to ensure understanding and compliance with the topic, and finally followed up by the feedback loop. Announced sessions usually work on one topic at a time, as opposed to the entire call, e.g., inflection used on introductions or, use your full name as opposed to just your first name. The process is to cement one or two skills/techniques at a time. It's just easier to do, and more effective. Please recognize that it is difficult to have the perfect call each and every time. You can also monitor for elements of a call for the entire department. This is the format recommended when a training need is identified:

- You have identified a need to work on *assumptive closing techniques* for the entire department.
- Classroom session to explain/review the topic.
- The instructor gives the example.
- Reps role-play the topic/lesson, talk it through, and rehearse.
- The instructor monitors only that topic for each rep by appointment, i.e., Alice: 10:00 to 10:45; Joe: 10:45 to 11:45, etc.
- Feedback for both at 11:45 to 12:10.

I would also recommend you get a list of pre-call plans (call objectives) from your rep for the four or five calls to be made for that session. Then camp* on the line and critique the calls at the end of the training session. Feedback should be immediate, i.e., shortly after the monitoring appointment is completed.

Camp on the line means you monitor the rep for the entire time scheduled, including time between calls.

You will also need to monitor the time expended between calls during these sessions. A stopwatch is a helpful tool. You will be surprised at the amount of time between calls. The question is why, and do they need help here as well?

Skills Depreciate Naturally. Can Peers Help?

It sounds like a big deal, but it isn't. It's fairly well known that peers, other selling representatives, have an immediate impact on the training event. Reps often go to other reps for clarification of anything or everything. Why is that?

- Convenience
- Admiration/perception of the peer's knowledge or success
- Concern for management's perception on the rep's ability or lack of same. (If I go to my buddy, no problem.)
- Laziness

You have a number of options available to you in what now is called peer monitoring/training.

- Option I: The rep to be trained listens to an experienced rep for a number of calls (5 or 6). The call objectives are explained, the mission identified, the objections are anticipated, etc. The reviews take place before the calls are made, and immediately after the session is completed.
- Option II: The experienced rep listens to the new rep based on the preparation noted above, and offers a constructive critique.

The results of peer training sessions are typically outstanding for a number of reasons.

1. It's real; not scripted role-plays.
2. Mistakes or missed opportunities happen to the best of us, and are not considered as devastating.
3. It's recognition and motivation for the senior rep that is doing the monitoring.
4. It's believable, real-world, as opposed to academic or instructional.

By the way, this process counts as part of the required 35% monitoring time for managers, thus freeing-up time for other tasks. You will find training is taken seriously because peers, unlike managers, tell it like it is. Mentoring is planned as opposed to go with the flow. Please remember that peers are using valuable selling time when assisting in the monitoring process and respect this important point accordingly.

How Often and Where?

I've stated my position on how often. "As much as possible, but no less than 35% of your available time." However, skip no one. Your best rep, who needs the least help, wants to be monitored. That rep wants to be reassured of your respect. That feedback is extremely important to an achiever.

As to where, I am looking to the real world. Side-by-side in most cases does not really get the job done as well as it could. Silent monitoring, from your office or a dedicated monitoring area does get the job done, and is highly recommended.

The monitoring benefits the ability to measure and take or make appropriate adjustments in a timely manner. If accomplished on a regular basis, consistency will be the desired result in your training program. The old sales or management moral is very true with reference to monitoring. *"You get what you inspect, not expect."*

Customer Behavior Styles as a Topic for Training

This turns out to be a fascinating topic, and one that is covered in great detail by author and publisher D. Forbes Ley, Sales Success Press, Newport Beach, CA 92660. His book, *The Best Seller*, is in its twelfth printing and in my mind is one of the best books ever written on field selling procedures and skills. Chapter Twelve covers the topic of Prospect/Customer personalities. Over the years I have found that if you understand how your customer prefers to buy, or negotiate, to do business, so to speak, your closure and customer retention rate increases substantially. I just never saw the concept published before the late 1980's.

With the above in mind, and with his permission to paraphrase, and adding my experience, let me suggest this topic is an important training issue. The explanation of behavior styles in Chapter Eight applies here as well. Thus, change your mind set from employee behavior styles to prospect/customer behavior styles. Simply stated, if you can forecast the customer's behavior styles from the conversation or other clues given on likes and dislikes, you will have developed a reasonable insight as to how long it takes for the customer or prospect to make a buying decision. You will note in Chapter 8, the below points were the key points to consider.

Behavior Style Summary

Drivers make-up their minds immediately or even yesterday. They are eligible for one-call closing attempts. Generally no other style will close in one-call unless you have accidentally called them just as the need occurred.

Expressive Persuasives want a few days to make up their minds, maybe about five days. They very rarely do any further investigation, but just in case, they will wait for a brief period of time, if possible. They just want to see if they stumble across a reason not to commit or buy.

Analytical types think in 30-day cycles. In other words, they need time to compare, review, plan, check-it-out. If you were to try to close your call objective immediately with one-call, there is a 90% chance it won't happen with these types. They like and want you to provide them with a ton of facts and details. They literally are contemplating purchase 30-days from now and are doing their homework early.

Amiables basically never make a decision in any defined period of time. It appears to be never, but, when they do decide in your favor, they become the most loyal customers that you will have. This group is the most difficult to understand and sell. They are good listeners, ask lots of questions, and still don't buy on a forecasted basis. They are not comfortable with change, thus their reluctance. Security is their overriding issue.

Some examples of Position Behavior Styles

Keeping all of the above in mind and thinking along these lines determines, how they enjoy performing the decision making process.

- Purchasing agents, engineers, chemist, finance execs. etc., are all generally analytical buyers (30-days).
- Sales executives are generally expressive persuasive buyers (about a week).
- Owners of businesses, entrepreneurs, top managers who make the difficult decisions, tend to be driver type buyers (today).
- Social Service types or groups, politicals, health care (nursing homes), librarians, customer service, human resources, tend to be amiable type buyers (months, weeks, certainly not quick).

Your marketplace, that is the decision-maker, may be heavily influenced (80%) by a specific behavior style, e.g.; your customers are nearly always purchasing agents. Thus, there is an excellent chance (80%) they are analytical. You should train your reps to recognize and respond accordingly. This information is very helpful when you are designing your call objectives. Although, this technique/skill appears to be soft and fuzzy, I have found it to be real and highly effective when planning the selling process.

Conclusion, Buying Behaviors

I would agree this is easier done in an account maintenance environment, as opposed to a "one-call, never talk to them again", environment. However, it's just one more tool to work with, and a valuable one at that. For training purposes, I would dedicate about an hour or more on the topic, and revisit it now and again. Role-play examples are helpful here. Also, have your experienced reps relate to the trainees the successful use of this technique.

Skills and Techniques, Initial and Ongoing

An investment in the initial training **is required**. Here is what it **is not** acceptable:

- Read this training book or watch this video and let me know if you have any questions.
- Sit with Dorothy for three days, she'll show you how we do it.
- You have pretty good experience from your last job, you shouldn't have any problems, and here is your account list. Go for it!

Training in telephone skills and techniques, and if required, sales skills and techniques, initially take about three weeks. It doesn't really matter if it's one rep or seven reps. You should plan for one week in the classroom (no less than 3.5 days) and 1.5 days for "one-on-one" training. Then, plan for two weeks of intense monitoring with feedback, training. You should be prepared to terminate the employee from day one, and at anytime during this initial training, if they are not catching on as quickly as your training experience suggests; cut your loses early on, and save time, money, and heartache. Your course content should be consistent. Don't attempt to build a training experience that covers "everything you ever wanted to know about this assignment, in three days." Information overload is your risk. This is an educational experience not a training program information dump or task. You should be after a solid foundation, one that can be added to, as opposed to a now or never agenda. Remember that information overloads help no one. Information overload only serves to enhance phonophobia. There are training topics over and above all other training topics previously mentioned. For example: The History and Culture of General Foods (your company) is important. So is "Where is the men's room, and what's your vacation policy." However, please not at the expense of actionable rep performance skills and technique topics.

If I stated that 80% of most organizations give very little attention to initial training needs, the techniques and selling skills, and that less than 5% have ongoing skills and techniques programs, would you be surprised? Product training, yes, techniques and sales skills training, no. When you stop and think about this situation, it's fascinating or stupid, whichever you prefer.

Think about this academic question. As stated before, an academic question is one that is designed to get you to think. When I perform our training programs for clients, I ask the supervisors and reps, "Which is more important, product knowledge, or selling and telephone communication techniques?" The answers from thousands of reps fall into these categories and corresponding percentages. Out of 100 instances,

1. Product knowledge only   65%
2. Both product and sales skills   25%

| 3. | Sales skills and techniques only | 5% |
| 4. | Don't know | 5% |

Obviously, both product knowledge and skills and techniques are important. Most likely, and in practicality, you would find it truly difficult to separate the two. I would also say that the question needs some specificity for inbound calls, compared to outbound calls. My answer, and I would hope you would agree, is that for inbound calls, product knowledge has the edge. However, for outbound calls sales skills and techniques have a bigger edge. Number 1 in the above survey is totally incorrect. Why is that?

It's the call objective. On an inbound call the objective is established by the caller and we react or respond accordingly. However, skills do come into play quickly, i.e., confidence building, probing sequences, negotiating skills, needs determination, etc. But if we can't get through to a decision-maker on an outbound call because of an administrative screen or voice mail, or we announce, as opposed to determining needs, we are quickly up that famous creek without a device to propel ourselves. Thus, skills play at least a 51% of importance, and most companies are providing less than 5% of their training program to these topics. I rest my case.

Ongoing training is important too. Not unlike a recently waxed car or a newly painted home, the task completed does not last forever. There is one simple fact: skills of any kind start to erode as soon as the training program is completed. Training must be continuous. The various training societies and associations claim that trainers are happy if 15% of the topic is retained after the presentation. The manager can anticipate problems will occur if there is no ongoing training program, and the definition of ongoing is continuous.

There are about 100 topical issues that are covered in the initial training program. If one were to revisit 50 topics a year, for 35 minutes a week, I would suggest that you would be on the right track to develop and maintain a professional marketing unit, that is close to being all it can be. If you do your math, we are talking about a two-year program, before you start to repeat the cycle. Your hard cost should be no more than $80 per year, per rep, for program material, and that's a small price to pay to promote sales call center excellence.

There appears to be eight major categories for proactive groups to work on, other than product knowledge and how to use our business tools and equipment topics. They are:
- Sales Skills
- Sales Techniques
- Feedback Loop
- Competition Information
- Tracking Your Effort, ("What is a good day?")

193

- Database and How To Use Effectively
- Miscellaneous Topics

There are five categories for reactive groups. They are:
- Communication Skills
- Techniques, Order Entry/Customer Service
- Case Histories
- Problem Solving, Decision Making, Procedures
- Miscellaneous Topics

We think there are a myriad of topics that can be revisited, weekly, or every other week, for one year, with both proactive and reactive groups. With permission of both the *TSR and CSR Hotlines*™ we are showing you a sample of the topics used for weekly training sessions. See Figures 9.3 and 9.4. (Figure 9.3 is just a sample of the 79 topics covered in the *TSR Hotline*.)

Training To Issues

There is a third major category of training, after initial and ongoing. From time to time special issues will pop-up, and it will be a cause for supplementary training. With permission of Nancy Friedman, The Telephone "Doctor"®, whose address

Figure 9.3

TSR Hotline® Subject Index (To name a few)

1. Advertising (Yours)
2. Advertising (Your Prospect's)
3. Anticipating Objections
4. Assumptive Close
5. Attempts, Presentations, Completed Calls
6. Benchmark Tracking
7. Benefits, Features, Advantages
8. Interest Generators
9. Lead-in's
10. Buying Motivations
11. Buying Signals
12. Call Backs, How Often
13. Call Objectives
14. Call Objective Worksheet, How To Use
15. Call Report
16. Career Pathing, Do You Have One ...
17. Case History of a Major Sale
18. Close-ended Questions
19. Closing Techniques
20. Closing Signals Quiz
21. Complaints
22. Consultive Selling
23. Contact-to-Close-Ratios
24. Contained Choice
25. How to Control the Call
26. Courtesy (Phone)

Figure 9.4

CSR Hotline® Table of Contents

1. Back to Basics (Part I)
2. Back to Basics (Part II)
3. "Gee, How Do I Handle That One?"
4. Managing Your Time
5. How's Your Communication Style?
6. The Written Word, How Much, How Often
7. Why all the Fuss About Customer Service, Anyway?
8. Opportunity's Knocking (Cross Selling)
9. Sympathizing and Empathizing
10. First Steps in Complaint Handling
11. The Choice is Yours (Empowerment)
12. Complaint Handling 101
13. Maintaining Control of the Call
14. What Can You Say When You Can't Say Yes?
15. The Communication Process: Are You Listening?
16. Some Quick Fixes For CS Stress
17. Active Listening
18. Resolving Those Interdepartmental Conflicts
19. Stress and Customer Service: You Can't Have One Without The Other.

is 30 Hollenberg Court, St. Louis, MO 63044 (800-882-9911), let me give you an example of the third major category.

Personal Calls can be a problem. How does the manager handle the situation? By using a half-hour training session, then make it a regular part of your program. (See Figure 9.5.) Don't forget the feedback loop, i.e., "Was there improvement? Did you let them know?"

Figure 9.5

How to Control Personal Calls at Your Office

Do you allow personal calls at the office? Is the privilege being abused? Here are some ideas and tips to help control personal calls at the office... both incoming and outgoing.

1. **Eliminate all calls.** While somewhat drastic, this method is one way to keep personal calls out of the office. Designate one person (and a back-up) to handle emergency calls.

2. **Curtailment.** Designate the hours personal calls are allowed. Put a time limit on them. For example, allow personal calls from 7-8 AM, 12-1 PM and 4-5 PM, with 3 to 5 minute limits on the calls. Choose the hours when your office is least busy. This option enables employees to feel comfortable on the phone with a personal call at the allowed times.

3. **Open Forum.** Have an employee meeting -- state the problem and suggest the employees come up with a viable answer. You may be surprised at the outcome. Most employees realize personal calls are not management's favorite topic. They might be able to come up with a reasonable alternative and get the ball rolling. Plus, they take ownership of the program.

4. **Monitor Calls.** Many communication companies now offer the option to monitor number and length of calls electronically made to any extension within a company. These reports can identify the offenders by phone numbers. Other systems track outgoing calls and can be programmed to eliminate specific numbers. If you opt for this plan, let your employees know in advance. You'll avoid some ruffled feathers later on as well as so called privacy issues. You may also have a designated phone for this use.

5. **Train Your Employees.** Let them know your policy on personal phone calls (develop a policy if you don't have one). Help your staff follow your rules by giving them specific guidelines. Here are a few suggestions:

   a. Never let an in-person customer wait while an employee is on a personal call. (Even if it's a business call, they should acknowledge the customer -- even if it's only with a smile and immediate eye contract.)

   b. Sometimes employees just don't know how to tactfully tell a friend or relative they're at work and unable to talk. They may be embarrassed to tell them. Here's a Telephone "Doctor"® tip on how to handle that graciously: "Aunt Mary, I'd like to hear more about your trip but I'm at work now and need to get some things done for the boss. Let me call you later tonight when we can talk and I am not so busy. Thanks a lot for calling. Talk with you later. Bye."

   c. Let employees know that if they are approached by the boss (or anyone else), they are expected to put their personal call on hold. Personal calls can wait, office personnel shouldn't.

   d. Encourage employees to use a client's name during the call. It makes it easier for you and co-workers to realize it's a business call. (Using names also helps to build rapport with a client.) There's not an intelligent manager around who would interrupt a business call.

The Seven Elements for New Rep Training

There appear to be seven major sections to consider when training new hires.

1. Background of the medium (telemarketing/telephone selling)
   - Why is this function important to Acme Company? Your company and departmental history are also important; how you, the trainee, fits into the big picture.
2. Telephone Techniques and negotiation (sales) skills (two parts)
3. Buying Behavior Styles
4. Call Objective Planning
5. Putting it all together
6. On the phones (live calls), monitoring for skills transfer and behavior change compliance.
7. One-on-one adjustments and reinforcement via the feedback loop.

The above is applicable for both inbound and outbound sales representatives. The topics within the sections are of course job specific. Thus, dealing with an angry caller is more important to an inbound Customer Service Rep, but may have some modest importance to an outbound Account Maintenance Rep. How to negotiate with the call screener is an important topic for an outbound, cold call representative, but not very important to an inbound rep. Quite frankly, the topic agendas are exactly the same, except that there is no need for an inbound rep to go through a lead-in and/or interest generating statements. That only happens with an outbound call, thus it is a proactive skill requirement. The remainder of the agenda has varying degrees of applicability. The aforementioned steps are the bulk of a four to five day training session, including the live calling (both inbound and outbound calls), and planned monitoring of service and feedback scenarios.

When thinking about time allocated for training, here is a guideline. Let one day of training represent six hours. The ideal size of class equals 8 to 10 trainees:

% of Day	Training Topic
25	Company, departmental background, plus understanding your assignment, guest speaker
100	Communication Techniques
50	Sales and negotiating skills and techniques
20	Call objective planning
20	Customer buying behavior styles
40	Working interactive exercises (for the entire program)

2.55 Days Total classroom time

2.45 Days On the phones being monitored plus one-on-one coaching. (Remainder of the week)

5.00 Days in Total

197

Tips on Presentation Skills

Unless you have been trained or educated at a state teachers college your training skills most likely have come from on-the-job experience. Assuming that's the case, eight out of ten times the presentation is, "Here is what I do and how I do it." That's better than a "sharp stick in the eye", but believe me, you can do better.

There is no substitute for job experience, but there can be a problem in transferring that experience to others. With that in mind, the following guidelines are offered.

- Understand how information is passed to others by trainers. It's one or a combination of three methods.
  - Read the lesson
  - Write your understanding of the instruction
  - Perform the function yourself and repeat it until it's understood, i.e., rehearse
- You can identify visual clues in your class by watching your students absorb the lessons. Some examples are:
  - intense note taking, and the need to verbalize as well
  - no notes, participates verbally, but also should take notes
  - asks no questions about the lesson, but thinks about the topic(s) for 24 hours then asks questions
  - asks questions during breaks, but not in class
  - does well in class and poorly on live calls. This rep will need a structured environment
- and, much more.

Coaching Skills Guideline

Your best bet is to cover all the bases, and not try to uniquely identify individual learning shortfalls. With this in mind, use your coaching skills guidelines. They will work for your skills presentation. The Ten Steps are:

1. Identify the topic
2. Explain and define the topic, the where, why, when, how, and who
3. Give examples of the topics
4. Instructor demonstrates
5. Enlist discussion from the class
6. Get class to paraphrase and perform the topic or issue (all students.)
7. Provide positive feedback and adjustments
   - ask the class for their critique
8. Encourage special note taking where applicable
9. Summarize and close on the topic
   - questions
10. Move on to new topic

What About Quizzes, 35MM Slides and Interactive Computer Training Material?

I have not made a formal practice of giving a written quiz. I believe I can accomplish the same thing with verbal checkpoints or questions. Really, it's a matter of preference. Some students actually are motivated by getting a good grade.

What About Interactive PC Training?

I am a little nervous about this method for outbound sales reps. I am convinced that so much more can be accomplished in the give-and-take of a stand-up presentation, as opposed to the tight graphics content, of a machine. I think this method is more of a product, method, history, and understanding opportunity, as opposed to a communication and sales techniques training device. Customer and prospect conversations aren't that structured, and that's the real challenge.

Overheads vs. 35 Millimeter Slides vs. Computer Presentations

This one is easy. Never darken the room for any reason, except a movie. Overheads should be your medium of choice. I want to visually read the class for their understanding of my instructions. It can only be done by eye contact with each and every student in a well-lighted room.

If you prefer to use Power Point or another presentation program on the PC, be sure that you have a projector with a bright enough image so you don't have to dim the lights. Also don't go crazy with the presentation program so that it becomes the show. In today's environment where people under 30 years old have grown up with MTV, video and computer games, and all types of multi-media, it's to your advantage to spice up your presentation of material. But use it sparingly to keep attention, and always tie it into your training points.

Use Easel and Newsprint Pad/Writing Board

Why consider this? Because it is another method of learning. It's nothing more than the spoken word reinforced with written captions which are visual, and thus supportive to learning.

The second method is to get the students to do what you do. Have them write answers to questions on the newsprint pad. Your example could be, "What kind of objections could we get to our Celebrity Service?" "George, take a crack at it on the pad up here. Write all the probable responses and get help from your classmates if you want to."

The third method is that variety of instruction helps maintain interest in the event.

A Few Other Tips

- I recommend casual business dress for training sessions.
- Catered events work well, including before the session starts, morning, afternoon, and lunch breaks. Optional also, are refreshments after the day closes.
- Take longer breaks if staff is experienced and actually assigned to an existing task, i.e., twenty minutes is a good amount of time. The reason is that they can respond to voice mail, etc..
- No more than six total classroom hours per day. You don't need the information overload syndrome.
- Come down hard on tardy students early on. Let folks know you are in charge.
- Allow no side conversations while you are instructing. It's discourteous and distracting to other students.
- If you clearly have a mis-hire in the class, if possible, remove right then and there.
- Never leave a white screen, overhead light on, while discussing a topic. That too is distracting.
- When writing on a board or easel pad, never stand in front of the device. At the easel, if right handed, place right foot at the easel leg and vice-versa.

Classroom Tips and the Student Workbook

Do workbooks depreciate, and does the quality of the printing have an impact? The answer is yes. Handouts can be a nightmare. Copies of copies of copies indicate the lack of importance. And, make the investment to create your material on a maintainable word-processing disk. This allows for changes, updating, and true professional presentations. Three-ring binders make sense here. Also, they are easier to maintain and of course, for larger groups perfect. Spiral binding also offers a nice solution, even though somewhat more difficult to change or update.

Encourage students to take notes and/or write in their workbooks. The workbook is theirs, or should be. Finally, copyright your material. Examples of a training workbook agenda follow in Exhibit 9.6.

Final Training Thoughts

Never assume reps have learned anything. Nodding heads don't tell you anything. Continually perform a reality check. Ask a class member to re-explain a topic you have just presented if you sense a problem. Training should be fun. I spend a lot of time telling "war stories" that for the most part show the humor of the profession, and traditionally show that even the instructor can be placed in an interesting situation. The students love knowing that "the best of the best" can make mistakes as well.

Please review Figure 9.6 for your typical proactive training agenda.

Figure 9.6

TRAINING AGENDA

I. INTRODUCTION TO TELEPHONE SALES
- Definition
- What Customers Want Most
- The Selling Plan
- Proactive Sales Calling Methods

II. PHONE TECHNIQUES, INCLUDING
A. Phonophobia
  1.The six key Phobias: What they are and how to overcome them
B. Phone Courtesy
  - Ten simple but crucial points that are part of your professional phone personality
C. Telephone Techniques
  - Volume
  - Rate of speech
  - Tone
  - Inflection and accents
  - Dealing with a talker
  - Voice Mail
  - Creative Phonetics
  - Power of Silence
  - Handling the Irate Caller
  - Saving the order that's about to be returned
D. Listening
  - Why salespeople are traditionally not good listeners
  - How to be a good listener by asking questions
  - How to use taping to be a good listener
  - The 12 key listening points
E. The Call Objective
  - The importance of having an objective and planning the call (the ECE Call Objective) for both inbound and outbound events
F. Getting Though to the Right Person
  - Getting through the screen and voice mail systems

Figure 9.6 (continued)

III. COMPONENTS OF A SUCCESSFUL SELLING PRESENTATION

A. The Introduction of Company and Self

B. Lead-Ins and Interest Gathering Statements
   - The importance of creating, getting and maintaining interest
   - Exercise - Writing an interest gathering statement to fit your needs

C. Probing
   - Open-ended questions
   - Close-ended questions
   - Alternative Choice
   - The importance of qualifying the suspect/prospect/customer
   - Understanding the motivation to buy and how to use it to your advantage
   - The power of silence
   - Confirming your probing sequences
   - Exercise

D. Paraphrasing
   - The difference between real needs and anticipated needs
   - The importance of insuring mutual understanding
   - Objection verification
   - Exercise

E. Features and Benefits
   - What is a feature?
   - What is a benefit?
   - How to determine benefits that correspond with features
   - Which benefits will sell your products/services?
   - FAB's
   - Exercise

F. Objections: The Inevitable and Essential Part of Selling
   - Price
   - Information
   - Time Stalls
   - Silence
   - Guttural Utterances
   - Exercise

G. Closing Techniques
   - Direct
   - Assumptive
   - Contained Choice

Figure 9.6 (continued)

- Recognizing Buying Signals and Trial Close Techniques
- Exercise: "Soft" Role-Play between Instructor and ISR

H. Summary of Skills Presentation

IV. BUYING BEHAVIORS

A. Why This Skill is Important (an Overview)
B. The Behaviors
- Expressive Persuasives
- Drivers
- Analyticals
- Amiables
C. Pulling This Skill Together
- Exercise

V. ESTABLISHING THE FIRST CALL OBJECTIVE FOLLOWED BY "LIVE" CALLING

A. Regroup and Review
B. Establishing the Second Call Objective Followed by "Live" Calling (INSTRUCTOR'S NOTE: During "live" calling sessions, your instructor will provide you with assistance and help where needed, on a "one-to-one" basis.)
C. Review Summary and Close

NICE TRY, BUT I'M AFRAID YOU CAN'T GET CARPAL TUNNEL SYNDROME FROM YOUR HEADSET

Chapter 10
Training:
Workbook Design, Format
and Examples

Introduction

When it comes to selling not much has changed over the years. Products and services have changed, however selling techniques have not. The skills I learned as a new sales representative for Dun & Bradstreet in the late 60's are the ones still taught today. Marketing has changed, sales channels have changed, but not selling skills.

Selling is all about needs determination. If a rep can find a need and the product or service offered fulfills that need, then we have the opportunity for a completed business transaction, a sale.

With the introduction of new sales channels, a variety of new sales channel techniques have become a training requirement, a need to be fulfilled, and/or unique topic to be addressed. E-mail, web sites, fax, catalogs, direct mail, broadcast, television, field selling, inside sales, or telemarketing applications all have become tools and/or selling resource assets to accomplish the business mission of selling something to someone. The technology around selling has greatly improved. How did the sales department ever exist before the fax machine was developed and made affordable to the entire business community? How did individual sales reps service account structure without contact management software? Sales and marketing productivity issues are enhanced every day. Yet, with all of our advancements, it still comes down to people conducting business with people. Dun & Bradstreet's logo in their first 140 years was, "Man's confidence in Man." Although it is probably politically incorrect these days, the message is the same. Selling negotiations are conducted between a comfortable buyer and seller. Closure does not take place until a need has been established or found in tandem with trust.

Selling is not as easy as it sounds. And, there are skills, methods, rules, and understandings to learn in order for the representative to be successful. Reps who do not learn their trade quickly end up as casualties. Their career field is one that is objectively measured. Success is determined by sales completed. In other words, no sales, no job. The motivation to being a good selling representative is twofold: Greed (you can make some good money here), and fear (no sales, no job). The professionals know exactly what they are doing and they tend to be students of their profession. Reward systems for this group tend to be very good.

On the other hand, telephone sales techniques are new in one form or another. They may or may not be winning techniques. There are selling rules and sales techniques, i.e., good business practices, for telephone sales channels. All of the above affords training opportunities, and that's what this chapter is all about. What is the best way to train business-to-business inside sales representatives, no matter if they are inbound or outbound? The phone is the tool, and we ask these folks to operate in a blind environment. We can't see the body language. Communication techniques become paramount in their importance.

For Whom Is The Training Book Written?

Strange question isn't it? However, it helps the entire training process if you think this one through. The answer in priority is, the instructor first, then the student.

The instructor drives the presentation. The instructor needs a device that lays out the course of instruction. The training workbook also provides the lion's share of the narrative on topics addressed, as well as room for notes and completed exercises and lessons to be learned. The diary (workbook) belongs to the rep, and the publication can be used for reviews, reality checks, and/or as a desk sale reference tool. When one takes notes in a workbook it becomes one's own. As the workbook material is presented, the pages are turned, thus the device is a combination lesson plan and guide, as well as a student workbook. The workbook, on a stand-alone basis, is of no value. You could not read the workbook and learn to sell. The workbook is of great value when it is used by the instructor as the course guide. It's also valuable to the student who interprets the verbal, written, and practical exercises via notes, underlining, etc. Therefore, a properly designed workbook is a major key to your training success. It's the foundation, the basics, the visual, if you will, of planned performance(s).

The Workbook Itself

Although these topics seem to be basic or oversimplified, the book addresses each topic to be learned, or related topics, with the following methodology.

There are five "stuffs"

- There is stuff to see, read, and listen to
- There is stuff to interpret
- There is stuff to do
- There is stuff to write
- There is stuff to try

Every overhead or computer slide used in the presentation should be in the workbook, along with a dedicated page for notes, which are used to note the student's interpretation, or as a reminder device. Examples are provided in later pages. The note block can even be used to present a few quick questions that will elicit student comment, as well as to keep them on their toes. Supporting your topical overheads, are written explanations of a topic using examples as well as definitions. However, if it is a simple point, the overhead plus notes are probably enough. If you plan to have your students create scripts, dialogs, write examples, etc., then you should have an exercise page on that specific topic. In most cases the note block can also be used for that purpose. When questions are asked in the note block, we can provide the answers in code or small print. This then becomes an instructor aid, as well as hints for the students. Examples follow shortly.

We will provide as a working example, the actual workbook pages from our generic, phones sales and techniques workbook, as well as the complete training agenda. (See Figure 9.6) Our books are maintained on computer, in MS Word, the latest version. This allows maintenance and updating at will.

I have found that the material is excellent for the new representative. Class sizes of at least four, and no more than twelve are recommended. You should leave no place to hide, and encourage – even demand – participation. Remember, the instructor for these sessions is perceived to be a very powerful, important person. The instructor assumes expert status.

Summary

There are two reasons these skills will deteriorate,

1. Lack of use

2. Tendency to revert to layman, or non-sales behavior

Because we, as professionals, know that selling talents or skills are not God given, and that there is truly no such thing as a natural born sales person, we have to understand that these elements of training must constantly be refreshed, revisited, and/or maintained. Once the basics are learned, it becomes a training challenge to keep the rep on track and sharp.

Secondly, because all trainees have been given the same foundation of skills and techniques, it becomes much easier to build on that foundation. Second level skills plus critiques from an objective point of view, as opposed to a subjective view, are easily added once the foundation is in place.

Training companies like Zenger Miller, Learning International, Casset Corporation, and others are successful to the tune of $250,000,000 each annually, based on consistent and tested training methodology. They prepare the materials and train the trainer. Planning and implementing your new workbook gives you the same opportunity for success that these organizations have. Presentation material is a key to the success of their programs, and it is the same for your programs.

What follows is a rather large exhibit of:

1. Business-to-Business

2. Outbound and Inbound

3. Inside Sales and Field Sales

4. Training workbook for new employees, or employees who have not had formal sales and techniques training. Sections of the book may also be used as topic refreshers, e.g., *closing techniques*.

It covers topics previously mentioned in this and preceding chapters. The presentation should provide you with an excellent guideline to create your own workbook, specific to your own needs. Please be reminded that product knowledge, other than product referenced as real examples, is not to be included in this training element. Our recommendation is that product knowledge training is presented before your sales skills and techniques program. Please remember this material is copyrighted, and permission to use it must be secured from the author. Permission may be granted, and often is, so don't hesitate to ask. This material is available on disk, and may be purchased for a reasonable price [1(800) 682-5432 or www.vanvechten.com].

Finally, after completion of this training, it's on to the phones, or as Mr. Firestone once said, "Where the rubber meets the road."

TELEPHONE SELLING WORKBOOK MODEL

Figure 10.1
(All 44 pages)

Provided by

F.G.I. & Affiliated Publishing Companies, Inc.

51 Hampton Drive

Freehold, NJ 07728-3148 USA

1-800-682-5432

www.vanvechten.com

Author's Note: This is a 44-page example of a 150 page-training workbook. It is provided to demonstrate methodology and concentrates on communication technique topics in this proactive selling career field. Actual sales skills and techniques are available but not present for this work. (LRV)

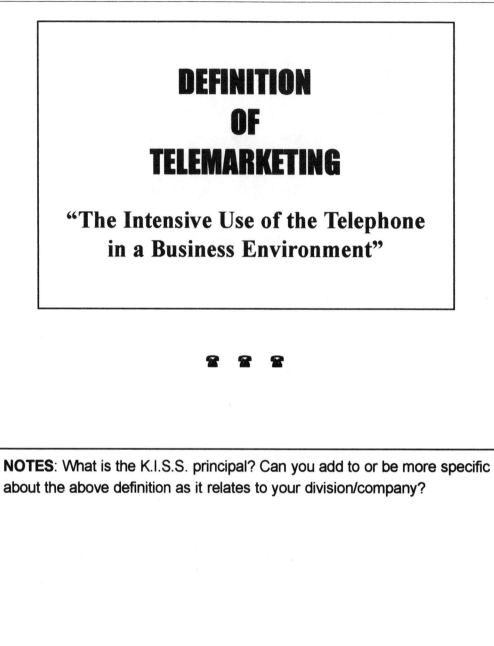

DEFINITION OF TELEMARKETING

"The Intensive Use of the Telephone in a Business Environment"

NOTES: What is the K.I.S.S. principal? Can you add to or be more specific about the above definition as it relates to your division/company?

What you need to know and background

Remembering that the telephone is only an instrument for communications and that it is also a sales and marketing **medium**, the definition of telemarketing becomes important, especially when training staff to perform in a professional manner.

Telemarketing: is the intensive use of the telephone in a business environment. What you do or accomplish when using the phone is what you do. Therefore, the tasks listed below are all telemarketing applications.

- ☎ End-user or pull-through call missions
- ☎ Lead qualification routines
- ☎ Order Entry and or Customer Service
- ☎ Collection of accounts receivable
- ☎ Set appointments and confirming appointments
- ☎ Marketing research (the gathering of business information)
- ☎ **Proactive (outbound calling) sales activities**
- ☎ Purchasing
- ☎ Planned/seasonal promotion activities . . . . . to name a few.

It is a curious but factual comment that how you sound and what you say is what creates your telephone personality. If you don't sound good or you handle yourself poorly over the telephone the process stops dead in its sales and marketing tracks.

We all have had the experience of talking to customers and prospects on the telephone long before we have met them in person and are surprised that they look different than they sound. Respondents to our telephone sales calls tend to "manufacture" images of the inside sales rep (ISR) depending on how they sound. Needless to say, the reverse is true. Confidences can be shaken or intense risks perceived by the caller (customer/prospect) or if the customer service/service representative or sales rep doesn't sound quite right or have a good phone personality. Equally important is the Company is impacted by the professionalism (or lack of same) that is demonstrated in any one call.

Easily 68% of all successful phone calls are dependent on how you sound. 32% of the success is based on what they say or know. It's hard to believe but a fact, never the less. This is especially true in the first 21 seconds of an outbound call (seven-second increments). *

A sales rep needs to be able to use the phone effectively in order that time may be managed effectively.

☎ ☎ ☎

* (Introduction, lead-in, interest generator, request for time, first probing sequence.)

NOTES: What is important about seven second increments? Is there a difference between a new call vs. ongoing relationships?

A THOUGHT

You may have talked to many people on the phone today,
But, the next time will be the first time you'll be talking to the
next customer or prospect today.

How will they perceive you?

Thoughtful?

Professional/Courteous?

Great Personality?

Willing to help?

Do you really sound interested?

NOTES: What does the above message really mean? Paraphrase please.

CUSTOMERS TELL US

The Best Sales People

- Try to help me with my interest, even if they are unable.

- Remember me and call me by my name.

- Allow me enough time to make up my mind.

- Tell me about a variety of programs in different price or quantity ranges.

- Remain pleasant and professional even if I don't buy or subscribe at this particular time.

The Worst Sales People

- Act Condescending or patronizing.

- Interrupt to disagree with my opinions.

- Make adjustments without telling me.

- Pretend to know more about the products or service than they actually understand.

- Become unpleasant or "short" when I don't buy or make up my mind quickly.

☎ ☎ ☎

NOTES: What is the message here?

THINK OF YOUR CALL OBJECTIVE, WHAT MUST BE SOLD FIRST?

☎ **OUR SERVICE/PRODUCTS**

☎ **SAMPLES/PROGRAMS**

☎ **SET APPOINTMENTS**

☎ **LEAD QUALIFICATION**

☎ **COLLECT MONEY**

☎ **TAKE ORDERS**

☎ **SAVE CANCELLATIONS**

☎ **UPGRADE AN ORDER**

☎ **MOVE INVENTORY**

☎ **MARKET RESEARCH, ETC.**

☎   ☎   ☎

NOTES: A trick question? Does the medium used (field or telephone) change anything?

EXAMPLE OF TYPICAL INBOUND CALL SITUATIONS

INQUIRY CALL: "OPPORTUNITY MISSED"

TSR: Good morning, ABC & Co. This is Alice, how may I help you?

PROSPECT: Yes, this is Harry James of H.J. Interiors. Do you folks still provide support for large contract assignments?

TSR: Yes, we do Mr. James, and we have a variety of design samples appropriate for every designers' budget, if this would be suitable to your needs.

PROSPECT: Do you also provide or have a good choice of early American graphics with coordinating fabric?

TSR: Yes, we do.

PROSPECT: Do you have any memo samples or cuttings I can see and can you send me a price list?

TSR: We sure can. Let me have your address and we'll get that information right out to you. Then call us back if I can be of further assistance. My number is ...

☎ ☎ ☎

NOTES: What is wrong with the above scenario?

EXAMPLE OF TYPICAL INBOUND CALL SITUATIONS

INQUIRY CALL: "OPPORTUNITY MISSED"

TSR: Good morning, ABC & Co. This is Alice Duncan, how may I help you?

PROSPECT: Yes, this is Harry James of H.J. Interiors. Do you folks still provide support for large contract assignments?

TSR: We certainly do, Mr. James, and we have a variety of packages to fit a variety of client budgets, along with a wonderful selection of fabrics and wallcoverings. All of our products, for the most part, are carried in our inventory so that you can see what is available and can be shipped on a fairly quick basis. May I suggest, we review your needs and then I'll offer you some solutions.

PROSPECT: Well, how about just sending me a few samples and your price list.

TSR: Sure we can do that. In fact, that's an automatic. I have prepared one and it will be in this afternoon's mail. However, I am sure we can provide you with the information you need in less than ten minutes. I need just a few minutes to gather some information about your application so that we can fulfill your needs more accurately. It should save you a lot of time in your information search in the long run.

(Start the probing questions)

☎ ☎ ☎

NOTES: What is the basic difference from "Opportunity Taken" and "Opportunity Missed?"

DON'T FORGET...

☎ **YOU ARE THE COMPANY! Not just an employee of the company.**

☎ **USE THE CUSTOMER OR PROSPECT'S NAME (people doing business with people).**

☎ **MAINTAIN CONTROL OF THE CALL! Successful selling is all about control of the sales call.**

☎ ☎ ☎

NOTES: What is a key technique with call control? What does "empowered" mean and which of the above statements does it apply to most?

THE CLASSIC MISTAKE

The major pitfall that telephone sales reps seem to fall into is the announcing vs. selling problem. Reps seem to think that if they continue to talk, tell "stuff," provide as much or all the information they can think of . . . the prospect/customer will pick out the information they need and buy something. It just doesn't work that way.

Selling only occurs if there is a need and you have found it. Furthermore, that your products/services fulfill that important need. Needs are heavily related to benefits and ever so slightly to features of your products. Thus, the case example below speaks for itself. Although, it's out of our industry, it is vivid. Imagine (if you will) a material handling sales rep attempting to sell commercial/industrial shelving.

ISR: "Hi David, and thanks for taking my call. Have a special for our customers that I would like to run by you; won't take more than three minutes. David, we have purchased a "ton" of metal shelving from a large distributor who went out of business at an unbelievably low price. They come in 6, 8, and 10-foot lengths and the width selection is 6, 12, and 18 inches. They are industrial grade and are rated at 750 lbs. per square foot of shelf. The height is basically your call, I've seen them as high as 36 feet. They bolt to the floor or wall or both to meet your OSHA safety regulations. They come in "gun metal gray", warehouse blue or institutional green and we can ship in one-day FOB Philadelphia. David, do you need shelving at your facility?"

David: "No. Thanks anyhow." (Click)

☎ ☎ ☎

That was an announcement and it's worthless!

Same situation, the correct way, *selling!*

ISR: "David, thanks for taking my call. I may have an opportunity for you and your company. However, I need to ask a couple of questions first. Is this a good time?"

☎ "Do you store finished goods or anything else at this location? It would be helpful if you would describe how that's done."

☎ "How many times do you turn the stock in your warehouse?"

☎ "If I can show you a way to ..."

That's how you find a need!!

☎ ☎ ☎

NOTES: Thinking about your previous experience, do you announce or determine needs?

PHONOPHOBIA

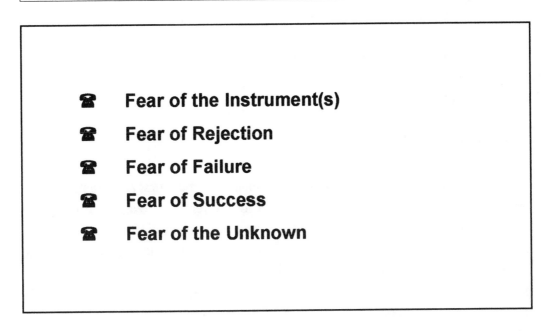

- ☎ **Fear of the Instrument(s)**
- ☎ **Fear of Rejection**
- ☎ **Fear of Failure**
- ☎ **Fear of Success**
- ☎ **Fear of the Unknown**

☎ ☎ ☎

NOTES: Instruments include all tools used in the performance of your job: software, hardware, phones, office equipment, laptops, computers, etc.

PHONOPHOBIA

Phonophobia, or fear of the phone is basically broken down into five areas:

- Fear of the instrument(s)
- Fear of rejection
- Fear of failure
- Fear of the unknown
- Fear of success

In order to correct the situation (the phobia), we must first analyze just which fear we are addressing, either for ourselves, or for our reps. The reason this is crucial is because the problem, once identified, becomes a problem half-solved. The most common claimed fear is of the phone itself, but in reality, it is not the instrument but one of the five underlying causes, i.e., rejection, unknown, etc. If the real cause of phonophobia is not identified, countless hours of coaching and counseling will result in short spurts of improvement at best. The real problem, which hasn't been addressed, will continue to linger.

First of all, who has these phobias? Everyone, at one time or another. The new rep, or the rep who has had umpteen turn-downs, the final close, the follow-up call to a big account, the pressure times when everyone's scratching to meet accountability and so forth. The manager who is calling to save the contract (the big one) or who is trying to set an example for a new rep. Even the president of the company who is seeking financial assistance for a new loan or is trying for some deserved public relations with the media. No one is immune.

Real Fear 1. Fear of the Instrument

To begin to understand this "fear of the phone" (or other equipment) we should absolutely, completely disregard fear of the instrument as being a concern. The instrument is just that: an instrument, it can do nothing without people. Consequently, it is not the instrument, unless the "how to operate, use or function with" is a factor. Remember, that with all tools, i.e., computers, software, the copier, or phone, it is ourselves or others that cause this fear, phonophobia. Briefly, we would like to cover the real fears as we have encountered them and later offer not a panacea, but an outline or guide as to how these fears may be overcome.

Real Fear 2. Fear of Rejection

Accepting the negative feedback to one's presentation of product or service as a personal attack on oneself.

Real Fear 3. Fear of Failure

Another variation of the "me" syndrome. No one is a robot and erasers are on pencils for a reason. People do make mistakes, you and or your client. To fear failure is to fear success. We become successful by correcting failure, much like a torpedo or rocket whose guidance system uses negative feedback to correct its course. Failure is what stimulates the correcting mechanism within us. It also is a positive motivator when managed.

Real Fear 4. Fear of Success

This is harder to explain because some people "believe" they will fail. To not fail runs contrary to their life plan and is not consistent with their role in life. Selling is a magnificent occupation for these people to prove their own ineptitude because it demands measurable performance. The definition of success is often reaching and or exceeding goals which, when done, is quite pleasurable.

Real Fear 5. Fear of the Unknown

Here we touch most everyone's lives. Few have truly accepted the fact that change, i.e., the unknown, is the only constant we possess. However, because it is the unknown or is mysterious, it is the "stuff" of what books, pictures, and stories are all about. The "thrill" of the unknown is equally measured by the "fear" of the unknown. How it effects one is simply a matter of where one is "psychologically set" and "current events," i.e., what's happening now.

Here then, we have the real causes of these fears: rejection, failure, success and the unknown. All are "I" or "me" oriented. There is really nothing about "the phone" itself or the prospect or client that causes the phobia the caller is the cause. Here are some tips on how to help uncover, discover and neutralize these fears. If properly diagnosed, you can either correct them or find another assignment, there is no middle course.

Fear of the unknown will rapidly dissipate. The reason? We are involved in highly predictable events. There will be a few who will say yes and a predictable number of no's. With that being said, the unknown becomes known.

Overcoming fear of rejection also takes mental toughness. To form the foundation for mental toughness means understanding that there are more no's than yes's.

If there weren't so many customers and prospect no's involved as part of selling, we wouldn't need the services of a salesperson. Another way to look at it: We pay the rep a salary to find and tolerate the no's. We reward them with commissions for getting the yes's. Then for exceeding their goals we provided bonuses and other incentives. In essence, a rep is being paid to take no's and is rewarded for yes's. Lastly, the no is personal: it is no to what the rep is presenting at a particular point in time. A "no" represents a "I don't see a need for what you have presented at this time." The "value to me" is missing.

Overcoming fear of failure requires a small but significant shift on how failure is viewed, i.e., to fail at something, a particular attempt does not mean either that one has failed at the task or is a personal failure. To illustrate this, a baseball player with a batting average of 300 has failed seven out of ten times at bat but is obviously successful at the task. Although the ball player knows that statistically he was less successful, rather than more successful when at bat, each time up was a "whole new ball game." The key here is to review the unsuccessful attempts, make corrections and then forget it: don't dwell on past mistakes/failures. A helpful hint to kill the fear of failure is to concentrate on past successes. Relive and dwell in the positive and the negative will have no room.

Overcoming fear of success seems to originate from this untrue perception. "If I have a good day that's okay. If I have three good days in a row, I'm in trouble; management will expect this of me all the time, I better slow down." Remember, we are in a statistically prevalent field. Good days and bad days are predictable. When you are on a roll go forth. This must be understood before starting the process.

Overcoming the fear of the unknown is best accomplished by making the surrounding environment as stable as possible. Bringing in the sales budget is always a challenge and occurs each and every hour, day, week, month and year. It doesn't go away and the market knows no mercy, knows nothing and cares less about anyone's problems. However, when the work environment becomes too tense or unstable, all sorts of future fears pile up. Reps should understand 96% of the unknown becomes known within the first four weeks of their employment.

In summation, phonophobia, or fear of the phone is really fear of rejection, and failure, which are jaded perceptions that can be altered through coaching and counseling by yourself and your supervisor. Fear of success is a time bomb that should be defused as quickly as possible, and fear of the unknown is merely a statistic.

We trust these guidelines have given you some ideas as to how you might help your reps to overcome these particular types of phonophobia(s).

PHONOPHOBIA SOLUTIONS

☎ **BE PREPARED**

- Master the skills of your profession
  - Telephone Techniques
  - Consultive Selling Skills
  - Understand the Sales Process
  - "Know Thy Customer"

- Product Knowledge
  - Know the top ten conceptual uses of products/services/promotions inside and out
  - Know where to find the other information you may need and quickly

☎ **KNOW & UNDERSTAND YOUR CALLING NUMBERS**

- Data should be Measurable & Realistic . . .
  Example:
  - 60 Dialings or Attempts
  - 30 Completed Call Objectives
  - 6 Closes, or Completed Call Objectives

NOTES: Give examples of your "numbers" for a typical week.

PHONOPHOBIA SOLUTIONS
(Cont.)

☎ **KNOW WHO YOU ARE CALLING BY CLIENT AND TYPE OF BUSINESS FUNCTION**

- **Clear and correct pronunciation of business and decision makers' name**

- **Business class, a Customer**
  - ♦ **Active and productive customer over past 12 months**
  - ♦ **Active and less productive over last 12 months, considered small or marginal**
  - ♦ **Inactive, has not purchased in last 12 months, but... can purchase (needs some work)**

- **Business class, a "suspect"**
  - ♦ **A probable, but we really don't know if they can or cannot buy**

- **Business class, a "prospect"**
  - ♦ **Can definitely buy, but hasn't yet**

- **Business Class, "Orphaned"**
  - ♦ **A customer, but not yet assigned to a sales rep**

NOTES: Are presentations to active customers equal to presentations given to inactive customers or even prospects?

228

PHONE COURTESY

1. **No food**

2. **Smile**

3. **Answering the phone**

4. **Who are you talking to?**

5. **Taking a message**

6. **Transferring a call**

7. **The hold/mute feature**

8. **The telephone as an interruption**

9. **Useless information**

10. **Hang-up last**

Source: Bell Telephone of Pennsylvania,
Operator Training, 1970

NOTES: Is it professionalism or courtesy? Is a better title for the overhead, "Why people stop listening?"

PROFESSIONAL TELEPHONE MANNERS
(AKA: WHY PEOPLE STOP LISTENING)

Although we all use the phone constantly, day in and day out, we may think we know everything there is to know about Phone Courtesy, but let's review ten small but basic points to insure a professional phone appearance and experience.

1. **No food.** Regardless if you are placing an outbound call or receiving an inbound call, you should not have anything in your mouth. Yes, that includes gum, candy, toothpicks, or cough drops!

2. **Smile.** It may not be necessary to have mirrors on our desks like the telephone company suggested to us years ago to remind us to smile. But... you can hear a smile over the phone.

3. **Answering the phone.** You should answer the phone like a professional: state your department or company name first then your first and last name and then pause. Then... "How may I help you, how may I direct your call?"

4. **Who are you talking to?** You should never feel uncomfortable about getting correct spelling of a customer/suspect/prospect's name. The same goes for their company name or any other information you need to obtain... to do your job more effectively.

5. **Taking a message.** I do not know anyone personally or professionally who likes picking up a telephone and not knowing who is on the other end of the line. "Tanya, call on line 1... pick up," no one appreciates. Therefore, it is perfectly acceptable to say in response to "Tanya Husk, please...", "I'm not sure where she is, may I tell her who is calling?" In that way you have accomplished an important thing: you are not saying it matters who it is to see if she is busy or not, and no one will get offended.

6. **Transferring the call.** If your phone system has the capability, try to insure the phone transfer is complete, i.e., so stay with the caller so the person does not get disconnected and feels comfortable with the transfer. If a disconnection is possible, make sure the person can get back to you so you can try again.

   If you are on the receiving end of a transfer, pick up the continuity of the call if it's possible, i.e., "Hello Ben, this is Tanya Husk. Laura tells me that you had a couple of questions on the product samples we sent you. Let me help you out." In that way, the customer does not have to restate his interest again (maybe for the seventh time).

7. **The "Hold" or "Mute" button.** No feature of the phone equipment has caused as much consternation as that little hold button. Here are some pointers about using it.

    a) **Use it.** don't plunk the phone down, cover it with your hand or any other part of your anatomy. People are not interested in your office structure, your office environment or your personal assessment of their problem.

    b) **Let people know you are going to use it.** "If you have no objection, I would like to put you on hold. It should only take a minute." Then get back to them and let them know what is happening. "Unfortunately, it is going to take a little longer than I anticipated, may I put you back on hold or should I call you back?"

    c) **Avoid terminal hold at all costs.** Regardless of jokes, music, radio stations, no one really enjoys being on hold, no one!!

8. **The telephone as an interruption.** You should never pick up the phone until you have an opportunity to compose yourself. If that means making sure you have a piece of paper and a pencil, or you sit down and catch your breath, make sure you do it. You don't have to answer the phone on the first ring. A good rule of thumb is to give yourself three rings to compose yourself. Remember, first impressions are lasting impressions and you want a professional one. On an outbound call speak slowly for the first 7 to 14 seconds. Allow the target to acclimate to your voice and call objective. This will drive off many problems that can show up later in the call.

9. **Useless information.** Don't tell your customers about the structural, organizational and reporting problems your company is now experiencing in the wake of the current move/reorganization/restructuring/reassignment. They are not interested. Determine what they need to know and make it short and simple. Also, no weather, "How are you," or other time wasters.

10. **Hang up last.** You are the professional. Make sure you hear the "click" before they hear your "click". Oft times, something else will pop into the customer's mind and he may remember same as you are hanging up in his ear.

Hopefully, as you've read this, you've gone through what trainers call the **Ah-Ha**, syndrome. If you did, that's good. That means you are at least aware of what you should do. Now the question is... are you doing it?

TEN BASIC TELEPHONE TECHNIQUES

☎ VOLUME

☎ RATE OF SPEECH

☎ TONE

☎ LISTENING SKILLS

☎ INFLECTION

☎ ACCENTS

☎ VOICE MAIL

☎ BUYING SIGNALS

☎ INTERRUPTIONS

☎ SILENCE

☎ ☎ ☎

NOTES: Can you think of any more telephone techniques?

BASIC TELEPHONE TECHNIQUES

Volume

It is important to speak at a volume that will allow the other person to hear you with little or no difficulty. This will normally be the same volume that you would use to speak to someone who is seated across a table from you.

Speaking too loud or too low will have serious and negative results on your ability to sell. If you speak too softly, the customer or prospect will not be able to hear you and will soon lose interest in what you have to sell. On the other hand, if you speak too loudly, the customer will move the phone away from their ear and thus put distance between you and your target.

Holding the phone properly can also affect the volume of your voice as it is transmitted over the phone. The mouthpiece should be directly in front of your mouth and should be about one inch to one and one-half inches from your lips. (The width of two fingers.) Closer for a soft speaker, three fingers if a volume communicator. Use of headsets solve this problem, if one exists. Field reps will find that planned calling hours while on the road or in their home office will be more efficient if they use headsets.

Rate of Speech

Just as volume is important when speaking to your customer on the phone, so too is your rate of speech. If you speak too rapidly, you will tend to lose the customer and you will also lose the call objective. The converse is also true; if you speak too slowly you have a tendency to bore the person on the other end and will again endanger the call objective.

The ideal rate of speech is between 180 and 190 words per minute. This rate will allow the target to understand what you are saying and maintain interest. This is the same rate of speech used by most radio and television announcers.

To determine your rate of speech, we will have you read the 180 word statement on the next page of your workbook. Remember, there is **no incorrect rate of speech!** Only a technique to allow for better communicating.

180 WORD STATEMENT

Most experts agree that the ideal rate of speech is between one hundred and eighty and two hundred words per minute. At this rate, people who are expected to listen to you will be able to hear and comprehend what you are saying. In the United States there are different patterns and rates of speech that are the product of geographic areas. In the northeastern part of the country, people tend to speak faster, while people from the southern states tend to speak slower than the 180 word rate. However, people in the mid-western states will tend to speak at the one hundred and eighty word rate and without accent. To test yourself note your start and your finish time. Use the second hand of your watch to do this. If you read the statement in less than a minute, you may need to adjust for the first 21 seconds and slow down. However, if you read this statement in more than a minute, you may need to be sensitive to your rate for the first 21 seconds when communicating with your customers and prospects on the telephone.

☎ ☎ ☎

*We noted that your rate of speech is important in the first 21 seconds of the conversation with reference to an outbound call. Do you know why?

BASIC TELEPHONE TECHNIQUES
(Cont.)

Tone

The tone that you use on the phone is your telephone personality. Your tone is one of the most important elements of your call since it is the audible indicator of your enthusiasm for your product, service and company.

While tone is a very important part of your call, it is the most difficult to self-evaluate. Usually we are so involved with the call that we forget about our tone and aren't aware of its quality.

To judge your tone, you should do two things. First, ask a co-worker to listen to you while you are on the phone. Then have them evaluate your tone. A second way to judge tone is to self-tape record your calls. It's not necessary to tape both sides of the conversation as you are only interested in how you sound. Then, before you forget about the call, listen to the tape and evaluate your tone of voice. Exciting, fun to listen to, good vibes, etc.

We know it's an old rule but if you smile while talking to your customer, your tone will improve and, quite frankly, so will your sales.

Ability to Listen

The first three basic telephone skills are related to how you talk on the phone. Just as important as talking is your ability to listen. Many times customers will be giving us *buying signals but because we don't listen, we miss opportunities for closing the sale.

Before you can improve your listening ability, you must first understand the reasons why it may be difficult for us to listen. There are seven reasons and three categories.

— Environment-Physical   — Fatigue   — Impulsiveness
— Personal Problems   — Laziness
— Emotional Words   — Intolerance

But, you *must* overcome these reasons and listen. (See page 236 for more details.)

We have found that there is no better way to listen than getting involved with the call.

SEVEN REASONS WHY PEOPLE DO NOT LISTEN

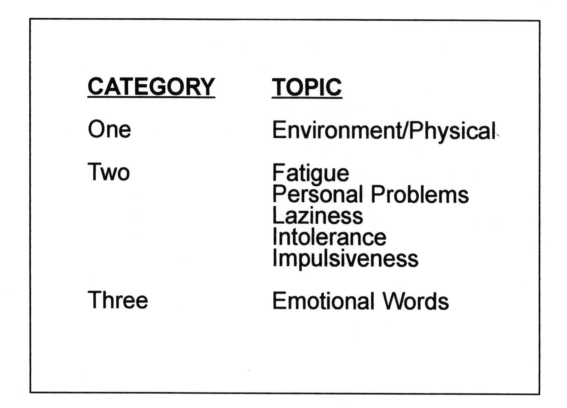

CATEGORY	TOPIC
One	Environment/Physical
Two	Fatigue
	Personal Problems
	Laziness
	Intolerance
	Impulsiveness
Three	Emotional Words

☎ ☎ ☎

NOTES: Category Two deals with perceptions, most likely the real cause is what?

INFLECTION

Voice Technique and Control: The art and skill of creating the perception of confidence, knowledge and experience through the use of voice inflection (up and down). Well known television announcer examples:

 "This is CNN"
(James Earl Jones)

 "NBC News, now more than ever."
(Unknown)

 "Watched by more people than any other Network, ABC."
(Unknown)

Fully 80% of your phone conversations will inflect downward to include your introduction (even your questions).

NOTES: Example: "Can you tell me who is responsible for creating your promotional programs?" Try this question with a downward inflection.

CUSTOMER ACCENTS

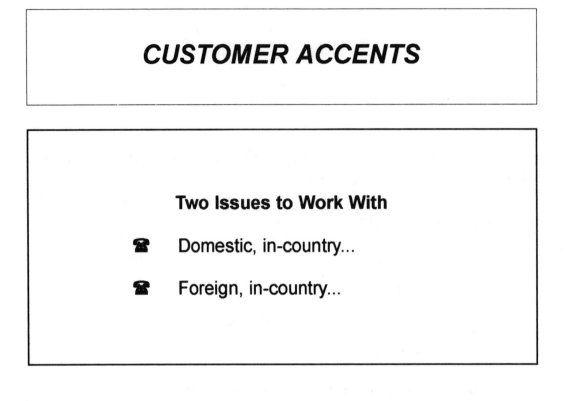

Two Issues to Work With

☎ Domestic, in-country...

☎ Foreign, in-country...

NOTES: What should you *never* attempt in-country? What is the most important technique to assist understanding with the foreign accent?

CUSTOMER ACCENTS
(Cont.)

☎ As we approach the new century, accents have become more of a challenge to all sales professionals.

Years ago it was only of modest concern. Accents to work with were southern, northern, western, mid-west, and West Coast. Some trainers recommended you should imitate the accent as best as you can to make the customer feel the call was from a friendly or someone from the area (establishing trust). Rates of speech were also suggested as a part of the technique (as in imitation). In this case imitation is not flattery, but often turns out to be insulting, a ploy, and definitely recognized for what it is, a fake. No help to your presentation for sure.

Interestingly enough, those of us who work a specific piece of the country do tend to pick-up both the flavor and sectional language just because it's there. What is the difference? First the latter is fine ... the former is a no-no! Secondly, you learn one naturally, thus it sounds reasonable and the other sounds put-on and offending.

It's interesting to note that when the TV networks hire anchor news people that they are nearly always from the mid-west. Even the major talk shows have mid-west personalities.

David Letterman, Tom Brokaw, Peter Jennings, Dan Rather, Johnny Carson. Why is that?

> a) No accent
> b) Slower rate-of-speech

The feeling is they are acceptable to the rest of the nation and are easily understood (reason, a and b above).

☎ However, the off-shore accent attempting to communicate in their new language is another story. The natives (us guys) are often not very patient and we revert to what we always do when we appear to be having difficulties in being understood, we speak louder, i.e., **"When in doubt, scream!"**

CUSTOMER ACCENTS
(Cont.)

Here is a fact you can take to the telephone sales bank. These people are **not hard of hearing**. Thus, increasing your volume is exactly the reverse of what you should do.

The techniques you should employ are:

1. Speak more slowly
2. More calmly
3. And at a lower volume
4. Apply patience

Remember, these people are being screamed at all day long by us natives. Anyone who practices slowly, calmly, lower volume and patience will enhance customer relations. Why? *Because you care.* If the tables were reversed, where would you do business? With a screamer or with an understanding, patient ISR?

FOUR RULES FOR VOICE MAIL

1. **Call back at different times. Don't save your "call backs" for 4:00 p.m. each and every day.**

2. **Call before the business day starts, at coffee breaks (in their time zone) and or the traditional lunch hour or after the business day ends, e.g. 5:18 p. m.**

3. **Don't provide a message that states what your call objective is all about.**

4. **Be as brief as possible!! Example:**

   ☎ **"Hi Ben, this is John Graystone over at ABC & Co. Time is 10:30 a.m. Thursday morning. I need to phone visit with you briefly today. Please call me at 800-780-7020. Thanks."**

☎ ☎ ☎

NOTES: Can 800 numbers cause a problem? If so... why?

BUYING SIGNALS
What Are They?

THEY ARE QUESTIONS ABOUT ...

FEATURES AND BENEFITS OF OUR PRODUCTS, SERVICES OR MARKETING PROGRAMS

EXAMPLES:

TIMING, PRICE, SIZES,

QUANTITY AND AVAILABILITY

OF PRODUCT(S)

☎ ☎ ☎

NOTES: Can you think of any more buying signals?

A CLASSIC MISTAKE
Interruptions

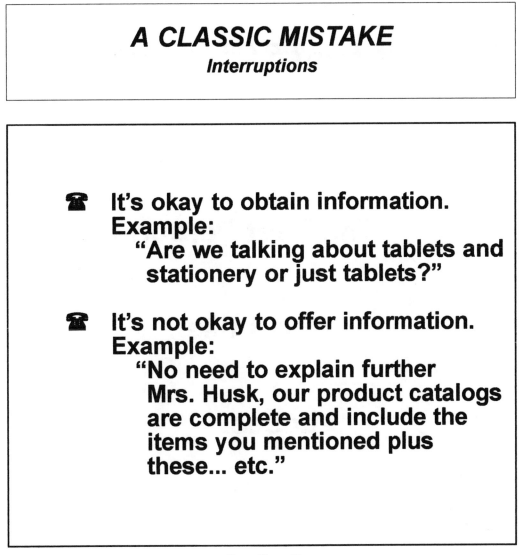

☎ It's okay to obtain information.
Example:
   "Are we talking about tablets and
   stationery or just tablets?"

☎ It's not okay to offer information.
Example:
   "No need to explain further
   Mrs. Husk, our product catalogs
   are complete and include the
   items you mentioned plus
   these... etc."

☎ ☎ ☎

NOTES: The problem usually occurs after an open-ended question. Do you agree?

THE POWER OF SILENCE

"The First Person

Who Talks

Loses."

NOTES: Does the lack of conversation, by either party, create positive pressure?

"THE FIRST PERSON WHO TALKS LOSES"

No matter what your telephone application is, i.e., lead qualification, customer sales, accounts receivable, etc., the age old problem of training the inside sales rep (ISR) to go through the "strategic pause" is difficult.

Example: "Mr. Patton, it looks like we have identified a unique need for our product to satisfy your needs. Would you prefer a product sample or can we place an order today?" (Strategic pause... a.k.a. silence, a.k.a. **keeping your mouth closed!**)

In our ISR training session we coach that: *"The first person who talks . . . loses!"*

In the above example, the buyer has a choice of a sample or the actual product. Either choice is a positive action for a purchase, or sale, or close. But, if the rep becomes uncomfortable with the silence after the question and talks or continues the conversation, they lose, i.e., no sale opportunity. However, if the customer responds in the positive or asks another qualifying question, the movement towards a sale closure continues. Thus, the first person who talks after a position is presented or taken, in effect and specifically the sales rep, loses the opportunities to close on the call objective.

No matter what the call objective is, once an action is requested by the ISR, **SILENCE IS GOLDEN!**

The methods we will use for this training are role play and or taping the actual conversations. Monitoring is a tool as well. However, monitoring is perishable. Taped role plays and tapes of presentations are never lost and are almost visual when this technique is heard. The role-play will be specific in each of the situations that might develop.

Example:

- "Mr. Hunter, if we can supply more than 60% of your battery and flashlight needs, would you be interested in our annual purchase discount?"
- "Frank, your objection appears to be cost. If I were to meet that concern, would we be able to do business?"
- "Do you use product displays for all your retail outlets or just those opened in the last twelve months?"

245

All examples require the **strategic pause** after the question is asked and literally, the first person that talks . . . loses! ISRs traditionally continue to talk when it appears there is an opportunity to have their CALL OBJECTIVES slip. Why? Discomfort!!

Also, because they are on the phone and not reading body language. Believe me, this skill can be learned. Ten seconds of silence on the telephone seems like an eternity, but the pressure is equally as uncomfortable on both ends. Save your tapes and note the footage where the good and poor examples exist for future peer training and self critiquing exercise.

NOTES: What are some of the situations that may require you to employ a strategic pause?

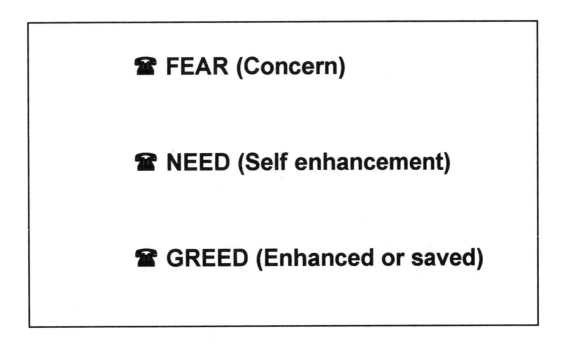

THE THREE REASONS WHY PEOPLE ARE MOTIVATED TO BUY ANYGHING

☎ FEAR (Concern)

☎ NEED (Self enhancement)

☎ GREED (Enhanced or saved)

☎ ☎ ☎

NOTES: Are the above motivations related to the benefits of our products and services? Give examples.

HOW TO HANDLE SCREENED CALLS

☎ **VOICE MAIL: Leave only your name, Company, time and phone number. No messages!**

☎ **CALL WHEN SCREENER IS NOT THERE**
- **Before the business day starts e.g. 8:00 a.m.**
- **During the traditional coffee-break, lunch and afternoon break, e.g. 10:15 a.m., 12:00 to 1:00 p.m. and 2:45 p.m.**
- **After the business day ends, e.g. 5:15 p.m.**

☎ **WORK WITH THE SCREENER**
- **Review in-depth "Getting Through The Screen"**

☎ ☎ ☎

DO ISRs SET APPOINTMENTS?

Field Sales Representatives (FSRs) do because they don't want to chance a customer, prospect visit unless it's expected. The days of "smoke stacking" (calling on customers and prospects because they are there as opposed to being expected or completing a scheduled appointment call) is long gone and a thing of the past. No one has the time anymore and it is very, **very** expensive to the company doing the cold calling as well as annoying to your target.

It's not any different for **inside sales representatives**. Time is the issue and he who wastes a customers time soon loses a customer.

Five Rules of Appointment Setting

Rule One: Determine when and seek agreement for the return call.

Rule Two: Be specific! Example: Let me call you back in two weeks. Does Tuesday the 14th make sense to you, Ben?

Rule Three: Determine best time in the day. Example: Ben, is it better for you in the morning or afternoon. (Field reps usually set an exact hour, inside reps select board ranges, i.e., morning or afternoon.)

Rule Four: Ask them to mark their calendar that you intend to call.

Rule Five: Forecast the time needed. Example: Ben, I won't need to take anymore than six minutes of your time, at best.

Summary: *Do not use* or *accept* these calendar-setting comments.

1. Call me next week   2. Next month   3. Next quarter   4. Next year

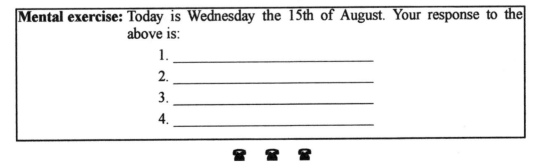

Mental exercise: Today is Wednesday the 15th of August. Your response to the above is:

1. _____

2. _____

3. _____

4. _____

Answers: 1. Monday, August 20th 2. Thursday, September 1st
3. Friday, October 1st,   4. Tuesday, January 2nd

"SELLING OFF THE BOTTOM"

 The action of selling minimums or lowest quantity before probing and determining the real or true needs of our customers/prospects.

 Example of Selling off the Bottom: ISR: "Right Doug ... you can order one case, that's our minimum, or ten cases and we will pay the freight."

 As opposed to satisfying real needs: ISR: "Doug ... I'm interested in your customers and their profiles. We may be able to address all of yours and your customers needs." (Probe, Probe, Probe)

NOTES: Examples?

HANDLING THE IRATE CALLER
TEN STEPS

1. Let them talk.

2. Don't Interrupt, "Let the spring unwind."

3. Use the terminology, "That's unfortunate," as opposed to "I'm sorry."

4. State... "I'm glad you called."

5. Offer to help.

6. Don't take it personally.

7. Understand WHY customers YELL...
    ☎ Their perceived expectation level has not been met.

8. I want to talk to your supervisor!!
    ☎ "Yes, I just need to collect some information first."
    ☎ Handle if you can, if not, pass call to the next higher authority.

9. Abusive language
    ☎ You don't have to take it.

10. "Shake it off" and go to the next sales call.

☎ ☎ ☎

HOW TO DEAL WITH A TALKER

☎ **Determine if this call is out of your control. If yes . . .**

☎ **Interrupt with questions about the size of business, type, location, number of employees, anything, even an address clarification, Zip Code confirmation.**

☎ **As soon as the answer is given... end the call quickly with your exit option...**

- **"Thanks for calling . . ."**
- **"Oops my other line just became active... need to run, and thanks for your... etc."**

☎ ☎ ☎

NOTES: Is it rude to break away? How does a smile help?

CREATIVE USE OF PHONETICS

When spelling names of anything. It creates interest and enhances listening when you use imaginative examples.

EXAMPLE

☎ **"B" as in Benefit**

☎ **"C" as in Creative**

☎ **"D" as in Dividend**

☎ **"E" as in Excellent**

☎ **"F" as in Feature**

☎ ☎ ☎

NOTES: Example: Your last name, how would you accomplish using the above technique?

COMPONENTS OF A SUCCESSFUL TELEPHONE SALES PRESENTATION

☎ **Introduction of Self and Company**

☎ **Interest Gathering Statement**

☎ **Probing**

☎ **Paraphrasing**

☎ **Features, Advantages and Benefits**

☎ **Answering Objections**

☎ **Summarizing**

☎ **Closing**

NOTES: Are all eight of the components used in each and every call or presentation?

No

Chapter 11
Performance & Performance Appraisals

Introduction

I am reminded of the once a year event that occurred at Dun & Bradstreet the world famous information agency. I was learning my craft, selling and sales management. My boss would bring the dreaded inter-office, craft envelope, with my 32 job descriptions, and request that I do a performance appraisal or every member of my staff. I hated that time of year.

I knew deep down in my heart that no one did anything with this stuff and it just seemed to me to be a waste of time. Of course, I was wrong. The real problem was that no one explained what they were for, or how I could use them to the employee's advantage as well as mine.

Over the years I have found one common desire by my staff and me as well, as it related to the managers that I worked for. It was the answer to "How am I doing?" When you think you have the job under control, you want others to agree with you. It's important to feel that someone is doing less and you are doing more. You want to hear it. Its called recognition. Recognition is a motivator. Accolades are the fuel that feeds enhanced performance. A critique of your performance is always a way to seek and claim perfection. It is a vehicle to aid in your career development. And most likely, it is the most mismanaged event in the business world. Conversely, the performance appraisal is the best tool a manager has, to develop staff so that they can be all they can be.

Action and Reaction

Your staff may hate the process and they often are disappointed at the outcome. The disappointment stems from the surprise and/or disagreement with the appraiser and the appraisal. The "tell them something good, something not so good, and then more good stuff" process may not be the best way to conduct the appraisal, however, it is a necessary event, and it should be a frequent event. The employee needs to participate in the process, otherwise they have no ownership and it is a complete waste of time. The more I consult with organizations the more I am convinced that the appraisal process is the most valuable element available, to bring out the best in your employees' performance.

When appraisals are formally conducted only once a year it leads to other problems. One problem arises if the annual salary increase is perceived to be attached to the appraisal. The evaluation becomes a potential adversarial event. We have all been there and drawn the conclusion that it is being picky so that there won't be the full deserved annual increase. Secondly, even if the appraisal is deserved the employee can't recover for one-full year or more. Thus, the objective of the annual appraisal is lost and follows the laws of physics, i.e., for every action there is an opposite and equal reaction. Low morale issues are often the case after performance appraisals.

What is Needed for an Appraisal?

Work, assignments, and the job must be defined. If the job is not defined there is no way you can conduct the appraisal process.

The Required Basics

All assignments have definitive objectives, conditions, expectation levels, tasks, responsibilities, directions, targets, and accountabilities. If I understand the job description, or if I have reviewed the operations manual (the part that effects me), and I am able to perform to these guidelines, I am in good shape. If the response is, "You're doing just fine, you're great", then I am going to feel good about myself. The first task then, is to ensure the job is documented and current. This task is done via the job description.

The Job Description (JD)

The JD needs to be alive, and a viable document. The JD is not a human resources (HR) tool, it is only housed in the HR files. It's your management tool, and it needs to be reflective of the assignments as they relate to today's environment. They should be updated daily if necessary, and published and re-explained no worse than quarterly. Jobs and job content in this day and age change on a monthly basis. We need

257

to stay on top of those changes, deletions, and additions as they occur. Don't lose sight of the objective. In order for me to appraise, manage and critique, we will both have to know what your job is today. In order for the employee to respond to the JD it will make a lot of sense to review the document frequently.

In the late nineties, we initiated the process of maintaining all job descriptions in a database. It is accessible to all managers and employees on a real time basis. That is to say, if the JD changes, it can be revised accurately and quickly with the appropriate approvals. This is important because I am going to be dealing with performance appraisals on a frequent basis, not once a year, but weekly, or no less than monthly, and in some cases daily. I'm going to answer your question, "How am I doing?" We won't review job descriptions here. Please see the chapter Finding and Hiring Staff for your JD guidelines and exhibits.

Sales Reps Performance Appraisals

Compared to other staff, sales representatives have very objective data available for performance appraisals. So do their supervisors and managers. Although impossible to eliminate, subjective evaluations should be used with caution. An example of a subjective statement is, "I think you should improve your attitude." The difference between the two (subjective vs. objective) is that the task can be measured with statistics and hard facts, as opposed to subjective opinions, which are usually where disagreements occur. The examples are:

- attendance
- number of dials
- number of presentations to decision makers
- number of sales
- number of sales dollars
- number of calls to existing account structure vs. calls to prospects
- number of calls to information requests
- number of calls to reactivate inactive account structure
- margin contribution against objective
- most product sold
- and much more

This data is available daily, weekly, monthly, quarterly, and yearly. Management reviews this data all the time, and in effect is performing performance appraisals covering specific periods of time. The process becomes formal when it is reviewed with the employee. To aid the process we have introduced what is called a Territory Management Program. An explanation of this program is at the end of this chapter.

The Five Basic Reasons Why People Perform as They Do

If the manager understands the five basic reasons why people perform as they do and consistently pursues answers to, or provides solutions for the employee, it will greatly improve employee results. A colleague of ours has given permission to reprint an article she wrote for our management report a few years back. It is brief, to the point, and very meaningful. Thank you Peg Fisher.

HOW TO USE PERFORMANCE EVALUATION TO INCREASE EMPLOYEE PRODUCTIVITY

Like quality control systems in manufacturing environments, good performance evaluation systems in business helps management do the best job of shaping people and operations for success and positive goal attainment.

by
Peg Fisher

Why do people perform as they do? Why are some employees successful and others not? How can I use performance evaluation to help identify the "real" reasons for under-performance? Or to congratulate the employee for their outstanding performance.

These are all-important questions faced by anyone who manages others. There are no mysteries to getting the answers when you know how to approach the performance evaluation process. There are five basic reasons why people perform as they do. The five reasons relate to these performance evaluation elements:

1. job description and job standards
2. management feedback to employees
3. events and conditions
4. skills and competencies
5. motivation

When you understand how each of these evaluation elements relates to employee performance, you can use them to identify "real" reasons for performance or performance problems. Once identified, the proper corrective action can be taken. Corrective action may require addressing management issues since performance problems are often the result of inappropriate systems and procedures, which are the purview of management. The following is a review of the five performance elements and their relationship to successful and unsuccessful job performance.

260

1. Job Definition and Job Standards

- Successful performers understand the job, know what is expected of them and are measured against realistic and appropriate job standards.
- Unsuccessful performance can result if the job and its standards are not properly communicated to insure employee understanding, or if information given is incomplete or in error.

2. Management feedback to Employees

- Successful performers have sufficient feedback to know what behavior on their part achieves desired results.
- Unsuccessful performance can result when employees do not know what they are doing wrong, or what they should start doing that they are not doing or what they should change. Ongoing management feedback is needed to help employees be successful. There should be no surprises during a formal annual evaluation because ongoing feedback identifies and corrects performance problems as they occur.

3. Events and Conditions

- Successful performers are not negatively impacted in their job performance by factors beyond their control.
- Unsuccessful performance can result when the work environment prevents job achievement. For example, time-consuming paperwork prevents getting primary tasks done; poor product quality results in returned goods and low sales volume; lack of support systems causes staff to waste time.

These examples demonstrate events and conditions over which employees have no control and cannot be held accountable. It is management's role to identify any work environment situations that reduce employee productivity and prevent primary task achievement. Once identified, management can take the action needed to neutralize or eliminate the problem. Thus, with obstacles eliminated successful performance can and should occur.

4. Skills and Competencies

- Successful performers have the required knowledge, education, experience, and skills needed to do the job; they receive training as needed to learn new skills and refresh others.
- Unsuccessful performance can result from mis-hires caused by lack of recruiting specifications or lax methods; training on-the-firing-line is a hit or

miss proposition at best. Close analysis of the recruiting process and training offered to new-hires and existing employees may find the real reasons for poor performance.

5. Motivation

- Successful performers have the desire to do the job.
- Unsuccessful performance can result if staff is not motivated to perform. ***Remember...*** You cannot motivate people because people motivate themselves. But, you can appeal to the things that do motivate them by putting in place the systems needed to make them feel important, provide job variety and challenge, assign responsibility and the authority required to do the job, and properly reward for desired performance.

Summary of Employee Productivity

Employee productivity and motivation are the goals of good performance evaluation systems, but the system doesn't stop there. A good system helps management do a great job of shaping people and operations for the desired success. Creating a dynamic performance evaluation system will help your sales staff to obtain World Class selling practices.

Peg Fisher, President, Peg Fisher & Associates, Inc., 414-633-1675. Copyright: Peg Fisher & Associates, Inc. Permission to republish granted to FGI & Affiliated Publishing Companies, Inc., January 1991. www.execpc.com/~pfa

Author's Note: We couldn't agree more with our colleague, Peg Fisher. I would only add one comment. Thinking about all the benefactors of employee performance evaluations, they are the employee, the company and let's not forget the most important group, the customers.

Using the Territory Management Program (TMP) as a dynamic tool to manage employee performance.

On the following pages you will find an exhibit of an installed TMP program. I believe it to be self-explanatory. Following one of my favorite axioms for management, "you get what you inspect not expect," you will see that the rep now has full definition on how to perform the assignment. The program is reasonably structured, and allows rep creativity to accomplish the objectives. Because there are objective measurements and goals, set in partnership with the first line supervisor/manager, the program creates rep ownership. Ownership of a program always encourages positive rep results.

The end result is that you have an ongoing performance appraisal process. The answer to the question, "How am I doing?" should now be easy to provide. Please review Figure 11.1 and customize to fit your needs.

Figure 11.1

"My Company"

TERRITORY MANAGEMENT PROGRAM

a.k.a.
TMP

TMP is a proactive sales representative program that specifically structures how your territory is to be managed and/or worked, to deliver for you and (your company's name), maximum sales results in the territory assigned, with the corresponding sales accountability.

FGI0199

Introduction

Managing a territory successfully is the key to customer satisfaction, personal recognition, and individual/departmental goal achievement. Achievement of goals also ties into your compensation and reward programs. Practically speaking the better your sales territory is managed, the better off your customer, your company and you.

Proper work habits and efforts ensure that targets of opportunity are addressed via a set of departmental priorities, that meet expectation levels for yourself, your immediate supervisor, your director, and your corporate sales management team.

TMP is a time management program as well as the tactical plan that will guide you through what is expected as it relates to your job performance. It provides you with clear and concise guidelines for overall goal(s) attainment.

TMP, as a program, is not a substitute for individual selling skills and learned sales techniques. Furthermore, it is to be considered as a guide, and not as a restrictive policy or program which takes away your individuality as a sales representative. Both your customers and your management team value your individuality.

Don't hesitate to ask questions, or make recommendations and contributions for program improvement to your manager. To borrow a well-worn phrase of the mid- to late 90's, the program should go with the flow, as opposed to being set in concrete.

Successful implementation of this program is part of your ongoing performance appraisal process. If there is anything that is not understood about your TMP program, your immediate supervisor will be happy to explain or assist you so that mutual objectives can be met.

PRIORITIES OF YOUR TERRITORY TMP

☎ As a sales representative your top priority is to reach, and/or exceed the mutually agreed upon sales goals and objectives for your territory. Any activities other than sales revenue activities always will have a far lesser priority.

☎ You will find that the 80/20 rule is alive and well in your territory. What that means to you is, close to 20% of your assigned account structure will deliver 80% of your territory revenue contribution. And, although the other accounts will need your attention, along with other tasks and objectives/goals, the aforementioned group should get the lion's share of your selling time. These high opportunity accounts need to be penetrated so that our wallet share of the total available business will be increased. Your investment in time with this group has a huge payback.

☎ Your second priority is to work new leads provided to you from a variety of sources. This will include leads from our promotional programs, marketing card deck leads, (these are usually small business opportunities and worked accordingly), space advertising promotions that provides a toll-free number for prospects to gather information about our products and services, field sales, and all other lead opportunities. Although we believe these leads are easier to close, the true challenge id to determine their real value to your territory. This evaluation sets your plan for call frequency. Thus, a $2,000 a year opportunity may be phone visited once or twice a year while a $20,000 opportunity may be called eight times a year. At any rate, leads depreciate quickly. Call them as soon as possible.

☎ Your third priority, and best source of new business, are firms that have not conducted business with us over the past 12 months. We call these inactive accounts. You should be able to reactivate 30 – 40% of these opportunities. You should request a report every month, of those accounts in your territory that have not been active in the past 12 months, and work this opportunity hard. This effort will also be very rewarding. In theory, if you are staying on top of this category you will know what is occurring with your account structure and respond accordingly, as events are happening. This list tends to become smaller and smaller because of your effort. However, they are still of value to your overall selling objectives. The reason for inactivity 46% of the time, is that the contact point or decision-maker has changed, and it's just a matter of re-establishing the relationship.

☎ The **"pull-through"** calls for your total account structure is your fourth priority. These calls need to be made to accounts who are not fulfilling their promised commitment, i.e., $10,000 a year commitment but only $1,000 recorded in the past six months. We have them on board, so to speak, we just need to create usage. That will be one of your call objectives.

☎ The final category is the selection of specific accounts, usually larger in nature, and working (selling) these accounts on the concept of, "We want to be your first choice, not your alternative choice." As your goal, select 36 accounts (three a month) for targeting, and bring in 18 of these accounts with greatly improved results. This effort also has large pay-backs to the AE (Account Executive).

The above is your assignment. It requires planning and commitment to fulfill. There are temptations all along the way that will attempt to interfere with your plans. The old expression, plan your work and work your plan is very apropos.

Not unlike a recent presidential campaign where the slogan was, "It's the economy stupid", we would like to adopt the slogan, "It's the territory top-line people, the top-line."

The Plan: In order to ensure the above activities take place, and as an ongoing training exercise, we have designed a worksheet that is to be completed every Friday afternoon, which plans your next week's work, and reviews the previous week's efforts. It's at this time your supervisor can provide constructive contributions, provide assistance where needed on your behalf, and take action on activities that are interfering with your plan. Again, we note that this program is a part of your performance appraisal process.

Note that your performance appraisals will be based on how well you are working your TMP, and of course, your sales production results. It's the top line team, the top line. Good selling.

KEY CODE ON CATEGORY OF CALLS FOR YOUR TMP PROGRAM PLANNING DOCUMENT

Category	Definition
1. _____	Account maintenance on top 20%
2. _____	Leads
3. _____	Inactive accounts
4. _____	Pull through, encourage usage
5. _____	Major account wallet share enhancement
6. _____	Miscellaneous (and must be defined) i.e., database maintenance, renewals, etc.

FGI0199

"My Company"
TMP Worksheet
(Weekly review)
For Emerging Markets
FGI0199

AE _____   **Week of** _____

I have planned sales activity for the below listed categories. I anticipated _____ dials per day and _____ customer contacts per day to accomplish my plan. This should accomplish my revenue goals of $_____ per day.

	My Plan			*The Results*	
Category	**Dials**	**Completes**	**Dials**	**Completed Av.**	**Daily Revenue**

1. _____
2. _____
3. _____
4. _____
5. _____
6. _____

Week's Total: $_____

Results worthy of notation by category

1. _____
   _____
   _____
2. _____
   _____
   _____
3. _____
   _____
   _____
4. _____
   _____
   _____
5. _____
   _____
   _____
6. _____
   _____
   _____

"My Company"
TMP Worksheet
(Weekly review)
(Cont.)

Territory Reconciliation

There are a total of _____ accounts in my territory.

_____ have been touched in the last six months.

_____ accounts have not been touched by me yet this year.

Reviewed by:

_____   _____

Supervisor   Date   Account Executive   Date

(To be placed on the reverse side of previous diagram)

Copy to Supervisor
Original to AE TMP
Workbook

FGI0199

Publishing Results

Whether you should you publish individual sales results is a question often asked by call center directors, sales managers, and even the representatives themselves. There are two answers.

Inbound calls are often out of the control of the inbound sales representative. Traffic is driven by other stimuli. Direct marketing, customer service topics, and/or artificial deadlines can all cause inbound traffic, which for the most part is distributed randomly to the representative. Thus, individual results are governed by the call distribution process. If results are to be published they should be by unit, group, or department. That's the only fair way to do it. Special kudos or mentions to individual reps are recommended, but not in comparison to other reps, i.e., the best to the worse scenario.

Outbound, inside sales results should be published on a fairly frequent basis and in a variety of formats, because the reps do control what is happening. The competitive factor, as well as the recognition factor are enjoyed and wanted by the players.

To this day, I still have sales bulletins from years ago showing myself as the top performer for the week of September 14th while performing as a young sales representative for Dun & Bradstreet. Nearly every year I think about throwing these sales performance sheets away, but somehow they manage to survive just one more year.

It makes sense to publish in a variety of formats as well. That gives reps a variety of ways to be recognized as an achiever. Examples would be reports showing:

- Most sales by dollars
- Most sales by numbers of transactions
- Lowest return rates vs. high rate of return
- Number of dials, high vs. low decision-maker contacts, etc.
- Average order value
- Anything else you can think of.

These reports are visuals of, "How am I doing?" They are also kept, taken home, shown to friends, family, colleagues, etc. The reports motivate the bottom-listed rep to get off of the bottom, and the top listed rep to stay on the top.

We recommend these reports have wide distribution. It's not unlike having ones name in lights on a Broadway marquee or, "my fifteen minutes of fame." The behavior style in these positions enjoys these devices.

Finally, publishing data is a commitment. Once you start the event you will have built a rep expectation level. Publish consistently and on time, or you will lose all the benefits of the program.

Summary

Appraisals and performance are directly related. Job descriptions, understanding the job, and providing the tools to get the job done as planned (the TMP) are the manager's major challenge. More frequent is better than less frequent. Objective vs. subjective is a must. The question, "How am I doing?" needs to be answered in order that you may have a healthy, productive department.

☎ ☎ ☎

I SEE YOUR OVERACHIEVER HAS FINALLY DECIDED TO HONOR US WITH HIS PRESENCE

Chapter 12
The Sales Center Facility

Introduction

Your selling facility is an important part of the success formula. Like everything else in this book and the real world, the topic can be confusing, and here is why. Call centers and proactive sales centers are two different kinds of animals. Management, unfamiliar with the topic, tends to think along the lines of, "One size fits all." This topic is like our previous discussions about HR policies in Chapter 6... are they different? They **are** different. Sales staff is not task-driven or operations-formatted. Anything we can do to enhance sales results has a direct payback in a number of areas. Here are a few examples that I have noted:

- Reduction in turnover
- Call productivity increases
- Enhanced sales results, total, and average order
- Selling representative acquisition, e.g., it's a great place to work
- Reduction of fatigue, stress, tension, and boredom
- Enhanced morale
- A positive visual for customers' tours
- And much, more.

There are a few simple rules to think about, and they don't need to cause your company a big increase in expenses.

LVD Issues

Lighting, ventilation, and distractions (LVD) are the key issues for your sales facility. If you have the chance to build a facility from the ground up the architect will ask you for input on these topics. When converting space, or allocating new space, you should pay attention to these details as well.

Lighting

Lighting falls into two categories: 1) at the sales position or station, and, 2) the overhead or ceiling lighting. GE lighting engineers note that for the best results and the least eye fatigue you should not be able to see the source of the light. To demonstrate this point, we never, ever look directly into the sun. You just can't do that because serious eye damage would be the result. Here are your rules:

- All overhead lighting should be incandescent as opposed to fluorescent. Fluorescent lighting is a pulsating lighting device, and causes eye fatigue after three hours. Incandescent is slightly more expensive to operate, however well worth it.
- The lighting fixtures should be recessed into the ceiling, and egg-crated or grilled to shield the light source. It's easier on the eyes.
- Station, cubical, desk, system, furniture etc., deserves task lighting. These are usually located under an overhead storage cabinet that is suspended from a partition wall, and the light flows down onto the desk surface.
- The desk surface should have a light colored, dull finish, e.g., oak as opposed to a dark finish like walnut. The reason is because contrast and reflection of light landing on these surfaces is hard on the eyes. If you will note the next dark desk surface that you see, it likely will be covered with paper to break-up the contrast. That is what the desk occupant does, and yet there is no need for that, if you planned properly.

Ventilation

Cooler is better than warm, and enhanced airflow is better than standard airflow. Stale air causes physical fatigue at four-to-five hours into an eight-hour assignment. That's why you see overhead fans working in the sales center, and I think that, too, is a fine idea.

We recommend the building or facility engineers, or HVAC specialists, be advised that you want additional airflow in your quarters. If possible, try to have your own thermostat and have it under lock and key in the center of the facility.

Distractions

Have you ever noticed how managers like to be located at the rear of the facility as opposed to next to the entrance? I'm inclined to think this is a leftover business culture thing, with the boss in the back corner office.

Visitors to the department should not be able to walk through the department to get to any destination or to use it as a thoroughfare to some other building location.

All management offices and office machines should be at the front entrance of the facility, room, or area.

Partitions should be four and one-half feet to five feet high, not six feet, not wall-to-ceiling, and definitely not offices with doors. We need a social structure here not unlike a bee hive or ant farm setting. Some light noise is conducive to the effort, but distractions are not. Cubicles should not be aligned in rows, but in groups of four to six stations. Pinwheels are good with four to five stations to a wheel. You should be able to see only one other rep from your station (see Figure 12.1).

Carpets, warm colors, light colored desk surfaces, and acoustical ceiling tiles all help the selling environment with reference to LVD. Windows, although sought after by all staff, are not required in the selling area. In break areas and conference rooms windows are desirable, but they are not needed on the sales floor. Again, they're nice, but not really necessary.

Break rooms close by or in the sales area are O.K. More than five minutes away for anything turns out to be a problem. It doesn't take long for you to lose your staff for periods of time not associated with the traditional break. Everything close by is better.

Location, Employees and Staffing

The center does not need to be located at headquarters, or at any other company facility. The unit can be anywhere. There is no need for big time capital equipment, e.g., ACD's, T-1s, mainframe computers. We just need trunks, lines, and phones that are connected to our networked or stand-alone PCs. Overhead expenses can be impacted favorably by not being in the corporate high rent district.

However, if you are in the company facility, locate the sales room away from other activities. There is no need to be in conflict, or to disrupt their culture. The objective is to keep your group out of harm's way. Sometimes sales teams, not unlike professional sports teams, act a little crazy, and we don't need to cause problems for other operating units.

Employees and Staffing

As of this writing, finding sales candidates, or a pool of available candidates, is very difficult to do. Dun and Bradstreet, Inc. quickly realized that the solution to the problem of being located in New York City was to move to the hills of North New Jersey. They also realized that locating operating centers in small cities like Allentown, Bethlehem, and Scranton, Pennsylvania, made the employee pool 100% better. You can do the same thing. I try to be mindful of five conditions; easy to get to, great parking, regional airport, next to colleges and universities, and in towns under 200,000 in population.

Summary

There is nothing earth shattering here in Chapter 12, just a lot of common sense. Your facility and how it looks, feels, and helps productivity, turnover issues, and morale are what this is all about. These are all soft topics, but hard issues. Take the time to consider all of the aforementioned discussion. In my opinion taking care of these business issues has a full 6.5% return on the investment.

Figure 12.1

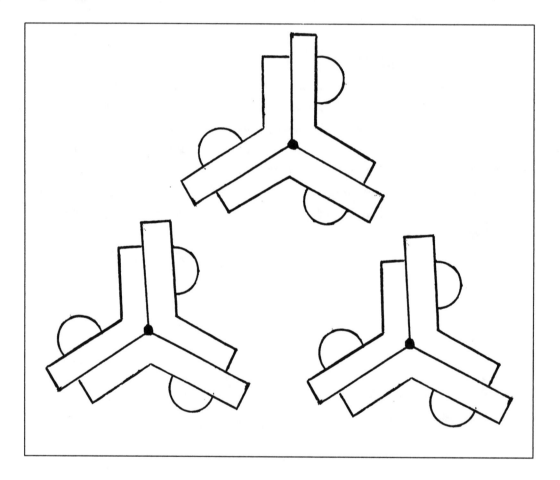

Chapter 13
Conflict Resolutions

Introduction

There are a few topics that are worthy of a brief discussion. As if the inside sales manager's job isn't hard enough, issues that can cause conflict are within every sales unit that I have ever visited. The manager should anticipate these issues, and be prepared to deal with them now or whenever they come up. There are eight topics that just seem to go with the territory. Here they are, with our response based on all of our experience with units like yours.

How Do We Know an Inside Sales Unit Is Really Worth It?

Occasionally other management in your company (including the CEO) will question worth, or return on the investment. This usually stems from the inability to truly track the sales results of your effort. We mentioned earlier in this book that if you can't track it, don't do it. The reason we said that was to anticipate this problem. It's called the challenge. Operations people, financial execs, CEOs, and nearly every other management person accountable for anything, do not fully understand what you do, and how you do it. I am not suggesting that the relationship is adversarial, but occasionally it appears that way. In effect, what all the management positions are saying to you is, "You say it works, but we have no hard data that this program is working or what the true incremental value is." That is both the symptom and the problem itself. Some examples:

- The direct mail manager states that his/her unit would have gotten those sales anyway. You are only cannibalizing direct mail sales production, and on top of that you're paying unnecessary compensation dollars, e.g., commissions.
- The field sales manager states that you can't sell larger accounts on the phone, and gives you the dregs of the account list.
- The customer base, in a client survey, states they don't want to be telemarketed.
- Other managers see your reps off the phone and challenge your effort, and the obvious waste.
- Someone reviews the telcom reports, and in a management meeting asks you what your reps do all day, since they are only connected an average of two hours a day. (Incidentally, this is more time than field reps spend in front of their responsibilities.)
- Orders coming through order entry centers are void of credit for your account reps because you did not directly close the business on the phone and order entry did.
- Reps appear to be living off of inbound calls from their customers. They hardly make any outbound sales effort.
- And 20 other reasons that appears to challenge your contribution as a sales unit. What is a manager to do?

A Solution? A Control Group

You need proof of your contribution, and I see nothing wrong with that. The data must conclusively prove that this investment has a return that makes sense. That is where the Control Group comes in.

The control group is nothing more than a like entity, which does not have the benefit of a telephone selling activity. For example:

Territory #3, Control Group	Territory #6, ISR Active
• 500 active accounts	• Same
• 150 inactive accounts	• Same
• 1,000 prospects	• Same
• State of Ohio	• State of Illinois
• One field sales rep handling 100 major accounts over and above the 500 accounts	• Same
• Three promotional mailings per year	• Same
• No inside sales rep (ISR) is assigned	• One ISR is active

Conduct your overall sales activities as a normal practice for both territories. Make sure the control group was not recently active with an inside sales rep's participation. Three months vacant should do it; this will also eliminate residual sales from previous activities which can muddy the issue. Track for six to nine months, or a year if you can stand the anxiety. The areas that should be impacted by the ISR are:

- Inactive account structure (customer lifetime value);
- Average orders (should be enhanced by 30%);
- Active account structure that should be impacted by a positive 35% in the worst case;
- Information requests, i.e., catalogs, product specs, etc.;
- General prospecting.

The reason is simple: 20 to 30 more decision-maker contacts per day as compared to three or four.

It's true the overall sales volume from these contributions will be less, usually due to the size of the assigned account structure opportunities. But the percent increase of incremental revenue should be dramatic when compared to all other sales resources. And there is your proof. By the way, margin percentages tend not to be shabby either.

Control groups need not be run continuously i.e., day in and day out or forever. However, I do recommend a recheck now and again to prove your point. That will say, "It is worth it."

Parity Issues, Inside vs. Outside

From my previous discussion of control groups, it may look like I have suggested that smaller accounts are, and should be, relegated to inside sales. That's not necessarily true, and the hypothesis can be tested. Part of the existing problem here is the culture, traditions, chemistry, and sales comp plan of the field sales force. We have seen a number of companies move to an 85:15 ratio as it relates to maintenance of existing accounts, with inside sales having the 85% accountability. However, that is a top-down decision, and not the reverse. In fact, you won't get a decision here unless the top boss agrees to do it, and won't listen to any ifs, ands, or buts. Selling is expensive, and the customer must be the first consideration. If they are properly sold and serviced, etc., then it doesn't matter if it's inside or outside sales assets performing the work. Cost of sales is a big time consideration here, and inside sales is less expensive.

What is the Problem?

The problem is that for whatever reasons a **we vs. they** attitude often develops. The solution to this is simple. The inside-selling group should lose its identification as such. The group is an extension of all sales assets. This group should report to the sales manager. It should not be telesales, or tele-anything. It should be an extension of the overall sales organization. Be advised this too is a top-down decision. Field sales compensation culture is powerful, and no one wants anyone else to "mess with my income". Some field assets may even be concerned with job security. Here is a word of caution. A very strong, politically positioned field sales groups can doom an inside sales group. I saw this happen a number of times a case in point.

A Case Example

All large pharmaceutical companies have animal health divisions. Bayer has one, Schering-Plough does, and so do the rest. Let's just say at one of these firms, the top field sales executive asked for staff to assist the field to cycle through their active veterinarian account structure. This would relieve both the hard-pressed sales rep of the five-week cycle responsibility, as well as provide customer touch, thus protecting the account from competitive influences. That was the plan, and the plan was installed. The plan and its implementation were the result of a field sales downsizing and budget cut. They couldn't add reps, but sales quotas were increased. On the surface, this was a good idea.

Five customer service people were hired to call the accounts. The division trainer was to watch over the group, and handle the training for the division sales team. Eighteen months into the program, a consultant (me) was called in to help make the program more effective. The expense was healthy, and it was difficult to track the ROI.

283

These people were not allowed to sell, but they could take orders or make recommendations for purchase. They could make announcements about things, pass customer requests on to the appropriate field rep, solve perceived problems, coordinate stuff, but not formally sell. Really they were nothing more than proactive customer service people.

Guess what? The customer base bonded with the inside sales group. Usage of product was enhanced, and growth percentages were dramatic when compared to field growth percentages. They even were doing better in comparison to the field reps on new business.

Well, this made the field group nervous. They thought, "We can be replaced." That was the call to attack and protect the culture, traditions, and compensation of field sales.

The field group made claims such as,

- They don't know how to sell.
- They can't demonstrate the product.
- The competition was sending in field staff. We are going to lose the business.
- They don't make enough calls.

"They don't", was the cry for the next six months.

The Consultant's Advice to the Senior Sales Exec

I suggested, they expand their sales team to include this unit, drop the proactive customer service mission, install a selling mission, reassign the accounts with field sales accountability, (as opposed to shared), drop joint FSR participation, transfer quota to the inside, and adjust field selling quotas and missions to work large accounts (penetration), and large new business opportunities. Design comps plans for the inside group, and train the heck out of them. Most important, get them an inside sales manager that reported to the division president, because the top sales exec retired, and the replacement apparently despised the successful inside sales group. Turf and compensation was being impacted.

The result was 120% gain in everything – and although an uphill battle every step of the way – literally, a ripping success. However, the battle was not over. In another reorganization effort, it was decided to move the inside sales group to the distribution center in mid-America. Order entry reps, along with customer service would assume the East Coast responsibilities. Field sales won. The program reverted back to day one, and the threat was neutralized. The biggest loser was the customer.

Epilogue

The president of the division decided not to upset the culture of his field sales organization, and used the transfer of the facility as a way out. It was a complete disaster. The inside successful sales group was gone. They won the battle and the animal health group started to lose the war.

So it can happen. A strong field sales organization with a different set of objectives can kill an inside sales group if it so desires. Only the top executives of the division could have prevented the event, and they didn't.

Inside vs. Outside Sales

What you might not recognize is that I could be considered as a wolf in sheep's clothing. For twelve of my fourteen years with Dun & Bradstreet I was in field sales and field sales management.

I migrated to inside selling by accident and necessity. To me, use of the telephone, intensively, was simply using the phone a lot, not telemarketing. However, my management brought to bear the traditions and culture of field sales, and literally attempted to drive me away from the phone as a direct selling tool. The expression of the day was, "In order for you to sell you had to be nose to nose, toe to toe and belly to belly". That was the only acceptable way to sell your products and/or services in your territory.

The above being duly noted and recognized, the next 25 years were involved with inside sales, and in its defense I would like to address the parity issue or channel conflicts.

Inside vs. Outside

Simply stated, there should be no conflict. Selling is selling, period. If there is a conflict it is generated internally, from the so-called history of the medium (field sales), or company culture. Inside selling may also be guilty of creating conflict by segregating this effort, thus creating a we vs. they environment. Not good my friends, not good. Although over simplified, all selling activity should be under the coordinated leadership of a senior sales executive. This position coordinates all sales resources in tandem, to accomplish the sales and marketing plan and its objectives. Furthermore, the customers and the business belong to the company, not the sales department.

Finally, all jobs are not created equal. For example:

- Inbound sales/order entry is not as difficult as outbound sales or field selling.
- Outbound sales are not as difficult as field sales.

The above categories are rewarded by compensation commensurate with degrees of difficulty or risk. In this case, risk means you can earn more income, but you can also quickly lose your job if you do not reach your assigned objectives. Each job level has increased risk attached to the enhanced rewards. The company is interested in producers for these assignments, and will replace anyone who can't produce. Therefore, compensation parity is out of the question in 80% of these situations. A situation can be defined as multiple sales channels.

Sales Channel Conflict

Perhaps you have heard of sales channel conflict. Its cause is the internal competition for sales recognition, and in turn, compensation dollars. In order for this conflict to be eliminated, the organization needs to have a clear set of rules for engagement with the customers and prospects. It's just that simple, and equally as complicated.

Believe or not, fairness has nothing to do with it. Neither does history, culture, or sales department traditions. The only issues are the customer and the future customer. The questions to be answered are, "What is the best way to conduct our business with the sales assets available to us?" and, "How can we (the company) successfully partner with our marketplace so that we both can be successful and reach our mutual goals?"

Field selling is a difficult job. It's lonely and frustrating to many. It's not the high-life others perceive. Base compensation for FSRs should be more than ISRs. The accounts, by nature of their size are more complicated, and a loss here is a big chunk of revenue to recover. I feel the incentive rewards should be larger than all other sales channels as well. If we are unhappy with our incomes as inside reps, then we should apply for an FSR opportunity. Compensation parity is not the solution, nor should it be attempted.

Fear of Staff

The final conflict managers and management alike have, is fear of staff. The examples are:

- My top producers must be handled with kid gloves or we'll lose them.
- We can't fire them, they might sue us.
- It's hard to replace staff. Not only are they not available in this area, it takes a long time to bring them up to full contribution. I don't have that luxury or the time.

The above logic shows the cracks in the sales management armor. In my opinion, it will just be a matter of time before someone, or something, becomes a casualty.

Being predictable and consistent goes a long way here. The three aforementioned issues or fears would never occur on my watch, because I would jump on all three as quickly as the events started to become a problem. The team would know this, and the problem would then become a non-problem. Expectation levels for all players would be met quickly, as well as consistently. To reverse an old football saying, "The best defense is a good offense." Address these topics as they are occurring, not after they occur.

Summary

Conflicts are, for the most part, brought on by ourselves. "We have met the enemy, and they are us." As managers, we get paid to solve and/or prevent these problems. In one way, conflict is good. It's why we have our jobs.

Chapter Fourteen
Publications, Associations and Conferences

Introduction

In this field, I just don't think you can get enough information, and there are now countless sources. The entire area is in overdrive, high gear, and is in a state of rapid change. In fact, in one way it's discouraging. Because of my perceived position within the industry, I've tried to stay on top of the information glut, the technology, and everything. So, it's not unlike the Pennsylvania Dutch expression, "The harder I try, the behinder I get!"

I feel I am losing the battle. For what it's worth, here is the "Van Vechten Seal of Approval" on magazines, reports, newsletters, conferences, training devices, and associations. I know I will miss some excellent sources, and for that I apologize. As with all lists and sources these will go out-of-date the minute they are published. Here they are, and good luck. I would not list these sources if I didn't think they were helpful.

QUITE FRANKLY, I WAS HOPING FOR A MORE POSITIVE INCENTIVE TO STAY.

Magazines

Call Center Magazine; "Technologies and Techniques for Customer Service, Help Desk, Sales and Support": Miller Freeman, Inc.; 600 Harrison Street, San Francisco, CA 94107; (615) 377-3322 for free monthly subscription.

Lot's of call center technical stuff, i.e., software, telecom and hardware. You need a dictionary to understand all the initials.

Call Center Solutions, (formerly Telemarketing Magazine) "The Authority on Teleservices, Sales and Support": Technology Marketing Corporation; One Technology Plaza, Norwalk, CT 08654; (203)852-6800 for free monthly subscription.

Has been around since 1982, editorial direction moving more towards technology of call centers as opposed to staffing and operations issues.

Operations & Fulfillment Magazine, "Practical Solutions for Catalog and Direct Response Operations Management": Target Communications Corporation; 535 Connecticut Avenue, Norwalk, CT 06854; (203)857-5656 X165. Free subscription, monthly.

Great customer service and distribution mechanics stuff here especially for catalogers.

TeleServices News (a DM News Supplement): Mill Hollow Corporation; 100 Avenue of Americas, New York City, NY 10013; (212)925-7300; BPA audited; free, 10 times a year with supplements weekly.

Truly a weekly news publication with special interest sections as an added benefit. It is more business-to-consumer driven, however. I check it weekly and look forward to the supplement.

TeleProfessional Magazine; "The Forum for Customer Contact Information": Advanstar Communications; Call Center/Voice Group, 501 Sycamore Street, Suite 120, Waterloo, Iowa 50703; (319)235-4473, free subscription, monthly.

This is the best magazine for me, and I read it cover to cover.

Equipment Catalog Suppliers

Hello Direct, 5893 Rue Ferrari, San Jose, CA 95138-1857, (800)444-3556 for catalog. Great phones, headsets, etc., I've never been disappointed; free brochure.

Telephone International, P.O. Box 3589, Crossville, TN 38557-3589, (800)492-3685, (a newspaper type format).

This is a big second-hand, rebuilt, hardware supplier, (switches, PBXs, phones, and phone systems) with absolutely outstanding prices. I have not used this source but they have an excellent reputation. Free

Selling Publications, Videos, Programs

Telephone "Doctor", "Customer Service Training Products and Services to Improve the Performance of People on the Telephone": 30 Hollenberg Court, St. Louis, MO 63044, (800)882-9911, for free catalog.

Tapes and videos on all topics, the best in the industry. The founder, Nancy Friedman is also an excellent speaker for meetings, etc. They have absolutely outstanding production quality, and hard hitting training messages/practices. Highly recommended.

Telephone Selling Report, 13254 Stevens Street, Omaha, NE 68137, (800)326-7721; $109 yearly. Geared toward the rep and the rep's trainer/manager.

Published by Business By Phone Inc., it is really great stuff, monthly, and very helpful with online selling tips. They also sell other publications and training devices, have very good prices and products, and lots of experience in business to business selling. www.businessbyphone.com

TSR Hotline, "Proactive, Business to Business Sales Rep's Skills Maintenance Handbook": 51 Hampton Drive, Suite 101, Freehold, NJ 07728-3148, $79.00; to order call (800)682-5432. There are 79 skill packed chapters for individual or group training; author, Lee R. Van Vechten. www.vanvechten.com

Published by Business By Phone, Inc., revised 1996, with over 7,000 copies in circulation. It is a three-ring binder system, certificate course. I'm a little biased, because I wrote the publication, and I think it's equal to, or better than, anything out there.

Books, Publishers, etc.

The Best Seller: D. Forbes Ley; Sales Success Press, Newport Beach, CA 92660; about $40.00

Overall, this is the best sales skills book I have ever read, and I'm very critical. Even though it's field sales driven, there is a ton of good meat here.

The Complete Guide to Marketing and the Law: Robert J. Posch, Jr.; Prentice Hall Publishing Co., Englewood, NJ 07632; about $45.00 and revised frequently.

When I have legal questions this is where I go first, then to an attorney.

Direct Marketing Publishers: Bernard Goldberg Publications; 1304 University Avenue, Yardley, PA 19067; (215)321-3068; call for free catalog.

Lots of how-to books on direct marketing and corresponding call center resources. They are easy reading, clear and practical, and highly recommended.

Newton's Telcom Dictionary; The Official Dictionary of Telecommunications: 14th edition; Harry Newton; about $50.00*
Understanding Computer Telephony; How to Voice Enable Database from PC's, LANs to Mainframes: second edition; Carlton Garden; about $50.00.*
Flatiron Publishing, Inc.; 12 W. 21 Street (7th Floor), New York, N.Y.; to order call (212)691-8215.

(*) Two reference manuals that help the reader to understand the integration of phones with computer databases. I could not live without them.

Peg Fisher and Associates, Inc. (PF&A), 1201 S. Wisconsin Ave., Racine, WI 53403-1976, Phone: (414) 633-1675, Fax: (414) 633-1541, E-mail: pfa@execpc.com, URL: http://www.execpc.com/~pfa.

Lots of how-to books and articles specifically directed toward wholesalers, distributors and dealers as it relates to strategic planning for call center sales activity.

Performance Appraisals: American Management Association (AMACOM); 135 West 50th Street, New York City, NY 10020; About $11.00.

An in-depth how-to book, very good, you need it.

<u>Phone Power & Power Talking</u>: George R. Walther; G.P. Punam's Sons (The Berkley Group); About $24.00

Covers styles and techniques of communication over the phone. Any book by George is a good investment.

<u>Please Understand Me; Character and Temperament Types (MBTI)</u>: David Keirsey and Marlyn Bates; Prometheus Nemesis Book Co.; P.O. Box 2748, Del Mar, CA 92014; about $20.00.

This is the best book on the Myers-Briggs personality profile typing. It is great for staff selection background and interpersonal staff relationships.

Associations

The American Teleservices Association (ATA) formerly The American Telemarketing Association; 4605 Lankershim Blvd., North Hollywood, CA 91602-1891.

Call centers of all varieties are the topic here, including education, networking, and lobbying activities; about 2,000 plus members. Started in 1982 by "yours truly!" (818)623-5385, Fax: (818)766-8168, Toll Free: (800)441-3335 and e-mail address http://www.ataconnect.org.

The Direct Marketing Association (DMA) Telephone Council; 1120 Avenue of Americas, NY, NY 10036-6700; (212)768-7277, membership fees are based on corporate sales volume.

The largest and the oldest direct marketing organization in the world, it is a good group, great if you are a big direct mailer. However, it is really not applicable for non-mailers, because pure telephone sales and non-mailers have little to gain with their agenda.

International Customer Service Association (ICSA); 401 North Michigan Avenue, Chicago, IL 60611-4267; (312)321-6800; (800)360-4272.

About 3,000 plus members with local chapters. Customer service and Help Desk driven, it is a good group, with networking and education being the emphasis.

Summary

All of the associations and magazines offer conferences that are worthy of your review. I find the networking to be excellent at these events. Let's quote old Ben Franklin again, *"An investment in knowledge pays the best interest."* I can't say it any better than Ben.

Chapter 15
Marketing, Budgeting and Consultants

Introduction

If you have been reading cover-to-cover, this is the chapter you have been looking for, the last chapter.

These last three topics may not be placed appropriately in the proper scheme of things with reference to this book, however, the topics are short in nature. I have combined them for this final chapter, but that does not mean the topics are any less important.

In fact, conceptually, they may be the most important. You are expected to be a jack-of-all-trades in your management group. You are in either the most enjoyable position, or the most precarious position as it relates to your career field. You're going to find that you are the only one who really knows anything about this topic. Like I have said, that's both good news and bad news.

Marketing

It has been my experience that other management believes telemarketing to be a solution to any and all opportunities or problems that do not fit anywhere else, or that the medium is simple to apply and manage. Or that it's inexpensive to use and can solve every problem that now exists with sales and marketing departments, program, or missions. Well, that's just not true. The medium, not unlike a special tool, has its place in your business mix, and it may not be the miracle application others tend to think it is.

Thinking specifically of your sales environment, these programs fit best:

- New business applications, as long as they are in tandem with other mediums. No cold calls please.
- Account maintenance for existing active accounts.
- Reactivation of inactive accounts
- Inquiry follow-through and subsequent conversion to signed business.

There is room for specialization on all of the above, thus, I don't recommend that one rep be all things to all situations. Therefore, government and national account reps makes sense. That group will approach their assignments differently than the standard territory rep. I believe that active and inactive account assignments are similar, and that new business applications work well on a stand-alone assignment or basis. You can limit as well as focus the reps' efforts and attention on the topic or assignment, and in turn enhance your ROI.

It is easy for a territory rep who has total territory accountability to become involved with a major account. In turn, everything else such as dials, decision-maker contacts, prospecting, etc., suffers. The solution to that problem is making the rep one or another, but not both.

All other so-called telemarketing applications tend to be information driven as opposed to sales driven. For example, "We need to know if hospitals have specific programs to address network protection software issues. Get the sales team to call and find out what's what." Now my friend, if there is not a selling opportunity here, that project needs to be outsourced. Always protect your revenue flow. Never get in the way of a finely tuned sales organization. Just remember, these outsourced projects are also a part of your responsibility, not the Research Director, New Products Manager, etc.

Fight it.

Do not let the marketing or research interests send you on a wild goose chase. Do listen to them, recommend solutions, manage the program for them; but never be distracted from your main assignment: **SALES, SALES, SALES.**

Do keep the database in proper shape and maintained. It's the key to your ongoing success. You don't want to be calling the entire database for each and every new perceived opportunity.

Do test everything. Telephone selling is the most statistically significant marketing tool in the universe. Making 279 calls to anything on a consistent basis will forecast your future efforts and results. This keeps you out of high-risk activities, and enhances call-to-close ratios significantly.

Do force your supervisors to monitor consistently and frequently. This is how you build a world class sales center.

Do keep your managers informed and updated on everything, both up and down the organization. We are in the "rapid deployment of information" era. You can and should be the voice of the customer, and the voice of your company's impact on the customers to your other management partners.

Finally, ***do have fun and enjoy this management assignment***. Fun is contagious and so are sales budget victories. There has never been a day in my life that I hated to go to work in this area. It's just too much fun.

Budgeting

Not unlike the once-a-year task of completing performance appraisals, the second most dreaded task was preparing the annual departmental sales budget. I'll never forget the first attempt at this task with good old Dun & Bradstreet.

I counted everything as accurately as I could. I gave my best judgment on everything. I spent days, hours, weeks, on extensions of numbers and formulas, and with a great deal of pride presented the document to my boss. In less than one day, the budget package was back on my desk with this notation: "Lee, add $180,000 to your revenue line, and take out $76,500 in expenses. Resubmit by this afternoon. R. Horkey, Vice President."

So much for trying to do the budget using that methodology. Later on, I kind of understood this process, and in one sense had to lose my naiveté in order to respond to these exercises. No one ever told me how to low-ball the revenue line, or highball the expense line, nor that the first thing that your manager did was to send the sales budget back to you knowing full well that you were playing the "lowball/highball" game.

The Tested Formula

With the above noted, I searched for a formula that was less work and not a game, and took only a modest amount of time to get to the end result. I would like to share this formula with you. It tends to underestimate revenue and overestimate expenses. I believe the reason for this is what's called the function of numbers. However, I find the aforementioned is the best position to be in.

☎ Expenses First: Expense allocation seems to be easier to do than revenue forecasts. We would note that it's better to take a full burden of expenses in your budget, as this becomes ironclad proof when you are asked to defend the contribution. You should use direct expenses whenever possible and not allocated expenses. Use a worst case condition as opposed to best case condition. Therefore, figure your reps for all available commissions, as opposed to 80% of the available amount. These are the expense lines you will need:

- Salary/wages
- Incentives
- Contest awards
- FICA and company benefits (a percentage of the above)
- Utilities
- Rent
- Office
- Postage, Express Mail, etc.
- Phone, Fax, e-mail, etc.
- Hardware/software
- Equipment
- Printing, brochures, name cards, etc.
- All phone and phone related expenses
- Construction, consulting, training
- Staff acquisition expense
- Travel and entertainment
- Meetings expense
- Miscellaneous (a percentage of above)

NOTE: Only accept allocated expenses if all other sales channels (including direct mail) accept these expenses as well. It's the old "apples to apples" thing.

Revenue

Here is where the formula comes into play. I literally go out into the *orders completed box* and count and total the orders, eliminating the top five and bottom five, to determine an average order size or value, i.e., AOV.

- On new sales units I add 35% to the average order.
- With mature sales units I add 25% to AOV.

  Next I note that there are 47 available weeks to work (with a defined number of sales staff), five days a week.
- For each manager I add one-half a rep; for each support person I add one-quarter a sales rep.

Revenue Example Applied to the Formula

- Input: one manager, two supervisors, four support staff, and ten ISRs.
- Average order value is $1,000 plus 35% or $350.

Formula

1. Number of selling staff (times)
2. AOV plus 35% (times) orders per day (times)
3. 47 work weeks (times)
4. Five days a week (equals)
5. Forecasted sales revenue

1. $10 + 1.5 + 1 = 12.5$ staff
2. $1,000 AOV + $350 gain $= $1,350 X 3 orders per day
3. 47 weeks
4. 5 days
5. Revenue solution

Therefore: 12.5 (X) $1,350 (X) 3 (X) 47 (X) 5 = $11,896,875

The incremental portion ($11,896,875 minus $7,050,000) equals $4,846,875.

NOTE: The above formula assumes managers can, and do, leverage their sales results without carrying a quota, thus, the value of an additional 2.5 reps. The same is true for support staff; they allow the reps to stay on the phone. The $7,050,000 is actual reps, times the average order value, times weeks and days, for the results.

That's how I do it, and I am always correct to plus or minus 3% when the results are in. Try it. You'll like it.

Consultants

I don't want to be self-serving here, but consultants save you money, not cost you money. They will advise, bring you the latest methodology and cut start-up or adjustment time immensely. Time is money. I am not sure why there is so much apprehension when it comes to hiring a consultant, but there apparently is.

A few words of advice: The first thing an unemployed executive does after becoming unemployed, is become a consultant. I'm not sure that a broad base of experience comes to bear with that opportunity.

Secondly, there are many types of consultants out there. When mistakes are made in the consulting selection process, they appear to be in hiring the wrong discipline. Generally speaking there are six major types of consultants or consulting activities.

- Business-to-business
- Service Agency/Call Center
- Business-to-consumer
- Technical, as in phone, database, software, hardware, etc.
- Call Center vs. Sales Center
- Proactive vs. reactive

Thus, a business-to-consumer, inbound consultant is not suited for a business-to-business, proactive sales applications.

I am a business-to-business outbound sales consultant. I pass off all other applications. They're just not my expertise. The consultant individually who says that he can do it all is one to worry about, in my book. If he is part of a firm with multiple disciplines... maybe. The only way you will get a clue is to review and speak with their clients, and ask about their experiences. Thus, if you are selling batteries to distributors, and the consultant's client list is all banking and financial, you can anticipate a problem. Exactly the same experience is not necessary, but closer experience than the above will be helpful for sure.

Concerns?

Here are some clues to watch for, to see if you should be concerned about a potential consultant:

- Is available immediately (no work, and why?)
- Charges $350 a day (what are you getting?)
- Has no client list, or you're unable to reach listed names (you need references)
- Consulting on topics where there appears to be no experience in the field (a little too hungry)
- Has not been picked up by the industry press for articles and contributions

- Charges for travel time at the same daily rate as his consulting rate
- Is never in the office when you call; voice mail, etc., calls back a week later
- Demands first class accommodations (air travel, hotels, etc.)
- Tells you how to do it, but don't do it themselves
- Bargains daily rate when you ask them to sharpen their pencils; reason: Proposal pricing. Charging what the traffic will bear is unprofessional

I have found that it takes twenty-five years to build a reputation, and one day to lose that reputation. Honesty and integrity need to be there. Finally, there should be a match on personalities. I have respectfully withdrawn from proposals for this very reason. The client and consultant will become very close, and trust will be your key ingredient. You pay these people to tell you like it is, not what you wish to hear. I suppose the expression "caveat emptor," or "buyer beware," is appropriate here as well.

A Final Word

I have shared with you what I believe will be helpful, in your business and your business careers. I could not have done so unless over 350 companies like yours were willing to learn and share their experiences. I thank them for their help, and wish all of my readers success with this material. I welcome your questions, contributions, and debate. You need only write to the publisher for your response or contact us via the internet: www.vanvechten.com

By the way, GOOD SELLING!

Lee R. Van Vechten

Here Are Other Resources You Can Get Right Now to Help You Close More Sales Using the Phone, and Manage and Motivate Your Telephone Sales Staff!

Go to the Business By Phone Inc. website at,

www.businessbyphone.com

for free telesales tips and articles, special offers, and other resources. Also be sure to sign up for the free e-mail, weekly newsletter, "The TelE-Sales Hot Tips of the Week."

Get a FREE Subscription to the Business By Phone Catalog of Tapes, Books, Telesales Rep College Seminars, Other Training Materials

If you use the phone in any aspect of sales or service, you'll find something in this catalog to help you do it better. Also, especially if you didn't buy this book through Business By Phone Inc. (the publisher), you'll want to be listed in our database so you can be one of the first to be notified of new books and resources to help you sell more by phone. Call our offices at 1-800-326-7721, or (402)895-9399.

Have Information In Seconds With Business By Phone's Fax-Back Service

You can have detailed descriptions of plenty of sales-building products in your hands as soon as you want. Go the handset of your fax machine, call (402)896-9877, listen for the prompts, press "1,"and follow the instructions. When asked, press "101" as the document you'd like. This is our Fax Information Directory listing all of the brochures and samples available to you by return fax. Receive this document, pick the additional information you'd like, then call again to receive your choices. Or, simply use the document numbers on the next page to make your selections.

Sales-Building, and Management and Motivational Materials You Can Order Right Now

The *"TSR Hotline"* by Lee R. Van Vechten

TSR Hotline is a collection of 79, four-page lessons on a variety of telesales topics and skills ranging from planning and opening the call to closing and managing accounts. It's suggested that managers review these lessons with reps in a sales meeting (at the beginning of a week, for example), and then encourage reps to work on the skills and take notes during their week. Another meeting should be held to discuss the results and reinforce the skills. For each set you order, you'll get a *TSR Hotline* binder, the 79 four-page lessons, and tabs that divide the sections. It's that simple. **$79 per set, plus $4 shipping.**

The Monthly *"Telephone Selling Report"* Sales Tips Newsletter

Get sales-building, how-to ideas, tips and techniques delivered to your desk every month in the eight-page *"Telephone Selling Report."* Fax Information Document #110 for all eight pages. **$109** for a one-year, 12-issue, subscription. Also see a sample copy online at www.businessbyphone.com.

"Hello Success" Training Program, Everything You Need to Run Your Next 12 Months Worth of Training Meetings

Run a complete sales training session every other week for the next year using the step-by-step, word-for-word instructions, audio tapes, and newsletter/worksheets in Hello Success. Twelve separate, independent training topics. Manager's Kit Includes Leaders Guide, 12 audio tapes, full set of newsletter materials. Each Rep Kit includes newsletter/worksheet materials and three-ring-binder. Fax Information Document 113. **$149** for Manager's Kit, **$30** per set of Rep Materials.

To Order Any of These Items

1. Mail your check, U.S. funds only, to Business By Phone, 13254 Stevens St., Omaha, NE, 68137.

2. Call us at 1-800-326-7721, or (402)895-9399

3. Fax your order with credit card number to (402)896-3353. *(Overseas shipping billed at cost. Candian shipping 2x listed rate.)*

4. E-mail to arts@businessbyphone.com

5. Order online at www.businessbyphone.com

To Get More Copies of This Book:

To get additional copies of this book, photocopy or remove this form, or call, fax or e-mail us with the necessary information. *(Inquire about quantity discounts. Also, bookstore and dealer inquiries welcome.)*

Yes, please send me _____ copies of *"The Successful Sales Managers Guide to Business-to-Business Telephone Sales"* at $79.00 (U.S. funds) each (+$5 shipping in the U.S., $7 Canada, overseas charged at cost.)

Name_____

Company_____

Address_____

City_____State_____Zip Code_____

Phone_____

Fax_____

Method of Payment

❏ Visa/MC/AMEX/Discover

\#_____

sig._____exp._____

❏ Check /Money Order Enclosed *(U.S. Funds Only)*

Ways to Order

• **Phone** your order to **1-800-326-7721**, or (402)895-9399.

• **Fax** your order to (402)896-3353.

• **Mail** your order to Business By Phone, 13254 Stevens St., Omaha, NE, 68137.

• **E-Mail** your order to arts@businessbyphone.com.

• **Order online at** www.businessbyphone.com.